The New Paint Magic

The New Paint Magic

Jocasta Innes

Pantheon Books, New York

All rights reserved under International and Pan-American Copyright Conventions.
Published in the United States by Pantheon Books, a division of
Random House, Inc., New York.

Originally published in hardcover in Great Britain by Windward/Berger Paints, and
in the United States by Van Nostrand Reinhold Co., Inc. in 1981. A revised edition
was published in Great Britain by Frances Lincoln Publishers Limited and in the
United States by Pantheon Books in 1987. This revised and updated edition
originally published in Great Britain by Frances Lincoln Publishers Limited,
4 Torriano Mews, Torriano Avenue, London NW5 2RZ, England

Library of Congress Cataloging-in Publication Data
Innes, Jocasta.
    The New Paint Magic: Jocasta Innes.
        p.   cm.
    Includes bibliographical references and index.
    ISBN 0-679-74251-4
    1. House Painting.   2. Interior decoration.   3. Paint mixing.
    1. Title.
    TT323. 156   1992
    698'.14—dc20   92-54111
                                                                          CIP

Manufactured in Hong Kong
6 8 9 7

Facing title page Agreeably battered fresco-style walls combined with a floor of painted 'marble' flags give this country living room a Pompeiian feel to it. A close-up photograph of the wall is shown on page 35.

Contents

Foreword

Paint, colour and pattern are enduring elements of interior design but as with everything else we buy or select, in making our choices we are responsive to, and are influenced by, contemporary taste. A comparison of the three different editions of *Paint Magic* makes this vividly apparent. *Paint Magic* was first published in 1981. A revised edition, with a new cover and some new material appeared in 1987. A third, much more substantially reworked version is just off to the printers – better, I think, in that it is clearer and tighter as to the information and also more comprehensive. And visually it is wonderfully surprising; there could be no clearer record of just how far the 'paint thing' has travelled since the euphoric but uncritical 80s. Not merely the surface treatments, but the underlying mood and style have altered, and I think *The New Paint Magic* picks up on this loud and clear.

The first job in updating a book like this is to sift through all the original photographic material – room shots, close-ups, step-by-step sequences – deciding which pictures must go and which are still relevant or appealing. I anticipated that this would be difficult or contentious, but in the event it was obvious which were 'no-nos' and which pictures should remain. The choice was made unhesitatingly. As we progressed from rejects to new material, the essential differences between the 80s and the 90s look in interior decoration began, unmistakably, to crystallize. What looked sadly dated was an affluent, posh, overworked look, with too many 'effects', too many *things*, altogether too much going on. Keynotes of the pictures we retained, on the other hand, were freshness, simplicity and unpretentiousness.

What surprised me about *The New Paint Magic* as it came together, is that it looks much *younger* than its predecessors: lighter, larkier, relaxed. The newest paint effects look easy and lived in. They are, of course, the product of artifice but they don't look it; mostly the look they aim for is what I call 'integral'. In other words, as in traditional fresco painting, the colours are fused with the wall plaster itself, message and medium as one. The result of these strategies is colour and texture that looks honest, real in the way sourdough loaves and homegrown vegetables seem real. There are many routes to this type of effect, from true fresco work – not so much difficult as arduous – to colourwashing with homemade distemper. I believe the fresco look is central to interior decoration over the next decade and we have explored it extensively. Another 'real' paint effect which has become especially important recently in furniture painting is the layering of colour to mimic the somewhat battered appearance of old painted country pieces. Known as 'heavy distressing', this approach comprises a whole slew of tricks, and it is the main innovation in the furniture painting section. Believing that painted floors are an attractive

A glowing wash, wavering between rose and terracotta, makes a delectable cocoon of colour for a frosty pavilion of a bed draped in muslin and spread with embroidered linen. By way of contrast, everything else – floor, furniture – is dark, plain and shiny.

as well as thrifty proposition, I have made a lot of changes in the floors section, adding new text and pictures and rewriting existing material. And I have included several new examples of graining techniques in the woodwork section.

In the event the majority of the original photographs have been replaced, starting with the cover and working right through to the last section. Fundamentals (which should be read *before* you start paint magicking although it turns up towards the back of the book), where we decided to compress pages of text and line drawings about tools and materials into a few gloriously crowded colour spreads.

So much for the broad brush changes. But we have also worked on the details. Very few techniques have been dropped along the way but the 'how-to' has sometimes been pruned, partly because I think many people know about the basics of preparation for painting, and partly to make room for new techniques and ideas. Running my own studio classes in paint effects for the past year has provided invaluable feedback here. The new finishes have all been tried and tested in the studio by students of varying abilities and I include them not only because they are general favourites – verdigris, malachite, simple graining effects, for instance – but also because I know that they can be done by people who insist that they don't know one end of a brush from the other. Teaching is a great way to learn, I have discovered. Students open my eyes all the time, breaking the rules, attempting impossible colour combinations, upsetting preconceptions that I didn't know I had.

As well as asking me the standard questions about paint effects, people like to sneak one in about when I think the 'paint thing' will run out of steam – the implication being that we will all then return to the normality and security of magnolia emulsion and white gloss. I hope this book is proof that paint finishes are alive and well, indeed flourishing, in this last decade of the twentieth century. I would like to think that they have become a permanent part of the DIY scene, evolving in step with changing tastes and needs, but remaining irresistible to anyone with an eye to a good thing by virtue of the seductive cheapness and the dazzling versatility of paint.

Jocasta Innes

Introduction

Throughout a history reaching back to earliest times, paint has played something of a dual role. On the one hand it has had a practical application, acting both as a vehicle for pigment and a protection to the surface it covers. This is how most of us still see paint – coloured stuff bought in a can and applied with brush or roller, the important thing being to get the colour even and the surface smooth. On the other hand it has also fulfilled a creative and much more significant purpose – as a vehicle for the human imagination, a creator of illusions, the modest but endlessly pliable means of fixing a glimpse of loveliness for posterity.

The true originators in this field have always been the great artists. But close behind these masters of illusion came the masters of the applied arts – designers, architects, decorators, legions of craftsmen whose vocation was to reflect contemporary standards of beauty and harmony in buildings, rooms and furniture. Naturally they borrowed freely from the techniques and materials used by the artists, developing these to suit their own ends. Thus we have the use of tinted glazes to enrich colour and give depth, and a host of conjuring tricks with paint to suggest marble, tortoiseshell and other precious materials.

If one had to sum up the difference between this sophisticated use of paint and the approach of the do-it-yourself painter, it would be in a phrase beloved of traditional decorators, 'broken colour', or, more succinctly still, 'distressing'. As every decorator knows, flat, uniform colour is inert and unyielding, while distressed or broken colour is suggestive, atmospheric. Walls treated with distressed paint are volatilized, the brute facts of bricks and mortar dissolved in a fluent movement of transparent colour shadows and highlights. The plainest box of a room, built yesterday, can be transformed with the right distressed paint finish into a place with a soul.

This magical transformation of our surroundings is in no sense beyond the reach of anyone who can read or hold a brush. Paint is cheaper than wallpaper and distressed paint is often cheaper still, since it is applied much thinned. Maybe a certain manual deftness, a cool head, and an appraising eye are a help toward achieving professional standards first time off. But the most exciting and instructive effects are often won by operating in blithe ignorance of all the rules. What is chiefly needed is a dash of venturesomeness, the will to get the materials together, and the curiosity to try them out. However, it can be helpful to begin with some knowledge and understanding of the materials and tools involved. I suggest you read the Fundamentals section (pages 210–232) before you do anything else.

Watery blue, flat cream and tarnished gold makes a splendidly effective colour scheme with a strong Scandinavian neoclassical flavour. The dado has been stencilled. The blue grows softer as it goes upwards, at its most intense on the skirting, becoming more nebulous on the ceiling. The floorboards have been painted white and waxed.

Colour

To use colours beautifully you must *feel* them, fall a bit in love with them like that colourist of genius, Henri Matisse. 'Colours win you over more and more,' he said once. 'A certain blue enters your soul. A certain red has an effect on your blood pressure. A certain colour tones you up.'

Colour, not necessarily bright, but positive, is the most memorable feature of all the rooms and interiors I have enjoyed and envied, and is the first question that preoccupies me when I have a room to decorate because I know that it will affect me directly every time I walk into it. I am sure the same is true of almost everyone – young children react with uninhibited delight to colour, so isn't it likely that the need remains present in all of us, but that it has become inhibited, or simply crowded out by other concerns? It needs to be roused and encouraged. Most people take the easy way out when choosing a colour scheme, playing safe, painting everything white or cream, getting a beige carpet because it 'goes with everything'. Colourless rooms do have their own chaste charm, but it is a pity that they should be the rule rather than the exception, when for a modest outlay one can live surrounded by lusty reds, soulful blues and singing yellows, not to mention all the subtle shades between.

The most interesting discovery I have made about the use of colour in decoration is that colours that have been 'distressed' are more flattering to a room and its furnishings than flat opaque colour. It is not just the colour that matters, but the way it is applied. The flat, inert (some would say plastic) finish of a couple of coats of standard emulsion [latex] put on in the usual way, seems to depersonalise a room. Brushing a tinted glaze, or a wash, in a deeper tone or contrasting colour improves the look of the place at once, giving an illusion of depth that makes the walls appear to recede and the room seem larger.

There is no better way of appreciating beautiful colour combinations than to look – with a relishing greedy eye – at the paintings of great colourists such as Bonnard, Matisse or Monet. But paintings are only a start – almost any arrangement of colours is worth looking at in this analytical way. A market stall, a fine Bokhara rug, a scrap of Chinese embroidery – food for the eye is to be found almost everywhere.

When it comes to turning theory into practice – painting your own room picture – the only way to find out whether particular colours really work together is to try them out. Unless you are very rich (or very poor) your colour adventuring will probably be restricted by some expensive fixture that must be taken into account – usually a carpet. Never mind, it is useful to have a point of departure.

The most important colour decision to be taken in a room is about the walls. A room has a lot of wall surface and the colour must look happy with the fixtures you have. Tiny samples of wallpaper, or paint colour, are seldom much help since any colour repeated over a large area is intensified to an unimaginable degree. Begin, instead by making up a still-life arrangement out of bits and pieces in all sorts of colours first – sweaters, book covers, anything will do. Group them near a window so you can look at them by natural light, and squint through half-closed eyes at the colours against carpet, curtains and other furnishings. This is crude but it can help clarify the situation. Next buy a tin of suitable white paint, mid-sheen or emulsion [latex], mix up those colours you like and try them on the wall. A range of universal stainers [tinting colours or colorizers] will give you most of the lighter tints. For rich, dark or strong colour, use the stainers with water only – mixing dark colours in wall paint requires a base colour near the one you are after, which could be expensive until you are sure what that is.

If the idea of experimenting straight on to the wall shocks you, use large sheets of lining paper painted in different colours, and pin these in a position where you get a view of the colour juxtaposed with carpet or curtains. Then hang a picture over it, place a chair in front, and try out some different cushions. All this helps to suggest what the colour would look like as a background to the whole room. When you have whittled the possibilities down to one or two, leave these pinned up and just live with them for a few days. If one colour gives you renewed pleasure every time you look at it, that's the one. The delight of paint is that if you aren't happy with the result after putting on the colour, it can be quickly modified by superimposing one of the decorative finishes described in this book. Strident colours can be softened by dragging or sponging in a softer, or deeper, shade, or simply glazing with a creamy transparent oil glaze, 'thin' pastels can be made richer, drab colours given a lift, or dark ones lightened. You could lacquer the walls, or spatter them with black and white specks for a 'porphyry' effect. If this seems a lengthy way of finding a pleasing wall colour, remind yourself that Monet was not too proud or busy to mix crushed brick into whitewash until he arrived at the shade he saw in his mind's eye, and that all this experimenting has cost time rather than money, and is vital training for your colour sense.

Having got the wall colour settled, the bulk of your room is blocked in; the rest is filling in and fun. Go slowly, and keep an open mind. Coloured floors can look splendid. Stain plain wood planks dark green, or blue, as a background to old rugs. If you can't afford an old rug, paint one on the floor, in the mellowest, richest colours your imagination can supply. People tend to leave a room's woodwork white, or off-white – decorators hardly ever use pure white, they prefer it 'dirtied'. But woodwork painted to match the walls can look exciting, and dramatically alters the proportions of a room, tightening it up so that it feels more together.

Furniture, decoratively painted, is another way of introducing colour – paint is the best possible disguise for undistinguished furniture, or plain junk. Imagine a full but useful little table, or cabinet, given a tortoiseshell finish. Or stencilled with a small diaper pattern for a filigree Moorish effect. Picture frames, lamp bases, boxes and old trunks are naturals for decorative treatment– marbling, tortoiseshell, sponging.

The number of permutations derived from the basic primary colours is practically endless and some of the technical terms used in describing

Colour vocabulary

The tattered layers of limewash on the wall behind the bewhiskered Victorian worthy could well date back to the time when this 18th century Dublin terrace house was built.

them can be confusing. Hue for instance is what differentiates one colour from another – redness, blueness, and so on. It is used interchangeably with colour. The purity of a colour is its intensity, or the absence of grey in it. Pigment is what paint is coloured with, the raw material. Until the discovery of aniline dyes in the last century, pigments were made from natural substances, though these were often treated chemically to produce further colours. The oldest pigments were natural clays, found in different parts of the world, and refined, and powdered. Nowadays most pigment is either wholly or partly chemical in origin.

Primaries are the colours from which all other colours can be derived – red, blue and yellow. Two primaries mixed together give a secondary colour – red and yellow make orange, yellow and blue make green, blue and red make purple. Two secondaries mixed give a tertiary colour – orange and purple make russet, purple and green make olive. A tint is the result of adding white to a colour, while a shade is the result of adding black. Tone is used to describe lighter or deeper versions of the same colour. Thus a deeper tone of red would be crimson, a lighter tone pink. Value is sometimes used interchangeably with tone. Complementary colours are colours that when added together in equal proportions produce a neutral shade – for example, yellow and blue, magenta and green, red and blue-green – they are to be found at opposite points of a colour wheel. Some knowledge of all this is useful when making up paints from a limited range of stainers or acrylic colours. Mixing a little of one complementary colour with another has a softening effect – thus a little green mixed into a red will take the heat out of it, and vice versa. Any commercial paint colour that is too harsh can be softened by adding a little of the opposite shade on the colour wheel.

A useful division of colours from a decorator's point of view is into warm colours – those tending toward or containing yellow or red – and cool or cold colours – those inclining toward or containing blue. However, this division is not so straightforward as it might first appear. There are warm blues (those with red or yellow in them, like indigo or duck egg blue) and cool reds (those with blue in them, like cerise), while almost every colour you can think of can be given a warm or cool cast by adding a little red,

Qualities of colour

Texture again is foremost in this detail of a colourwashed wall surface, only instead of resulting from 200 years of noble decay, this effect is the contemporary product of watery colour applied in a painterly fashion. Paint is used here to accentuate the grainy texture and bumpy surface of a rough plastered wall, and would make a superb background for rustic furniture and natural textures.

yellow or blue as the case may be. Even white tends to have a blue or yellow cast, depending on its pigmentation, and this can affect any colour you mix with it. Thus the 'brilliant white' paints sold everywhere today nearly always contain a high proportion of blue, to make the white look whiter, and are therefore to be avoided as a base for mixing other colours.

Most people know that warm colours cheer up bleak, north-facing rooms, and that light tints of the same colours make dark rooms look brighter too. The brighter warm colours are sometimes called 'advancing' colours – orange, red, yellow, magenta, emerald – as they seem to bring surfaces optically closer. The cold colours – dark green, blue, grey, purple – are 'retreating' colours, giving walls depth when they are dark, and a light, cool airy feel in their lighter tints. Colour preferences are highly subjective, but on the whole warm colours are easier to live with, and easier to mix together successfully. There is something high-strung and formal about many cool colours – sharp, pale blues, greens, pinks and cerises – which seem to demand lots of fancy plasterwork and stiffly elegant furniture. But a clever mixture of the two is often very effective. A splash of ice blue, blue-pink or lilac can refine warm earth colours in the brown, russet, ochre range, while the colder blues and greens cry out for a bit of red, a strong Chinese yellow, or a rich brown. For ideas, look at such masterly examples of polychrome decoration as Persian and Moorish tiles, oriental rugs and batiks. The quest for the one colour that will make a room sparkle is one of the fascinations of decoration.

Colour media An important aspect of colour is the way it changes character according to the medium, or vehicles, with which it is combined. Colours in a medium that dries flat, without shine or the slight 'fatness' given by oil or synthetic resins, look quite different from the same colours mixed in a high-gloss medium or one that dries to a sheen. People make the mistake of trying to reproduce colourful folk designs in today's 'fatter' paints. These never come across as vividly as the originals, which were invariably done in a thin, flat, dry-textured medium, the simplest linseed oil paint or, often, distemper. I have got close to these folk textures by using acrylics in water, ground pigment in linseed oil and in turpentine (which counteracts the oil), universal stainers [tinting colours] in undercoat or matt emulsion [latex].

Colour made transparent, by thinning it with water, or oil, or varnish, produces another effect again. Some colours are inherently more transparent to begin with – raw and burnt sienna, raw umber, Vandyke brown, Prussian blue, ultramarine, crimson and scarlet lake, viridian green, for example. All these are excellent for colouring transparent oil-based glaze (see pages 223–24), or for tinting varnish.

Pure white Other colours pass in and out of favour, but white, plus all its variations, will always remain many people's first choice. It goes with everything whatever the colour or style of furnishing or decoration, and its reflective qualities make dark places lighter and small places appear larger.

Pure white looks best under a brilliant sun when its reflectiveness is fresh and dazzling, but its character changes dramatically in the northerly light of colder climates. It can look bleak and chilly, unless warmed and enlivened by strong colours and friendly textures. With pure white, it is essential that the paint is thick. Three coats is the decorator's minimum requirement, and perfectionists claim that between five and nine coats, depending on time and inspiration, give a white of pristine perfection. But it must be a white white, not the commercial 'brilliant white', which contains a tinge of blue.

Most people, however, find off-whites easier to live with as they provide a better foil to furnishings and pictures – offering the luminosity of pure white without its chilliness. Off-whites are a large and varied family, consisting of all the tones that can possibly be achieved by adding a little of this or that colour to basic white. The most appealing off-whites are the warm pearly, or cool silvery, ones. Warm off-white shades are produced by mixing in a little yellow, red or warm brown. Silvery off-whites are achieved by mixing in a tiny amount of one of the many blacks available (ivory or lampblack for preference), plus a tinge of blue or a cold earth shade such as raw umber. An infinitesimal amount of tinting colour has a disproportionate effect – hardly visible in the can, it throws a subtle glow or shadow on the walls which can alter the character of a room.

Shades of white

Some of the most popular paint effects are the ones which combine whites with off-whites to give a discreetly luxurious surface – pale but not passive. Warm creamy white mixed in an oil glaze and ragged or rag-rolled over a plain (but not 'brilliant') white, gives a delicate vellum or parchment finish, which is a wonderful flattering foil to other colours and textures, and looks good in rooms of slightly formal quality.

A different sort of sophistication results from mixing textures as well as tones. For instance, stencilling an overall pattern in matt white over shiny off-white and vice versa, produces a damask or brocade effect, which makes a pretty, luxurious finish for a small, feminine room. A simpler way of arriving at a similar contrast would be to use shiny cream (possibly lacquered) on walls and frosty white matt paint on both woodwork and ceiling. Contrasts like these are discreet, not noticeable at first glance, but pleasing to the eye as they gradually become apparent.

While the warm-toned off-whites add liveliness to a room, the cool, silvery ones create a gentle, Quakerish calm, especially suited to eighteenth-century rooms, or panelled rooms with interesting joinery.

The late John Fowler, doyen of British twentieth-century decorators, favoured the use of 'dirty whites', in two, three or more subtly graduated shades, for accentuating the different planes and mouldings of traditional joinery. The magical quality of his work came from his use of lighter shades on prominent surfaces, darker ones on recessive surfaces, and intermediate shades on intervening mouldings. A similar effect can be achieved using three shades of opaque flat colour, or three tones of glaze dragged over the same white base.

Walls

W alls not only define and shape the given space that is a room, they also make up the largest surface area, so that what you add to them in the way of colour, pattern or texture is bound to have a considerable effect. Too many people, however, make the mistake of thinking that treating the walls to the most lavish finish they can afford – handprinted wallpaper, adhesive-backed felt, pine cladding or panelling – will make the room come together and look good, regardless of shabby furniture and ill-assorted carpet and curtains. What happens in fact is that the room appears unbalanced and uneasy, with the favoured walls making themselves oppressively felt. Furthermore, should the lavish finish turn out to be an expensive mistake, which can happen even to old hands at the game, you are stuck with it. A wall finish should be cheap enough to let you approach decisions about colour and texture in a relaxed frame of mind, which is the state most likely to produce the right decisions. And it should be flexible, so that if the colour does turn out to be wrong for the room, or just difficult to live with, you can retrieve your mistake without too much labour. What is more, you should be able to change it all quite easily every few years – walls get a lot of wear and tear and one's tastes alter.

The short answer, as you may have guessed, is to stick with the time-tested, traditional solution to all these problems: paint. Paint is the most practical, the most flexible, and, I am increasingly convinced, the most interesting, beautiful, and, in some mysterious way, the most appropriate way to cover a wall. 'There is no limit to what you can do with paint', a master-decorator friend is fond of saying. I don't think the claim is exaggerated. By paint, you must understand, he does not mean simply the standard 3 coats of emulsion [latex] paint with which most of us are familiar. Emulsion paints are useful of course, but sticking with them exclusively does limit the range of decorative possibilities. Paint imaginatively and knowledgeably used, as it is by a professional decorator (in the manner of an artist rather than a do-it-yourself expert), can be made to produce a quite breathtaking range of effects – subtle, extraordinary colours, textures and patterns.

One advantage of not being an expert (that is, someone who trained as a decorative painter and who also has considerable experience of working professionally) is that one can approach the subject unhampered by tradition and come up with some unorthodox ideas. In the various dry and technical treatises I have read I have never seen it mentioned that most of the finishes I shall be describing go on more rapidly than a conventional paint job, that they give an elegant effect for a ridiculously small outlay, or that doing them is engrossing, even exhilarating. Nor is it mentioned that you don't need to use specialized equipment – improvised tools and materials can produce equally good results, though perhaps at some sacrifice of slickness and speed. And none of the books emphasize what to me was the most surprising discovery about these finishes – that they are not at all difficult to do. Possible exceptions are the higher flights of trompe l'oeil and mural painting, although even there you can bring off

Previous page Stencilled designs, especially ones as gutsy as these, often look most effective on walls with a distressed finish. Here, two thin gouache washes, each a vivid but slightly different orange, were slapped loosely over one another above a white emulsion [latex] base, to produce a deliberately brushy effect. The stencilling on top is a modern version of an 18th-century wallpaper pattern.

unexpected successes if you are not over-ambitious, and cheat a bit.

Learning to use these techniques has other, practical advantages. The more you know about decorating, the more powerful (in the sense of being able to control your environment) and independent you become. Take choosing a colour, for instance: knowing what to use to make your own colours opens up exciting possibilities. You can mix up colour to match or complement a favourite picture or rug, play about with different glazes to create a totally new and personal colour effect, blend woodwork colour to match walls, or add a squeeze of this and that to transform a commercial paint that turned out five shades brighter then you expected. It's a nice feeling to know that with a tin of suitable white paint – or a pot of transparent oil glaze [glazing liquid], if you can get it – and a battery of stainers [tinting colours] you can achieve just about any colour scheme.

As you go along you pick up all sorts of useful decorator's tricks. You find that some finishes make a room look larger, or sunnier, while others give the meanest little box of a place a sumptuous air. Try a rosy sponged-marble effect in a bathroom, or a tortoiseshell one in a cramped corridor. If too many cupboards and doors are the problem, 'lose' them by dragging them to match the walls. You can emphasize good proportions by stencilling an elegant border in a contrasting colour at ceiling level, above the skirting or baseboard, round doors and windows. Or, conversely, if achingly empty expanses of wall are the problem, break them up visually with stencilled borders at chair-rail height, or borders and motifs painted to suggest panelling. A fine collection of old prints, photographs – any pictures in fact – gain enormously in significance when hung on walls dragged two ways to suggest coarsely woven silk. It is a fact that 'distressed' colour finishes are more flattering than solid colour as a background to polished wood, gilt, rich colours and textures.

Versatility is the keynote to these finishes. If you are going for a cottagey freshness and simplicity, they can be as artless and understated as you like. Colourwashing – applying transparent coloured washes blurrily over white – is one of the prettiest and airiest effects I know; dragging or stippling gentle colours on a white ground looks appealing too. Alternatively, by applying several layers of different coloured glazes on top of each other, you can achieve a lustrous colour which would not look out of place in a Venetian palazzo.

Most of the techniques I shall be describing are traditional, and have been used by decorators as well as artists for centuries, although as yet they seem not to have percolated through to the do-it-yourself level, remaining part of the repertoire of exclusive interior decorators. I only became aware of the more recherché uses of paint by accident when I came across a painter in the middle of dragging a room and questioned him about what he was up to. It looked simple enough, and the result was so attractive that I was fired with enthusiasm to find out more. The result – some years later and after much experiment – is this book, which I hope will leave readers better informed to tackle this most fascinating aspect of interior decoration than I was on my first attempt.

Making good and preparation

There is no denying the fact that conscientious preparation pays off, ensuring a longlasting, professional-looking paint surface. Top decorating firms allow considerably longer for 'prepping' than for the final paint treatment. Thorough preparation means that repainting later will be much less onerous. Amateurs are perfectly capable of matching professional standards if they can spare the time and don't begrudge the physical effort or domestic disruption, but if you just want a rapid colour change, or a quick upgrading of your surroundings, you may prefer to settle for less than perfect underpinnings.

A decent minimum

Washing down painted surfaces and filling are the two basic minimum requirements of a respectable redecorating job. Washing down ensures that surfaces are cleared of grease, dust and dirt, all of which would interfere with the bonding of new paint, while filling cracks, holes, chips and other blemishes gives a sound, streamlined foundation for your work. Rooms in reasonable condition will need little more than this. Tougher measures may be indicated, however, if the plasterwork is crumbly or the paint on woodwork or mouldings is layers thick and really unsightly. A heat stripper [heat gun] gets rid of old paint with less mess than blow torches or chemical solvents and the hard work is rewarded by newly smooth surfaces and crisp detailing.

Old whitewash or distemper, usually on ceilings, can be dealt with in two ways. It can be repainted, using the same kind of paint – see page 210

More of an allusion to stone than a serious imitation of it, this elegant finish with its random spatter and discreet blockwork depends for its effect on perfectly smooth walls, filled, sanded, primed and undercoated to exacting professional standards.

for information here. Or, where you wish to switch to an emulsion [latex] paint, it should be scrubbed off with a scrubbing brush and warm water, and sealed with a stabilizing sealer. Emulsion paint will not adhere properly to old powdery paint surfaces.

Washing down

Where possible, clear the room of furniture, curtains, pictures and picture hooks, mirrors and so forth. If taking up the carpet is too difficult, try to roll it back from the skirtings [baseboards] and cover with plastic dust sheets. Begin by sucking up as much dust as possible with a vacuum cleaner attachment, paying special attention to picture rails, cornices, the top of cupboards, and door and window architraves. Use a broom to clear any cobwebs. Make up a bucketful of hot water plus a little ammonia, soda crystals or standard cleaning fluid to cut grease, and use a large sponge to swab down paintwork on walls and woodwork, starting at the top and working downwards, and changing the water frequently. Rinse with clean water if the surfaces are really dirty. Clean the ceiling as well. Open the windows, leave some heating on and let the room dry overnight. The surfaces will now be ready for filling.

Papered walls

Wallpaper makes a satisfactory base for paint as long as it is well stuck down and sound. Simply brush down to clean, paste back any loose edges, and level holes or gaps with filler [spackle] – see below. Wallpaper in tatters is best removed with a steam stripper, but be prepared to find crumbly plaster beneath.

Patching plaster

Remedying seriously defective plaster is a job best left to a professional, but the odd holes – even quite sizable ones – can usually be patched up with a proprietary all-purpose filler [spackle]. Lining paper can rescue plaster which is beginning to go, providing a taut clean surface for decoration. Fill any holes first and sand them flat, then paste on the paper with butt joins, and brush a thin coat of decorators' glue size over the paper to seal it before painting.

Rubbing down paintwork

Gloss painted surfaces need rubbing down with abrasive paper before repainting, especially if a water-based paint is being applied. This roughens the surface and gives the paint something to grip onto. Aluminium oxide paper or wet-or-dry sandpaper used with water will speed an arduous job. You should rub down gloss paintwork even if you are repainting with a gloss or oil-based eggshell paint, and wash it down thoroughly using an extra strong cleaning agent such as sugar soap.

Filling

Use an interior grade of all-purpose filler [spackle] to fill all cracks, chips and holes. Brush out loose material to make sure the filler will bond. Mix the powder with water to a smooth but stiffish consistency, and fill with a metal scraper, overfilling to counteract the shrinkage as it dries. Sand level with walls when dry, and spot seal with emulsion [latex] or undercoat. Filling gaps between walls and skirtings [baseboards] or door and window frames is time consuming but yields a visible improvement. Professional decorators are adept at gauging the proper consistency of filler [spackle] for this (a little sloppier than you might think) and at smoothing the filler with a damp rag at just the right moment, after it has begun to harden but before it is too dry – test by running your finger along first. Alternatively, get yourself a caulking gun, which operates rather like a cake icing nozzle and bag.

Applying undercoat and primer

When using emulsion [latex] paints on previously emulsioned walls, there is no need for a special undercoat, unless a radical colour change is involved. Usually two coats of the new colour will give a sufficiently opaque cover; three coats may be needed when applying a pale over a dark colour. Use an oil-based undercoat under oil-based or alkyd paints. Consult your dealer over the most suitable undercoat for the new water-based eggshell paints. For speed, you can apply by roller (see page 228), using a brush for the top and bottom of the walls.

Before painting with emulsion new plaster can be primed with a fast drying acrylic primer or with a proprietary primer sealer or simply with thinned decorators' size to reduce absorption and make the paint go further. Emulsions or distempers are the only paints suitable for new plaster; for any other paints the plaster must be six months old or the residual moisture will cause flaking and other problems.

Painting

An oil-based eggshell, or the newer water-based eggshell, remains the preferred and most efficient ground for any oil-based glaze work, because it is less absorbent and thus allows the glaze to stay 'open' and malleable for longer. Emulsion [latex] paint is too porous, consuming vastly more glaze over the same area, though I have found vinyl silk emulsion to be a satisfactory compromise. The highest quality work is still done with a brush, but rollers undoubtedly save time and muscle power. These are, however, better suited to emulsion [latex] than oil-based paints.

Equipment

You will need: an appropriate roller and tray (see page 228) or decorators' brush (wide enough to speed application, but not so large and heavy it tires you to handle it); a small brush for cutting in; a light aluminium stepladder; plastic paint kettle; rag for wiping up spills; plastic or cotton dust sheets; a dusting brush.

Method

Decant paint into the plastic kettle or roller tray rather than working from the tin; not only is this lighter to hold, but less paint is exposed to the air this way. Spread dust sheets over the floor. Make sure the stepladder is stable. Start painting from the top corner of a window wall. Don't overload the brush or roller; two thinner coats are still preferable to one thick one. When using a brush, hold it by the handle for emulsion [latex] paints, by the stock for the thicker, more resistant oil paints.

Cover the wall area a block at a time, moving down and then across. As one patch of wall is painted move on down to the next, brushing it into the first. Painting should always be done methodically, but speedily, to keep the 'wet edge' going so that one patch doesn't begin to dry before you can get around to blending the edges in with the next. If you have to break off before finishing a room, try to stop in a corner, so that there is no obvious join when you start painting again. A first coat can be quite sketchy because the second will even things out. Try for a smooth texture, however, softening pronounced brushmarks with a nearly dry brush (wipe it on a rag) or rollering in all directions to spread paint evenly.

Walls are painted after ceilings but before woodwork. It is usually quicker to 'touch out' colour that has strayed onto a ceiling with the ceiling paint afterwards, than to stop short of the ceiling and tidy up with a smaller brush. Always allow one coat to dry thoroughly before applying the next. When using oil-based paints, rub the surfaces down lightly when dry with a fine grade abrasive paper to remove 'nibs' or flecks of dust trapped in the paint. This is particularly important for a superfine finish and 'faux lacquer' effect.

Varnishing

To varnish or not to varnish is a question that worries many people exceedingly. There are no hard and fast rules, other than those suggested by common-sense considerations. Decoratively painted woodwork is commonly varnished on the assumption that it will need wiping down often and get rougher treatment. The more fragile wall finishes, either glazed or colourwashed, last longer if protected by a varnish. One or two coats of matt or mid-sheen clear alkyd is the usual choice over oil glaze work. Over the popular 'washy' water-based effects, a coat of clear matt alkyd or an emulsion glaze which comes in a matt finish, gives some protection without spoiling the airy, chalky look which is their special charm. Alternatively, you may prefer to settle for repainting more often. Polyurethane varnish provides the toughest protection but gradually yellows and darkens, which matters over pale colours or wherever you might need to shift pictures around frequently. Hallways, kitchens and bathrooms take a beating one way or another, and are probably better off given one or two coats of a tougher polyurethane varnish. (See pages 214–15 for more information on varnishes.)

Whatever varnish you choose there are some rules for successful application. Use a clean, soft varnish brush or 'glider' kept for this purpose alone. Thin the first varnish coat with the appropriate solvent (white spirit [mineral spirit] or water) in roughly 3:1 proportions. Check that the room is as dust-free as you can make it, cleaned and vacuumed first, then when you have finished, shut off the room until the varnish is dry. Try not to leave 'skips' (unvarnished areas) and check the walls in a good light. Varnish, even matt varnish, looks wet and shiny on first application so skips are easy to spot. Any varnishing will look better lightly smoothed over with fine abrasive paper when hard dry to remove the inevitable grit, dust, and hairs that get trapped in the surface.

Special Paint Finishes

The most interesting development in decorative painting over the past few years is undoubtedly the rise in prestige of those effects based upon different ways of applying and tinting plaster. The most prominent craftsmen specializing in this work are nearly all Italian, Italy having a tradition of skilled use of plaster reaching back to Roman times and beyond. It is only fair to say that the resurgence of interest in these wall finishes has much to do with their exclusivity. Though the materials used, such as lime plaster, powdered pigment, beeswax and so forth, are readily available (if you know where to go), the secrets of application are not. And even if they were, most people would be deterred by the sheer physical effort involved in trowelling on plaster, never mind the need to hack away at existing surfaces to create the right conditions for a reliable bonding between old and new plaster.

Despite these real drawbacks I still think it is useful to know something about these recondite finishes: they are interesting in themselves and have a beauty and integrity that may persuade more people to embark on serious study and research into their application today. Moreover – and this is the nub for the amateur decorator – their combination of purity and depth of colour with subtle textural variations points the way decorative painting is moving today. These qualities can only be successfully realized when the original process is understood.

There exists considerable confusion over the meaning of the term fresco, which in Italian simply means 'moist' or 'fresh', in this context referring to the dampness of the freshly applied lime plaster on which the pigments were applied. From ancient times onwards, the technique was widely used for mural decoration, for its beauty, simplicity and permanence, so that the word 'fresco' has become almost interchangeable with painted mural decoration, at least among laymen.

Buon or true fresco describes one technique only, where lime-compatible pigment in powder form of absolute purity, is mixed with water and painted onto freshly applied and finely textured lime plaster. On wet plaster the watered pigment glides off the brush, such is the absorbency of the base. A base coat of coarse lime plaster, known as the *arriccio* was applied first; the late medieval and early Renaissance masters of fresco, Giotto, Masaccio and others, roughed out their mural schemes in charcoal and red pigment on this surface. Then the second layer of plaster, using finer sand and more lime putty and known as the *intonaco*

Fresco

Buon fresco

Pure and vivid colours juxtaposed under the Mexican sun. The extraordinary scumbled texture of the blue exterior wall was arrived at by applying three successive layers of blue paint, washing some of the colour off again each time.

was trowelled over the base coat. Only a relatively small area of *intonaco* was applied daily; this area was known as the *giornata*, and might be a metre square or more, depending on the delicacy of execution needed. A madonna's head, with its gold-leafed aureole, might require a whole day, whereas a much larger area of straightforward drapery or background could be completed in the same time, often with the help of apprentices.

To modern eyes, the revelation of the fresco technique in this its simplest form is the astonishing beauty of colour which results, so clean and pure as to be almost incandescent, but relieved from inhuman perfection by the minute variations in the *intonaco* surface. The brilliance of the colour has to do with several factors – the purity of the powder pigment itself; the fact that the lime surface on which it is applied dries naturally to a dazzling whiteness, so creating a reflective base without equal; and the manner in which the wet pigment is sucked into and bonds with the drying plaster.

A fresco finish can last 2,000 years, though this hardly recommends it to the modern interior decorator, given the speed with which clients weary of any scheme devised for them. If, as a devotee of pure colour, you do feel moved to try fresco work, you will need to find an adventurous plasterer and to start with an old and dilapidated shell of a room, hacked back to brick or stone masonry, or stripped down to lime plaster on laths. From here you could create a lime plastered room onto which pigments can be brushed quite plainly, with perhaps a simple contrasting border top and bottom. If you have artistic skills you might attempt a more elaborate scheme, maybe inspired by the fresco painting which survives from Roman Pompeii, where marble dadoes, trompe l'oeil niches, swags and draperies and other visual conceits were used to expand and elaborate on the neutral architectural spaces. Marbling on lime plaster works remarkably well, as the Romans discovered; while the plaster is moist the crude veining can be trowelled further, to produce adventitiously softened and blended effects, which nonetheless dry with a pure brilliance that lends them extraordinary presence and dignity.

Mezzo fresco and fresco secco

In cool, damp northern climates a freshly plastered room's surface can be kept suitably moist for up to two weeks, according to fresco painters working in these conditions today, but in the Mediterranean it often happened that the *giornata* surface quickly dried to a point where it no longer absorbed colour cleanly and evenly. In these situations fresco painters resorted to other expedients. The first was *mezzo fresco* where the same pigments were diluted in 'lime water', the clear liquid that settles on a body of slaked lime, best used while the plaster was still on the moist side. Although less integrated than *buon fresco* colours, these applications were still to some extent absorbed into and bonded with the surface. *Fresco secco* is the term used for any work done on dried lime plaster surfaces, for which the usual medium used historically was egg tempera, where egg yolk was mixed with dry pigment. *Fresco secco* was used to apply the blue pigments lapis lazuli and ultramarine, because these were adversely affected when used on wet lime plaster, the colour darkening and becoming discoloured. It was also used for details, highlights and other additions which were applied once the whole work could be seen and evaluated. Sadly, the blues, such an essential note in medieval fresco work, being *secco* and therefore more fragile, have suffered most from time and wear, leaving so many Madonna and Child subjects bereft of their original colouring.

Faux fresco

It seems a pity that we should not be able to enjoy something of the quality of true fresco without going to the lengths of a complete replastering job. This is a challenge which has exercised many decorative painters, myself included, and we have come up with 'effects' of varying degrees of complexity, which convey something of the subtle flow of colour which is luminous, yet matt and a touch chalky, of the ancient *buon fresco* method. The techniques are chiefly borrowed from the *fresco secco* method. They are all done with water-based paints, for although it is also possible to imitate the fresco look with oil-based media the colour is not so pure and tends to alter over time.

Watercolours on a skim coat

One simulated fresco effect decorators have been experimenting with, and which gives something of the requisite chalky colour and texture without going to the lengths of replastering, consists of applying a 'skim' coat of various plaster-type substances to create a 'thirsty' surface which takes up watercolour like blotting paper.

An easy 'skim' compound for amateurs to handle is a standard filler, [spackle] mixed up with water to a creamy consistency and skimmed over the existing wall plaster with a trowel and metal scraper.

Preparation

The existing walls should be well washed down to remove grease and grime; glossy paint may need sanding to create tooth for the skim coat, but fillers are obligingly adhesive and will spread out thinly and smoothly (though some people prefer a bit of roughness in the texture) without further assistance in the way of sizing, primer or undercoat.

Materials

Standard filler [spackle]; plasterer's trowel; metal scraper; paint kettle or other container for skim mixture; abrasive paper; face mask; colour pigments in powder form or gouache or acrylic colours; a selection of artists' brushes for the decorative painting; stepladder.

Method

A disadvantage of filler in this context is its drying speed; don't make up a bucketful, or you will find it setting solid before you have covered one wall. Make up enough to fill a small paint kettle to start with, scoop it onto the wall surface with a plasterer's trowel and use this together with the scraper to spread it out thinly as far as it will go. 'Thinly' means 2–3 mm, [$\frac{1}{12}$–$\frac{1}{8}$ in], just thick enough to obliterate the previous surface and give a fine new one. With a little practice you will find the skim goes on as fast as paint.

Above Applied colour and wall surface are totally integrated in the ancient technique of *buon fresco* in which pure pigment dissolved in water is brushed onto wet lime plaster. As the plaster dries the colour bonds with it to create the most durable but also the most visually satisfying of all painted surfaces.

The samples shown here were painted in earth colours of absolute purity in the *buon fresco* method. A limited palette of colours are compatible with lime and thus suitable for *buon fresco*. Certain colours, such as the blue derived from lapis lazuli,

could only be added once the plaster was dry, and was applied in the technique known as *fresco secco* in which the pigment is bound with egg yolk.

Opposite, above Pompeiian ruins again serve as an inspiration for a mural in the fresco style painted by a young American decorative artist. She has worked out her own method of simulating *buon fresco* using acrylic colour on new white plaster skim (see page 32). When dry, the 'fresco' is lightly distressed with abrasive papers.

Opposite, below Pigments, plasters, soaps and waxes are just some of the traditional ingredients used by an Italian craftsman based in London. With these he and his team create an impressively varied range of surfaces which can be applied to materials as diverse as concrete and plywood. Many of his 'surfaces' derive from stucco techniques, relying only on depth of colour and subtly variegated texture for their effect, but this pomegranate motif is part of an atypically complex scheme using stencils and many soft colours for a look of old embroidery.

It is easy to create a roughened, old plaster surface if you want that. Simply ease up on the trowelling and scraping, leaving slight bumps and 'cracks' for instant age. Conversely, if you want an extra-smooth skim coat, you can abrade it with a sanding block (abrasive paper wrapped round a small chunk of wood) in just the same way as when filling cracks. But the fall-out will be considerable. Wear a mask and overalls, and run the suction attachment of your vacuum cleaner frequently.

When the skim coat is dry, you are ready to apply colour and/or decoration. The simplest, most authentic form of colour is pigments in dry, powder form, obtainable from good artists' suppliers (see page 233). These are used dissolved in water, and applied with soft brushes of varying size, depending on whether you want to cover the whole area with colour or build up some applied decoration with fine brushwork. The colour will dry several shades lighter. Once dry, further watercolour can be brushed on top to create deeper tones, patterns and so on. It is best to practise effects first on a skim coated board, or in a corner which will be hidden by furniture.

Gouache and acrylic colours, both of which can be diluted in water, may be used instead of dry pigments.

Other types of skim coating

A young American painter (see acknowledgements, page 240) has evolved her own faux fresco method based on a ready-mixed substance known in the USA as 'jointing compound'. This is trowelled and spread on walls or plywood panels in just the same way, but has the advantage compared with filler [spackle] that it will not set hard so rapidly and needs no mixing. She photocopies her design onto clear acetate sheet and uses an overhead projector to project it onto the wall area before lightly drawing out the design with coloured chalk. She has used this approach successfully to create mural designs based on wall paintings at Pompeii that were originally executed in fresco. She uses dry pigment in water for authenticity, and deliberately creates a slightly distressed roughness on the skim coat.

The closest UK equivalent to jointing compound is one of the proprietary textured finishes, available either in powder form or (more expensively) ready mixed. Though these are normally associated with systematically textured surfaces obtained by combing or stippling the material while still wet, they can also be applied smoothly using the trowel and scraper method described above. The chief disadvantage of this material is the difficulty of getting it off again, should you want to, as, when set, it is much harder than filler. On the other hand, properly applied, what it offers is a hard, compacted surface not unlike traditional stucco (the plaster or cement used to coat the outside walls of a house).

Coloured skim and plaster finishes

An interesting alternative to the effects described above is to mix the skim compound itself with pigment. In the sense that the colour becomes part of the skim coat, this in some respects more nearly resembles true *buon fresco*, though the colour achieved will not have the same luminosity. But people who like the honesty of unpainted plaster – and many do – are likely to find this approach appealing. There is something 'real' about built-in as opposed to brushed-on colour. The main snag is the difficulty of controlling the colour, as tinted plaster while wet is many shades darker than it is once dry. Some practice runs are clearly required here, using sample boards and varying proportions of pigment to skimming compound.

Method

Dry colour can be added by spoonfuls to the powder before combining it with water to make your skim. Acrylic colour should be added to the mixing water. In either case mix well to distribute the colour evenly. Remember how quickly this substance hardens, and only mix up a bowlful at a time, making a careful note of the proportions of colour to filler. Then apply with a trowel and scraper as above.

This approach need not be limited to skim made up of filler [spackle], but can also be extended to ordinary plaster. If you are employing a professional plasterer you will be able to arrive at an integrated colour by mixing pigment into the finishing coat before he applies it. But you will need a sympathetic plasterer, tolerant of unfamiliar procedures, and some time spent experimenting with colour beforehand. It is also important that the plasterer uses decorators' white plaster, rather than the commonly chosen 'pink thistle', for the finishing coat. Try out various colour mixes and leave them to dry before deciding. Earth colours, ochres, siennas and umbers are all authentic and pleasing as tints.

The mixed-up colour will seem almost to vanish as the plaster dries out, but it can be magically summoned forth again by applying a thin coat of soft white wax on top and burnishing this lightly with a soft cloth. This final waxing can also be used with the skim coat of standard filler, and will have an equally dramatic effect on its colour. In both cases the waxing will create a soft sheen, not unlike the texture of what Italians call *stucco lucida* or polished stucco.

Rubbed finishes

Colour can be rubbed onto, or off, walls to give further variants on the 'fresco' look. Rubbed on colour can be layered, colour on colour, to give greater richness of tone, and more options as to the final result. Suddenly tiring of my own pink rubbed walls I rubbed over the pink with a brownish red oil glaze [glazing liquid], to give a pleasing terracotta shade, matt and cloudy in texture. Rubbing off is both more arduous and less predictable – you need to make a sample board or patch of wall – but because the colour that remains is driven right into the plaster, it creates an interestingly grainy surface and mysterious bloom of colour that looks as old as Knossos wall painting. The two techniques are quite different.

Rubbed on colour

This goes faster, and gives greater control, done over a slippery base paint. A professional would choose an eggshell base, but I have used vinyl silk emulsion [latex], which is easier and quicker to apply for DIY

33

Above An easy way to evoke a sense of ancient fresco work is to paint large-scale patterns and borders with large bits missing as in this Italian villa. It is a case of knowing what to leave out as much as what to put in.

Right A faithful but spirited evocation of Pompeiian fresco has been achieved here with watercolour on white plaster over a backing of hessian [burlap]. Cracks and worn patches were deliberately introduced to soften and age the finish, using abrasive papers, scrapers and anything else that came to hand.

painters, with complete success. Any colours can be used, though those in the fresco range (see page 30) are particularly beautiful.

Materials Vinyl silk emulsion [latex] or eggshell paint as a base colour for walls; oil glaze [glazing liquid]; a little white undercoat; small container for holding the glaze; artists' oil colours, universal stainers [tinting colours] or dry colour which should be dissolved in white spirit [mineral spirit]; soft cotton rags; alkyd varnish; stepladder.

Method For the rubbed colour mixture the trick is to mix up a colour much darker than the final shade you are after, using a basic glaze formula (see page 224) and adding some white undercoat for a chalkier matt look. Tint with artists' oils or universal stainers and, optionally, some dry colour. I find dry colour helps along the required powdery look, but it needs to be very finely ground, and steeped in a little white spirit first. You should wear a mask when handling it, as with all powdery substances.

Have some cards prepared with your basic vinyl silk emulsion [latex] or eggshell wall colour to use as a reference while mixing and testing the rubbed on colour. Use a soft lint-free rag (old sheets, torn up, are ideal) to apply the colour, dabbing it on and immediately spreading it out finely to cover the base with a transparent film of colour. When the depth of colour is satisfactory make sure you have enough glaze. Very little is needed, not more than ½–1 litre [1–2 US pints] to colour a decent sized room. Start on a window wall, in the top corner, working down and across. Try to avoid patchy build-ups of colour and 'skips', or bald patches, standing back to check from time to time. Build-ups can be softened by teasing the colour out further while it is still malleable. 'Skips' can be evened out later by stippling glaze very finely over the bare spots with a brush. A second rubbed coat, especially if it is a deeper shade like my terracotta, will even out most irregularities anyway. Note that colour applied this way will tend to show up cracks, bumps and other imperfections, but this is the way people like their walls to look today, a little battered.

If you feel your first rubbed colour is too thin, you should leave it to harden for several days before rubbing a second coat of the same colour, or of another colour, over the first. If the first rubbed coat threatens to 'lift' while you are applying the next, the solution is to seal it with an isolating coat of extra pale matt alkyd varnish, then apply coat 2 of rubbed colour. This all sounds like a lot of work, but rubbing on is a very quick way to apply colour, much less laborious than painting.

Seal the rubbed colour with alkyd varnish. This allows a further chance to modify the rubbed colour, by slightly tinting the varnish itself. Use artists' oils for this, dissolved in solvent.

Rubbed off colour This discovery came about by accident. A painter friend rollered a terracotta emulsion [latex] onto walls in a passage in my house. It dried to a dark, stifling shade, and the only alternative to painting it out (two or three coats over that particular colour) was to rub it off again, which we did with handfuls of silicone carbide paper. Hard work. But after clearing a large patch we suddenly looked at it with new eyes, and saw that it looked superb just as it was. We used it as the background to a mural of dancing Greek figures. It may seem perverse to put paint on only to rub it off again; but it remains a greatly admired surface. Perhaps one to try over a small space?

My terracotta emulsion went straight over new pink thistle plaster, which being new would absorb more colour. I suggest you choose a colour many shades darker than the one you are after, roller it on and then sand off with sanding blocks. On walls previously painted with many layers of colour, rubbing down will produce surprising and fortuitous effects. To make sure these are acceptable, sand back a patch before you embark on any further repainting and rubbing back. An extra bonus is that the walls will come up wonderfully smooth, excellent for applying any further decoration on. I don't think there is any need to varnish this effect because it is more or less integrated with the plaster. If you feel you must, use the usual clear flat alkyd.

Colourwashing

Colourwashing gives a soft, delicate dapple of watery colour to a wall, suited to countrified rooms and the sort of unpretentious furniture, rustic checks and stripes and sisal matting that people today find congenial. A warm white ground colourwashed in apricot or yellow, gives a sunshiny look to a north-facing or underlit room, while colourwashing in pale blue turns a bright sunny room into a cool underwater place, like the sea with the sun overhead.

Distemper

The medium for this traditional pretty finish is old-fashioned distemper paint, which can be thinned liberally with water, is cheap, and dries to a soft, textured finish without streaking or hard edges. Distemper can be obtained from certain suppliers to the decorating trade (see list of suppliers, page 233). Or, more cheaply, it can be home made from readily available ingredients in the authentic traditional way.

Homemade distemper You will need some whiting, available from builders' merchants, hardware stores and artists' suppliers; it comes in 3 kg [7 lb] bags, or in larger amounts if bought from a wholesale trader. One bag should make sufficient distemper to paint a small room. You will also need rabbit skin glue. Make the glue according to the directions on the packet – they usually specify $\frac{1}{2}$ a kilo [1 lb] of size to 9 litres [9 US quarts] of hot water. Stand the glue container in a pan of hot water and heat slowly – a *bain-marie* arrangement which prevents the glue 'catching'. When warm and runny, it is ready for use.

Other requirements are cold water, a bucket, powder colour for tinting, a medium-sized spoon, and a larger bucket or tub of hot water.

To make your distemper, half fill the smaller bucket with cold water and pour in whiting until it rises to a peak about 100 mm [4 in] above the

Overleaf An attic kitchen in Spitalfields, London, seems a little closer to heaven thanks to the ethereal blue which has been washed over walls and ceiling so they look like a Mediterranean sky. Bands of deeper blue colourwash define windows and a former fireplace alcove. It is airy, insouciant and witty, a long way from the fitted kitchens of the 80s.

surface of the water. Leave it to soak for an hour or two and then stir vigorously to make a smooth paste. Next, dissolve some powder colour in a little cold water to make a concentrated solution and add this, spoonful by spoonful, to the whiting mixture, until you achieve your desired colour. Stir until it is evenly coloured. Now pour in your warmed glue, mixing thoroughly. Your distemper should be the consistency of ordinary thick paint. If it stiffens too much, as the glue becomes cool, stand the bucket in a larger container of hot water to warm it up.

Do not make up more distemper than you can use at a time – it will not keep longer than a day or two. Use the distemper as it is for the ground coat. For a colour wash to go on top, thin it considerably with water to the consistency of milk.

Alternatives to distemper

Other, more easily available methods, give a similar effect, and they are worthwhile experimenting with. One professional decorator's substitute for the old distemper wash is to use a glaze of much thinned flat oil-based paint or undercoat over a trade eggshell base (mid-sheen oil-based paint). This gives a similar transparency of colour, dries to a matt finish, and can be manipulated so as to leave no hard edges or brushmarks.

Another method is to use a wash of emulsion [latex] paint thinned to liquidity with water, painted over a clean, flat emulsion ground. This gives visible brushmarks and plenty of texture.

A third possibility, dear to the heart of some decorators, is to use a wash of pure colour and water, with a tiny amount of emulsion paint to give it just a little body. This gives a super-transparent colour, and lots of texture too; see the photograph on pages 18–19. The colour can be glowingly intense if richer and richer tones are used one on top of the other – working from light to dark red, for instance. Each coat of colour should be left to dry thoroughly before adding another, and slapped on fast to avoid dislodging the previous colour.

My own company, House Style, markets a proprietary colourwash; more information follows on pages 44–5.

Materials for colourwashing

Paints and colours A wash or glaze for colourwashing is thinned a great deal more than those used for the other finishes in the book – about 9 parts water, or solvent, to 1 part paint. The usual ½ litre [1 US pint] of paint should therefore be ample for at least two coats of colourwashing in a small room. See pages 210–213 for types of paint, and 221–226 for instructions on mixing, thinning and tinting washes and glazes.

As usual, oil paints are thinned with white spirit [mineral spirit] and tinted with universal stainers [tinting colours] or artists' oil colours; emulsion [latex] paints are thinned with water and tinted with stainers or artists' gouache or acrylic colours.

Other equipment You will need a bucket for the colourwash mixture – one or two (depending on how many of you there are); wide soft brushes, say 100 or 125 mm [4 or 5 in]; a stepladder; clean rags for mopping up.

The application is the same whatever type of paint you use. Dip your brush into the wash, then slap the colour on loosely and irregularly in all directions, trying to avoid heavy brushmarks and hard edges. Leave a good bit of ground colour uncovered. When it is quite dry repeat the process, brushing over most of the bare patches and also over some of the first coat of colour. This gives nicely varying intensities of colour, and a dappled effect.

Thinned paint of any kind will dry very quickly, but it is probably best to leave each wash overnight to become really dry before applying the next, or you may find you are taking the colour off rather than putting it on. If this happens the bare patches can be rescued by patting on colour with a sponge. Don't be alarmed if a very watery wash runs off copiously to begin with. It may need to be gone over assiduously with a soft brush to persuade it to stick. Put lots of waterproof protection on the floor and expect the first coat to look a mess. The next coat makes a miraculous difference – the colour suddenly comes alive, and the walls knit together with the inimitable radiance that watercolour alone can give.

Varnish A matt, slightly aged and non 'finished' look is the aim with colourwashing, but if you will need to wash the walls, varnish them for protection with a clear, matt alkyd varnish, which barely changes the colour of the paint.

Method

A crossways brush movement for colourwashing counteracts the liquid colour's natural tendency to run straight down the wall.

Proprietary Colourwash effects
Left, from top to bottom Proprietary Colourwash in a vivid yellow wiped over white emulsion [latex] for an instantly sunshiny effect.

Another proprietary Colourwash, Sea Blue, has been wiped thinly over a mid-blue matt emulsion [latex] to give a colour which almost matches the intensity of lapis lazuli.

These 'ancient' walls are the work of a few hours, using complementary shades of proprietary Colourwash, Lettuce Green and Terracotta, brushed over a stone coloured basecoat of emulsion [latex]. The colours neutralize each other and when dry create a mellow dappled effect like weathered stone or old parchment.

Right The washed out colour, like bleached and faded denim, is the result of applying thinned watery colour over a distemper base. The chalk of whiting in distemper drinks up colour like blotting paper, and dries with a powdery bloom ideally suited to old rooms of a rugged, rustic style.

Proprietary Colourwash One of my own products, devised in collaboration with a paint chemist, consists of concentrated transparent water-based colour which has some flexibility in use – it does not 'set off' the moment it hits the wall but can be teased and smoothed for longer than a diluted emulsion [latex]. Its formulation gives it clean and pure colour without any pasty-looking filler content. It is also odourless, and in the USA it is increasingly being used instead of oil glazes [glazing liquids] as a means of colourwashing a room. It is intended to be used sparingly, as a diaphanous colourwash rather than as a transparent paint, and gives the best results when used as a softening, blurry wash of colour over a matt emulsion base coat. The delicate swirl of translucent colour it imparts redeems the dead flatness of an opaque emulsion [latex] paint, lets it 'breathe' visually and adds a depth and glow which is gentle and easy to live with. There is no quicker method of humanizing a modern plastic paint surface, in my experience. And this type of colourwash in particular does have a feeling of fresco about it, though of course it is not authentic. There is a visual link, however. And the deep blue does score over the original fresco work in that, historically, blue was applied in the *secco* method using egg tempera, and so lost some transparency. The deep blue devised for this range of paint therefore seems to me a real addition to the pure wall colours available in a water medium.

Preparation Proprietary Colourwash can be applied over existing wall colours if they correspond to the shades described below, but the surfaces should be washed down to remove, grease, dirt and dust. If filler has been used on cracks or holes it should be sealed with the same base coat, for otherwise these areas will soak up colour differently from the rest of the wall.

Method Colourwash is available in ½ litre [1 US pint] plastic 'kegs'. 1 keg will 'wash' 50 square metres [60 square yards] of wall, applied with a decorator's sponge and smoothed out thinly, using a small standard decorating brush to soften or even up concentrations of colour where necessary. Over a white emulsion [latex] base two applications may be needed, over a coloured base one is usually enough. The paler colours in the range, white, buff and pale yellow, perform well over a warm, broken white base – not brilliant white. The mid-tones in the range are most effective over paler versions of the same shade, and the stronger shades of green and blue look stunning over cold light blues. The terracotta needs an ochre yellow or brick pink.

Starting in the corner of the window wall, apply a reasonably generous splodge of Colourwash straight from the container onto your sponge, and begin wiping on the colour, over as large an area as it can easily cover. Don't pat-pat the wash on, as you would with decorative sponging, but smooth it out to leave a transparent veil of deeper colour. Use the brush to disperse and soften places where the colour builds up. Try not to keep working over and over the same patch. Once the wash sets up or feels touch dry (and this varies with wall surfaces, room temperature and climate) it needs to be left to 'cure' for 24 to 48 hours before a second coat is applied. Curing here involves hardening, so that working over the top does not lift the first coat. Should this happen the remedy is to leave to dry, then stipple the same colour onto the bare patch.

Once you get the knack, the process should skip along. Cover the entire base colour, however thinly. Expect the whole effect to look a touch hectic at first before the wash dries matt and settles down. When you return the next morning you will be agreeably surprised.

Varnishing

I am often asked whether walls colourwashed in this product need varnishing to protect them. As usual the answer is – it depends. Colourwash hardens with time, so that it can be sponged down lightly. Over surfaces that will get considerable handling, like staircase walls, I recommend one coat of the palest matt clear alkyd varnish. Otherwise I prefer to leave the finish unvarnished, as sealing Colourwash tends to impair the delicate chalky texture which is its special charm.

Dragging

A dragged finish consists of controlled brushmarks, usually arranged vertically on walls, while on woodwork and other surfaces they echo the grain of the wood beneath. When a firm brush is 'dragged' through a tinted glaze it creates a finely striped surface with a subtle, slightly 'shot silk' appearance. Dragging looks most at home in well proportioned period rooms, with decent sized skirtings [baseboards] and cornices top and bottom. It is generally considered the most difficult wall finish because of the difficulty of keeping brushstrokes straight down a length of wall and of preventing a build-up of glaze at the start and finish of each stroke. Beginners find a rougher rustic dragging easier, and this can look very decorative too. Other variations on the theme include dragging first vertically, then horizontally (using two successive coats of wet glaze) to give the look of woven fabric, and using a brush with some bristles snipped out, irregularly, to make clumps of stripes of different thickness, like classic pyjama fabrics.

Some people suggest that the technique was developed in colour by the late John Fowler, as an extension of the possibilities of a basic graining procedure. It has also been claimed that dragging imitates the finely ridged surface obtained when brushing on lead paint. On walls it makes a dignified background to paintings and antiques, but latterly dragging seems to have been used chiefly on woodwork, in neutral colours, to make discreet colour contrasts and give a 'finished' appearance.

Colours

Pastel glazes dragged on white, or deeper colours dragged over a pastel base, always look effective. Blue on blue, green on green are popular wall colours, but dragging one colour over another – blue on green or lilac on grey – accentuates the 'shot silk' effect. Unusual colour combinations can also work well – grey-blue over orange, warm brown over light blue; I am fond of dragged red walls, using a darkish tone of red over a warm buff.

Preparation

For the best work, dragging is done in a tinted transparent oil glaze [glazing liquid] over a non-permeable eggshell base, and finished with a colourless alkyd matt varnish for protection. It is possible to drag other types of paint but the traditional formula still gives the most elegant effect. Walls do need to be in good shape for dragging, as it shows up bumps and cracks in an unappealing way. They can either be well filled and sanded before base coating, or lined, sized and base coated.

Materials

Professionals all have their favourite glaze formulae, but one based on a proprietary transparent oil glaze [glazing liquid] tinted with artists' oil colours or universal stainers [tinting colours], thinned copiously with white spirit [mineral spirit] and 'softened' with the addition of a varying amount of standard white undercoat, is widely used. The more undercoat is added in proportion to glaze the softer, chalkier and more matt the pinstripe brushmarks will look. See page 224 for recipes and page 220 for colour mixing instructions. Test out dragged colour schemes on card or paper before launching off, letting them dry before going ahead on the wall, because wet glaze colour calms down a lot as it dries.

   The quantity of oil glaze needed will vary with the absorbency of the base paints. 1 litre [2 US pints] of glaze will be enough for an average-sized room painted with a non-porous eggshell paint. Over vinyl silk and matt emulsion [latex] you should allow for greater absorption – $1\frac{1}{2}$ to 2 litres [3–4 US pints].

Dragging in parchment colour on white makes a soothing foil for the pretty green mouldings painted in trompe l'oeil, which do so much to improve the proportions of a turn of the century drawing room. Note the ingenious conversion of a problematic bay window into a sunny windowseat. The radiator underneath has been concealed behind an unusual cut-out grille painted in with the walls.

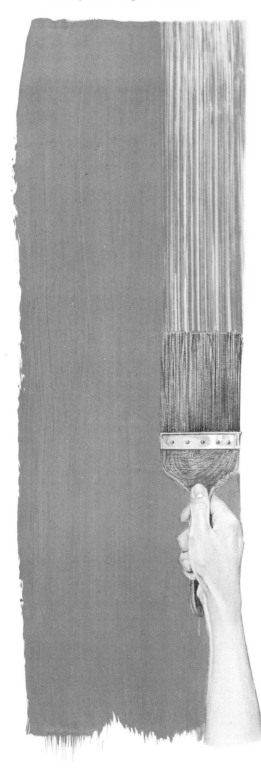

Hold the dragging brush in a firm but relaxed grip, and steadily draw it down through the wet glaze or wash.

Brushes The brush shown is a long-bristled 'flogger', much used in graining. It creates pronounced stripes, but most people find the longer bristles hard to control down the length of a wall, as they offer no resistance to speak of. A 'glider' or varnishing brush is a good alternative. A standard decorating brush, 10 cm [3 or 4 inches] wide, gives enough bristle to press against the glaze and produces fine, clear stripes. For more rustic, irregularly striped effects, a wide paperhanging brush is useful; beginners often feel more comfortable with this, which has shorter, thinner bristles. These are the ones to snip into for pyjama stripes. Being so much wider they make the dragging go faster too.

Other equipment The most important piece of equipment is a sturdy, light aluminium stepladder. To contain the glaze you also need a paint kettle with a wire handle, or a roller tray for the paperhanging type of brush. Rags, newspaper or kitchen roll are essential for wiping excess glaze off the brush now and then.

Method

Experts can drag-paint solo, but two people usually do a more efficient job. One person brushes on the glaze down one strip of wall at a time, usually about 45 cm [18 in] wide, and the other follows behind, immediately brushing down vertically on the still wet glaze to make the characteristic stripes. It is important that the first painter is already applying strip number two, which should just overlap with number one, before the first strip has been dragged, to prevent the glaze hardening up before the 'dragger' can deal with it. The 'wet edge' is especially important to successful dragging, and mistakes are hard to ignore – though, as with all these glazed finishes, hanging pictures and putting back furniture always 'knocks back' irregularities to a secondary plane.

It is important to get the glaze consistency right before starting. If it is too overthinned and runny the stripes will tend to blur and merge again. Correct this by adding a little more oil glaze. Let the glaze 'set up' for up to a minute before dragging, for very distinct stripes; for softer stripes increase the quantity of white undercoat. Too much glaze gives a 'jammy' look which is not attractive, though a slightly jammy glaze is good for the two-way dragging, as it gives a slight three-dimensional texture, like cloth weave. Dragged walls should be almost matt when dry, with the eggshell base well covered, but if you end up with a sheen you dislike, flatten it out with a matt, colourless alkyd varnish, which also gives protection.

The most difficult part of dragging is avoiding a build-up of denser colour at the top and bottom of each stroke, always recognizably the mark of a beginner. The trick is to use the lightest pressure on the brush at the start and finish of each stroke, without fumbling or smudging. This knack comes with practice, of course. One neat way round the problem is to make a positive feature of this colour build-up by painting it as a solid colour band afterwards. Colour which strays onto the ceiling or cornice is best touched out afterwards, but on the woodwork it can be wiped off with a rag by either of the painters involved. To avoid obvious breaks always stop at a corner, not half way across a wall. Wipe the dragging brush frequently on a rag to remove excess glaze. It is helpful to begin dragging where a vertical already exists, at a doorframe or in a corner, for example.

Rather than have two people alternately using the stepladder, it can be simpler and safer to have two ladders, or a lightweight stool. It is extremely difficult to drag even vertical lines without wobble on tall walls, while dragging from cornice to dado is quite manageable. A painted dado could be a solution, where there is no real one. Although with time the glaze itself becomes tough enough to wash down cautiously, professional decorators usually complete dragged walls with a coat of clear matt or mid-sheen alkyd varnish.

Stippling

Stippling has been practised by generations of decorators to soften colours and eliminate brushmarks from painted walls or woodwork. Using a large, fine stippling brush, the painter went over newly applied paintwork closely and quickly to distribute it as evenly as possible, creating a matt, just perceptibly grainy, texture. A decorative stippled finish can be achieved by pressing firmly against an area of thinly applied wet glaze with a stippling brush or soft wad of cloth or a roller, so that the glaze is drawn up into tiny pinpricks of colour, and the ground allowed to 'grin' through. Depending on the tools used, the effect varies from a fine freckle of colour to a soft mottling. Stippled walls make a flattering, uninsistent background to any sort of furnishings.

Brush and pad stippling Brush stippling gives the most delicate, even finish, like the bloom of colour on a peach. It is slow and tiring to do, however, and best reserved, I think, for small areas, woodwork or furniture. The brushes, too, are expensive as brushes go, though an ordinary painters' dusting brush makes a cheap substitute. Stippling with wads of soft cloth gives an effect halfway to rag-rolling, see pages 54–7, but tighter and more uniform.

Roller stippling A mohair roller can be used over wet glaze to create a broken, coarsely stippled effect, very quickly.

Stippling is usually done in transparent colours over a white or light-coloured base coat. Just enough of the base colour shows through to soften and lighten the glaze, so that raspberry red over white will appear as deep pink, coffee brown over cream as *café au lait*, and so on. Pastel colours are attractive and make a good background for stencils.

An interesting variant of the technique, popular in the thirties, was to stipple an opaque coat (usually white or cream) over a bright and shiny base colour, such as scarlet, emerald green or cobalt blue. An opaque coat used in this way is usually called a 'scumble' (not to be confused with the transparent oil glaze sometimes sold as scumble glaze). The effect of tiny

Overleaf Vellum and parchment were buzz words in 1930s decoration, and this interesting pastiche of a 30s interior makes use of stippling in shades of cream to give walls the air of having been papered with squares of vellum. The specially commissioned cabinet has been stippled to match, in handkerchief-sized squares. Aluminium leaf has been laid on the cornice and door frame.

Colours

flecks of shiny colour surfacing through a matt, opaque scumble is an appealing one, but it must be done with a brush and so is probably best kept for furniture – though it is a feasible way of softening a shiny wall finish you have grown tired of. Another thirties trick was to use stippling to blend and shade bands of different wall colour into each other, creating the cloudy pastel effects that were so popular in hotel powder rooms, cinemas and cocktail bars. Overall stippling – a brush would have been used – allows one colour to merge into another gradually and almost imperceptibly, with no demarcation line.

Preparation
Wall surfaces should be sound and reasonably smooth, though bumps and cracks won't be so obvious as with a directional finish such as dragging. It is important, however, that the ground coat be a non-porous paint for the stippling to register effectively and evenly. One coat of oil-based paint with a mid-sheen finish over one of undercoat gives the right kind of base. Roller stippling, being coarser and bolder, can be done over a ground of emulsion [latex] paint, but the results will be patchier since a water-based paint will soak up the glaze unevenly.

Materials for stippling
Glaze Transparent oil glaze [glazing liquid], or a glaze of thinned oil-based flat paint, undercoat or mid-sheen finish (see pages 210–213) can all be used for the stippling coat, depending on whether you want a shiny or matt finish. Exact quantities are difficult to give, but 1½ litres [3 US pints] is enough for a small to average room. Left-over glaze should be stored in a sealed jar for touching up later. For stippling ordinary emulsion [latex] paint, use a sponge. As the paint is brushed on, the sponge is used to break up the surface, which dries to a soft mottled finish. A marine sponge gives the most pleasing, random effect.

Use universal stainers [tinting colours] or artists' oil colours to tint the glaze yourself. See pages 223–24 for instructions on thinning and tinting. Note, glazes made of diluted paint tinted with stainers give a slightly different effect from tinted transparent oil glaze. They look softer, muzzier and less glowing, because of the white pigment on which most paints are based.

Tools These depend on which type of stippling you have decided upon. Stippling brushes come in various sizes, the largest being the most time-saving for wall treatments. A roller should be the textured variety, lambswool, mohair (or synthetic equivalent) or coarse polystyrene, *not* the smooth foam sort. These are so cheap that you may think it worth buying a couple of detachable roller heads to save time cleaning off the build-up of glaze. Stippling with a cloth wad offers plenty of scope for experiment. Using rags of different textures gives different effects – a soft finish with muslin, net curtains, glass curtains, or old sheeting; a crisper look with hessian, burlap, or sacking. Whichever you start with, make sure you have a plentiful supply, because the cloth pads will get hard with paint and have to be jettisoned fairly often, and changing the type of cloth halfway will give a marked change of texture to the walls. Some painters use crumpled soft paper. Try out various effects before you decide which method to use.

Other equipment You need white spirit [mineral spirit] for thinning; a paint kettle, bucket or wide flat tin to hold the glaze; a stepladder and plenty of clean rags.

Brush or pad stippling For this sort of stippling, two people definitely get on better than one. So when you have mixed up your glaze, one member of the team brushes it evenly and finely, no thicker than a film, over a vertical strip of wall while the other follows behind stippling the surface while it is still wet and malleable. Keep the pressure on the stippling brush steady and even. Efficient teamwork is important in brush stippling because this takes quite a time, and it helps if you can be stippling the top half of a wall while your partner is brushing glaze onto the bottom. Keeping a wet edge is always important for a professional-looking wall finish. If a glaze seems to be drying too fast to keep a 'wet edge' going, adding a little raw linseed oil acts as a retardant. Stippling with cloth pads is less tiring than brush stippling but needs the same quick, decisive touch.

Method

Remove surplus glaze from the brush periodically, by brushing out on waste paper or rags, to prevent it from overloading to the point where it puts on more glaze than it takes off. Change cloth pads occasionally for the same reason. Odd unevennesses can be touched out, if necessary, after you have finished a strip. Stand back for an overall impression. Darken light patches by picking up a trace of glaze on pad or bristle tips and touching the colour in lightly. But go easy, colour builds up faster than you expect, and take care to clean the brush before re-using. Build-ups of glaze, where you have gone over one place twice with a loaded brush, can be toned down either by re-stippling with a clean brush or rag, or, if very stubborn, by a brush or rags moistened with a little white spirit [mineral spirit] to soften the drying glaze.

Roller stippling This is a different animal. It takes longer to brush the glaze on than to roller stipple it off again, since a roller flashes up a vertical surface in no time at all. Simply roll the roller up and down over the wet glaze, using quite firm pressure, until the colour is evenly textured. Take care not to let the roller skid over the glaze, because this wipes off streaks of colour, which then have to be patched up and re-stippled. Clean the roller head frequently by rolling vigorously on waste paper to mop up surplus colour. It is more difficult to cut in neatly at the top and bottom of a wall with a roller, and glaze may accumulate here or smudge on to the woodwork or ceiling. Keep clean rags handy for wiping off smudges, and even out built-up colour by stippling over the area with a soft rag moistened with white spirit. Clean the roller at the end of the session by rolling on paper, then in white spirit – which has to be squeezed out by hand – then on clean paper.

Varnish If the walls are likely to need frequent washing down, varnish with a clear matt or mid-sheen alkyd varnish (if you have used a wash this is certainly necessary). Matt varnish dries almost invisibly and gives a tough finish that can be wiped clean.

Ragging and rag-rolling

Ragging leaves an elegant flow of softly variegated texture over wall surfaces. Rag-rolling is a striking variant of the same finish.

For a ragged finish, a bunched-up rag or chamois leather is pressed onto wet glaze. By varying the pressure on the rag, rolling it this way and that and re-arranging it from time to time, subtly varied impressions are left that create a pleasantly uninsistent but lively flow of textured colour.

For a rag-rolled finish, rags or leathers are rolled up into a small bolster shape. This is then rolled up (or down) the wet glaze to give a directional pattern of broad blurry stripes, reminiscent of watered silk. The rolling movement needs to be carefully controlled as the stripes must be more or less vertical, parallel and equidistant. Professionals often pencil or chalk in guidelines with a spirit level or plumbline.

Twisting rags into a loose rope, which is then knotted into a figure of eight and rolled up the wet glaze, gives a highly dramatic patterning similar to the bold 'graining' on eighteenth-century American country furniture.

The owner of this room, tired of her chilly white walls, rag-rolled them on the spur of the moment with sky-blue emulsion [latex] paint. No setting could be more delicately atmospheric, or could more perfectly complement the blue green of the painted chair.

Colours Because of the relative obtrusiveness of a ragged finish, I think it is best confined to softer colours. The more 'interesting' pastels – blue-green, brownish-pink, greyish-mauve – all look attractive ragged over a slightly 'dirty' white ground – that is, a white base tinted with a little raw umber for a cool greeny-grey cast, or a little ochre and raw sienna for a warmer cream. Colour on colour looks fetching if the colours are of similar intensity or tone. One of the most attractive ragged finishes I have seen was a warm duck egg blue – a greeny blue – ragged with a transparent faded-brick colour tinted with burnt sienna. In complete contrast a parchment-tinted glaze – a little white plus raw or burnt umber – ragged over plain white gives an ultra-refined, discreetly expensive finish.

Preparation As with most of the special wall finishes, ragging with a glaze is best done over a mid-sheen oil-based paint. If you use an emulsion [latex] paint for the ground coat, again a mid-sheen finish may help, as it is more difficult to keep the wet edge going on an absorbent base. A wash of thinned emulsion paint should be ragged over a flat or mid-sheen emulsion [latex] ground. Make sure the base coat is clean and dry.

Materials for ragging *Glazes and washes* Ragging with transparent oil glaze [glazing liquid] gives a very crisp pattern; thinned oil-based paint (mid-sheen, flat or undercoat) or a wash of thinned emulsion [latex] paint produce softer effects; see pages 210–213 for types of paint. As usual ½ litre [1 US pint] of full strength paint or glaze should be sufficient to rag a small room.

54

Thin glaze and oil-based paint with white spirit [mineral spirit], adding a little drier to thinned paint if necessary to prevent drips. Use universal stainers [tinting colours] or artists' oil colours to tint these glazes. Thin emulsion paint with water and tint with stainers or artists' gouache or acrylic colours. Thin and tint your glaze or wash in a pan, paint kettle or bucket, following the instructions on pages 223–24. Experiment on boards, or paper, or in a corner of the room to find the effect you like.

Above Ragging off by dabbing the bunched-up cloth onto the wet glaze.

Right Here the glaze or wash is being ragged onto the wall using a rag-rolling movement. Since it goes so quickly, ragging on is particularly suitable for applying a fast-drying wash.

Rags and brushes You need a wide, soft brush to apply the glaze or wash and a good supply of rags or a piece of chamois leather to distress it. Rags can be of varying texture (old sheet, gauze, or even hessian or burlap), but they must be well washed and lint free, and of course the same type must be used throughout. Rags and leather can be used dry or – with a glaze – wrung out in white spirit [mineral spirit] for a softer effect.

Method

Apply the glaze over a fairly large section of wall with a large soft brush. Transparent oil glaze needs to be worked over quite a lot to even out brushstrokes. The oil glaze made from the recipe on page 224 is easier to brush out than a proprietary glaze, though much slower drying. There are two ways of using the rag to make a pattern. Either bunch it up in one hand and dab and push it about on the glaze with a 'loose wrist', or wrap it into a loose but compact bundle and, using both hands, *roll* this about over the wet glaze in various directions like a rolling pin. The idea is to make an irregular pattern, but one that looks fairly uniform overall. From time to time you will have to change your rag, as it will become stiffened with glaze or paint. With oil glaze or oil paint chamois leather should be used wrung out in white spirit, as this allows you to clean it now and then.

If the wet edge dries while ragging with oil-based paint, try softening it with a clean rag soaked in white spirit. A wash of emulsion paint dries very fast so if possible have two people on the job. Paint a small strip of wall at a time and fade out the wash toward the edge of the strip so that the overlap is not too thick. If the wash starts to dry before it has been ragged, dabble it with a wet sponge to make it workable. A little scouring powder on a damp cloth should cope with a recalcitrant hard edge.

Varnish For protection, a ragged finish can be covered with a coat of clear matt or mid-sheen alkyd varnish.

Sponging is a really jolly decorative finish, quick and easy to do, and capable of infinitely varied effects according to the type of sponge, the way you wield it and the number of colours used.

Sponging

Sponging on or off The most commonly used sponging technique differs from most of the decorative finishes described here in that the sponge is used to dab the tinted glaze or wash *on*, taking up the colour from a large flat surface, such as a plate or tray. However, you can brush on a glaze in the usual way and then use a clean sponge to distress the wet surface – a sponge wrung out in solvent gives a very regular, prettily granulated appearance, like a close-textured stone, or knobbly knitting.

Sponging on with two colours The sponging-on method, done with two different coloured glazes or washes over a light ground, is a quick way of obtaining a marbled effect that can look opulent in a small room. For the most emphatic patterning, the wall surface should be painted first with a

Overleaf Sponging is the easiest and fastest of the special finishes to apply and can look particularly stylish when three related colours are sponged in separate 'continents', as in this young artist's flat, and then softened and blended slightly at the edges. The handsome wall painting is a crib from a museum postcard, done with fast drying acrylic colours.

light-coloured, mid-sheen or flat oil-based paint. An emulsion [latex] paint ground coat makes the most suitable base for sponged-on emulsion colours. The sponged-on colours should be thinned to transparency with the appropriate dilutent.

Materials for sponging
Glazes and washes For sponging on, tinted transparent oil glaze [glazing liquid] gives the most translucent marble-like effect. Otherwise use a glaze of thinned oil-based paint: mid-sheen, flat or undercoat, see pages 221–25. Flat paint and undercoat dry flat, of course, if you want a matt finish. Sponging off is more easily managed with a glaze; a wash will probably dry too quickly to be very successful. For a small room, 1 litre [2 US pints] of any of the above should be ample for sponging on or off. See pages 223–24 for instructions on thinning and tinting glazes and washes.

Use universal stainers [tinting colours], artists' oils, gouache or acrylic colours as appropriate for tinting. Thin transparent oil glaze and oil-based paints with white spirit [mineral spirit].

Equipment A marine sponge is essential for sponging-on; it doesn't have to be new. If this is too expensive, the best substitute is a pad of soft crumpled muslin or cheesecloth, held bunched up in the hand. (Change this when it gets hard with paint.) Cellulose sponge makes hard-edged identical prints that don't flow together attractively. However, it can be used for the sponging-off method, where it will produce a regular stippled effect.

You will also need a bucket or paint kettle for mixing the glaze; a clean, flat container to use as a palette; a stepladder; and plenty of rags or waste paper for wiping up.

Method
Sponging off For a simple, uniform, one-colour sponging, brush the thinned glaze out over a strip of wall in the usual way, then press the sponge – wrung out in white spirit [mineral spirit] – evenly over the wet glaze. This finish needs to be regular, so spend a little time working over thicker patches of colour to get the whole thing evenly distressed. You may need to wash out the sponge from time to time in white spirit if it becomes loaded with glaze.

Sponging on For two-colour sponging to produce a marbled effect, soft, transparent glazes and a light touch with the sponge help give the impression that the colour was floated on. Keep the glaze in a flat container large enough to dab the sponge into, and have waste paper handy to test the colour on before dabbing it on the wall. Thick wet prints mean the sponge is overloaded. Go on dabbing the paper until you get a soft cloudy impression; then dab over the wall surface with a light, 'pecky' hand movement, keeping the sponged prints fairly spaced out. A good bit of ground colour should show through the first sponged colour, say two-fifths of the total area. When the first glaze colour is quite dry, sponge on the second colour. Concentrate on the blank areas, but overlap with the

60

previous prints too, to give a dappled effect that must not be allowed to become too regular and predictable. Change the position of the sponge regularly, and wipe it clean now and then on clean rags, or rinse out in solvent – but take care to squeeze it out well, or this will make the next lot of paint very diluted.

Varnish Apply varnish after 24 hours, or when the glaze is hard, using a clear matt or mid-sheen alkyd varnish (thinned 3 parts varnish to 1 part white spirit).

Above Sponge on the glaze or wash using a light 'pecky' movement, to produce a soft, cloudy impression.

Right For two-colour sponging, wait until the first colour is quite dry, then apply your second colour in the same way, for a gently marbled effect.

Lacquer can look soft and warm as well as
hard and shiny, and this is the effect
achieved by layers of glaze, varnish and a
final waxing in an Arts and Crafts room in
London. The frieze – a typical Arts and
Crafts addition – was inspired by the
sophisticated folk style of Carl Larsson.

Lacquer finish

A rich surface gloss and depth of colour are the *lac-de-chine* characteristics that decorators are after when they suggest a 'lacquer' wall finish to their clients. I don't mean by this the sort of effect you get by simply painting everything with gloss or enamel paint. That is certainly shiny, but it looks thick and lifeless compared to more complex effects built up with matt colour and glaze or varnish. Lacquer-look finishes are a demanding background, unkind to shabby furnishings and oddly shaped rooms. Shiny colour needs a high degree of finish everywhere else – sound plasterwork, handsomely moulded cornice, well-painted woodwork, elegant furniture, velvety carpet – in short, an expensive effect. An exception to the rule might be a room where something nearer to worn old lacquer has been contrived, using dark base colours – crimson, vermilion, olive green, deep blue, chestnut – brightened with a little discreet gold stencilling and given a semigloss varnish for sheen rather than shine.

There are three ways to get a lacquer-type finish. The first, if you simply want *shine*, is to apply 1 or 2 coats of clear varnish (semigloss for sheen, gloss for a reflective high shine) over walls painted in your chosen colour. The second method, though similar, gives colour richness as well: you apply the varnish in the same way, but tint it to tone with the paint beneath. In the third method, the base coat is covered with a toning glaze, and *then* varnished. If you apply a number of coats of glaze and varnish, all tinted differently, you can get a wonderful depth of colour.

Preparation

A lacquer finish requires perfectly prepared walls. Choose the base paint colour to look good through clear varnish, or to tone with subsequent coats of glaze or tinted varnish. When it is dry, lightly sand it to remove dust, but don't grind away so hard that you cut through the paint. Dust the walls down, then wipe them over finally with a tack rag. As for any varnishing job, the room itself should be immaculate before you begin, to prevent dust from settling on the sticky wet surface. Remove curtains or draperies and rugs, cover furniture with dust sheets, and vacuum and dust everything. Keep doors and windows closed.

Materials for lacquering

For one coat of varnish (thinned 3 parts varnish to 1 part white spirit [mineral spirit]) for a small room – 3 by 4 m [10 by 12 ft] – you need 1 litre [2 US pints] of clear, gloss alkyd or polyurethane varnish.

To glaze the same room you need ½ litre [1 US pint] of mid-sheen oil-based paint *or* the same quantity of transparent oil glaze [glazing liquid]. Better still try making up the homemade oil glaze recipe described on page 224 (it is already thinned so you'll need about twice the amount). This glaze gives a beautiful glowing, transparent finish that shouldn't need varnishing, goes on very easily and doesn't leave brushmarks as the bought variety is inclined to do. However, because of the linseed oil content, it can take many days to dry really hard. Use universal stainers [tinting colours] or artists' oil colours for tinting. See pages 210–13 for information on paints and 223–5 for mixing and tinting glazes.

64

Other equipment Brushes should be fairly wide, 75 or 100 mm [3 or 4 in], and of extra-good quality. Varnish brushes should be kept for varnishing only (see page 232), as you don't want bits and pieces of old paint marring your smooth finish. White spirit [mineral spirit]; fine sandpaper; a stepladder; the usual pan, paint kettle or bucket for the thinned glaze, and plenty of clean rags are also required.

Tinted varnish To tint varnish, dilute a blob of stainer [tinting colour] or artists' oil colour in a little white spirit, than add a cupful of varnish. Stir well with a stick or spoon, then add the rest of the varnish, thinning as above. Try the effect on a patch of wall. Varnish should be applied with a full brush and brushed out fast, lightly and evenly to avoid brushmarks. Applied too liberally, varnish will 'curtain' or sag. Thick coats of varnish tend to wrinkle so two thin coats are always better than one thick one. Likewise try to avoid going over the same spot twice, as this can leave sticky deposits that dry darker. Although the varnish won't take long to dry, allow longer than the can says if the room is not heated – ideally varnish should be applied in a mildly warm room, to help flow and drying. One coat may be enough, if you are very careful, but 2 will give greater depth of colour and shine. Let the first coat dry really hard before putting on the second – it may take several days.

Glazing Apply glaze with a large soft brush over the entire wall surface, keeping it even and as fine as possible. Brush out well to avoid brushmarks – stippling over an oil-based glaze will eliminate them. Leave for 24 hours until it is perfectly dry, then varnish over, thinning gloss or semigloss varnish as suggested and using a clean brush.

Method

For an antique lacquer effect, the colours should be softened to the patina of old japan, not used hot and strong. This can be done by painting the walls with an antique glaze (see page 168) before or after stencilling, or by adding a little of the same antiquing colours to the final varnish. Try the effect of raw and burnt umber on a patch that won't show – raw umber is particularly flattering to greens and blues, while burnt umber is richer over reds. A speck of black can be added too, to age the whole surface down even more. One coat of varnish is enough, but 2 – both thinned – are better. I think semigloss varnish gives a softer, prettier texture than gloss.

Antique lacquer

Stencils Designs stencilled in metal powder can look splendid on a lacquer finish. The stencilled motif might be a simple fleur-de-lys or Tudor rose, which always look good spaced out on a diagonal grid. Or adapt the quaint chinoiserie figures that decorated eighteenth-century japanned pieces. You could perhaps alternate a flower-spray motif with a typical old gentleman standing on a humped-back bridge, or fishing from a sampan, and remember that the stencils can be used back to front for a slight change of emphasis. Alternatively, of course, you could limit yourself to a simple gilt border stencil.

Decorative Painting

Stencils are an essentially simple but versatile decorative tool, a way of painting repeat patterns which has been known for thousands of years. They were popular among the rulers of medieval Europe for 'powdering' painted walls by disposing a motif over a regular grid. (Henry III of England had green walls powdered with gold stars stencilled in this way.) A great revival of stencilling took place in the latter part of the nineteenth century when elaborate polychrome schemes were used to decorate churches, public buildings and the newer royal residences like Osborne House and medievalists such as William Morris and William Burges made frequent use of stencils in their interior designs.

Stencilling has also flourished at a different level as a poor man's

Stencilling

Left This lively diamond design was stencilled in yellow and silver by Vanessa Bell and Duncan Grant in their home, Charleston Manor. The overall pattern has a slight jazz-age feel to it and provides a vivid background to gentler decorative treatments on furniture and ornaments. A similar effect can be easily reproduced using two simple rubber stamps.

Opposite Stencilling like this was always done in imitation of wallpaper at a time when labour was cheap and wallpaper imported and expensive. Note how the bands of motifs keep to a wallpaper spacing regardless of cracks in the boarded walls. It is ironic that stencil patterns like these may be one of the best records of forgotten early wallpaper designs.

67

approximation of fashionable printed wallpaper as a means of imitating overall repeat motifs. One tends to find examples of this use in the remoter country districts, from New England and Scandinavia to Sicily. Stencilling is undeniably laborious, but the result can be delicious and it need not have the homespun simplicity of these rural examples. Some modern designers such as John Stefanidis and Renzo Mongiardino make use of highly sophisticated versions of the stencil-as-wallpaper idea, using many 'faded' colours, and much variation of tone to suggest antique embroideries or tapestry. Such ambitious schemes, sadly, demand the specialized expertise of these designers but stencilling with 'powdered' motifs is an easy and dramatic way to give impact to almost any decorating scheme, and it is perhaps surprising that few people experiment with these techniques. Strong self-contained motifs such as stars, fleur-de-lys, scallop shells, oriental seals and heraldic emblems are all suitable. One of the prettiest schemes of this sort, in Sweden, shows a sprig of coral a few inches high, stencilled in pale red on a pale grey ground, not closely, but at intervals at least a metre [3 ft] apart. After many years of timid floral borders, there are signs that bolder use of stencilled pattern is becoming popular, with ethnic and abstract designs appealing to younger people. There is a great range of pre-cut stencil designs to be found in art shops as well as specialist shops but if you have a pet design or want to devise one based perhaps on a chintz or a rug design, it is fairly easy to make your own; the process has been made vastly easier by photocopying machines, with their capacity for enlarging small motifs and vice versa.

Use stencils not just to decorate walls but to improve a room's proportions, draw attention to attractive or quirky features, or to add bold blocks of pattern. Deep borders top and bottom cut a room's height, and can substitute for a cornice. False dadoes were often stencilled at dado height, with different wall colours above and below, another device for shrinking height. For a neoclassical look, stencil pilasters at intervals between dado and ceiling, and marble the dado below. And don't overlook the possibility of stencilling on fabrics, floors, furniture, and even sisal matting. One tiny motif stencilled on a grid is a simple, if painstaking, way to add charm and interest to anything from a papier mâché box to a three-panel screen.

Oiled stencil card or acetate are used for cutting out stencils. Oiled stencil card, which is opaque, is much easier to cut with a scalpel or craft knife than transparent acetate, which tends to split very easily. Use carbon paper and a sharp pencil to transfer motifs onto stencil card, and a rapidograph drawing pen for drawing on acetate. I use layers of newspaper for cutting on, which I find less tiring than plate glass and cheaper than the cutting boards sold by art shops and picture framers. A light craft knife or scalpel is easier to wield than a heavy-duty craft knife. The knife must be sharp so blades need to be changed often.

Brushes and sponges Stencillers today rarely use the straight-cut hog bristle brush commonly sold as a 'stencilling brush'. This is tiring to use, with its 'pouncing' or stamping on of colour. A softer, rounded mop-like brush used in a looser, round-and-round action, gets along faster and gives a fine, dry image that can be as misty as the one achieved by spray paints.

Sponges, marine and synthetic, are used to stencil textured images, and are easy to handle. A felt painting pad is used by some people. Spray paints are less and less popular, because of fumes and ecological worries.

Spray adhesive is excellent for attaching stencils to any surface, especially useful in the case of fragile, lacy stencils which need to be kept as flat as possible to prevent blurring or tearing the stencil. A light pass with the spraycan over the stencil is all that is needed, and it can be peeled off again easily without damage to the wall paint beneath.

Paints A few painters swear by oil colours applied with an almost dry brush, but most people find artists' acrylic tube colours the most convenient because there is a huge colour range available, and the paint dries on impact, used correctly. It may be used on any surface, including floors and fabrics; floor stencilling gets its durability from final varnish. Although some people use emulsion [latex] for stencilling, I find it too thick to stencil with sensitively.

Other equipment: You will also need rags; a plate or two for a palette; masking tape; portable stepladder; plumbline; straight edge or long ruler.

Above The simplest rosette stencilled in distemper on a regular grid imitates wallpaper in a Swedish farmhouse, and makes a sympathetic background to a wonderful medley of paint effects: primitive marbling and graining plus a burst of folk exuberance on the decorated wall cupboard.

Right Stencils are moving away from floral and pastel designs. This close-up of a farmhouse kitchen wall, distempered a rich Venetian red, says it all – as well as making a handsome backdrop to a colourful collection of pottery.

Cutting stencils When using acetate, trace designs onto the acetate with a rapidograph; the material is transparent so simply lay it on top of the design. Transfer paper or carbon paper is used to transfer designs onto card, which is opaque. Card is much easier to cut smoothly. An expert, with a strong grip, can easily cut a fine, bevelled edge round each shape. Keep cuts as smooth, clean and lively as possible; with sharp blades you are almost drawing with the knife. One advantage of acetate is that when in use it can bend round corners, and is almost indestructible. Card gradually softens and wears out, so make spares.

Registration Positioning stencils accurately is chiefly a problem when superimposing different 'cuts' for polychrome effects. For such schemes, cut all stencils the same size with notches in the top corners which you mark lightly on the wall with chalk. Borders are simplified by overlapping the beginning and end of the stencil. Grids are best marked out lightly in chalk, or with a chalked 'snap line' available from builders' merchants.

Painting Put dabs of colour round the rim of your plate, with a splodge of white acrylic colour in the middle. Experiment with colours, mixing them up on the plate; you need very little colour. The cardinal rule of stencilling is to use an almost dry brush. Pick up colour, then work it up into the bristles

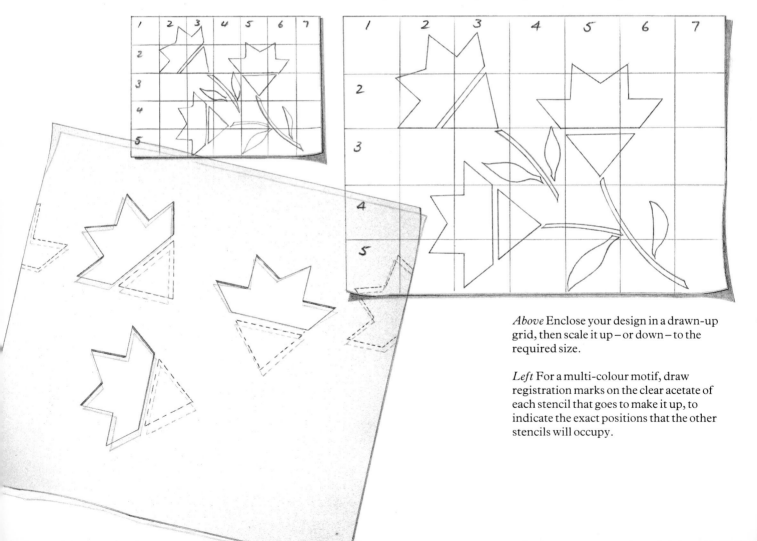

Above Enclose your design in a drawn-up grid, then scale it up – or down – to the required size.

Left For a multi-colour motif, draw registration marks on the clear acetate of each stencil that goes to make it up, to indicate the exact positions that the other stencils will occupy.

Right Begin cutting a stencil with the smaller sections, working up to the large ones, so that you don't weaken it unnecessarily. If you are using stencil board, try cutting a bevelled edge by holding the blade at an angle of 45°. This will help to prevent paint from seeping under the stencil, and give a crisper edge.

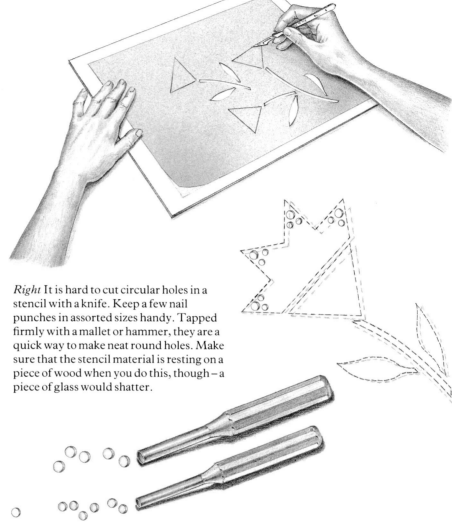

Right It is hard to cut circular holes in a stencil with a knife. Keep a few nail punches in assorted sizes handy. Tapped firmly with a mallet or hammer, they are a quick way to make neat round holes. Make sure that the stencil material is resting on a piece of wood when you do this, though – a piece of glass would shatter.

Above When you design your stencil, 'bridges' at frequent intervals help to strengthen it, as well as forming an integral part of the pattern.

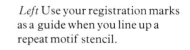

Left Use your registration marks as a guide when you line up a repeat motif stencil.

Left The freshness and charm of this rubber stamped country bathroom come from the simplicity of its design. The alternation of large prints with small leaves a pleasantly uninsistent pattern over the walls. The somewhat random positioning of the motifs adds to the pretty hand-painted effect.

Above A charmingly random mosaic effect using acrylic colours and our old friend the potato, carved here like a little waffle iron and used to print colour straight onto the walls of a small bathroom.

on a piece of newspaper. When the colour emerges soft, slightly transparent, without visible moisture, you are ready to start. Fix stencil in place with spray adhesive or tabs of masking tape, or hold it with one hand. Use a round scrubbing motion to apply the colour, like putting rouge on one's cheeks. Paint as fine as this is fun to shade with a quick further rub of another colour. Designs featuring two predominant colours (from two stencils) say, red apples with green leaves, work well when each colour is shaded with the other: red on the green leaves, green on the apples. This simple trick, you will find, prevents stencils looking 'jumpy' on the wall. Applied decoration must always 'lie down'. If you are superimposing colours within your stencil design, make sure that the first layer of paint is fully dry before applying the next colour.

Varnishing

On walls, most stencil schemes will not need varnishing. But a coat of clear matt alkyd will certainly prolong the life of an ambitious and intricate project. Stencilled floors and furniture can be varnished with matt alkyd or polyurethane for extra strength, though the latter should not be used over pale colours.

Rubber stamping

Not everyone realizes that the invaluable rubber stamp used for countless routine purposes also has immense decorative potential. Rubber stamp manufacturers, given scale drawings of suitable designs, will convert them into decorative stamps for a modest fee. Using quick-drying paints or inks, you can then stamp designs effectively and fast on to walls or furniture in any arrangment you favour.

The idea comes from the traditional method of hand printing fabrics with carved wooden blocks. Small floral motifs stamped in a regular grid look like hand-printed Indian cotton, especially if the same design is massed together to make a patterned border surround. A geometric motif, such as a simple diamond, can build up to quite a different effect – Art Deco-ish, or '30s' Bloomsbury style in the manner of Duncan Grant and Vanessa Bell. The scope for patterns is immense, but remember that it is the size and complexity which will determine the cost of the stamp.

The naive quality of small repeat floral motifs is perfectly suited to small cottage-style rooms. Here, instead of measuring up painstakingly and pencilling in guidelines, you can – if you feel confident enough – trust your eyes when it comes to positioning the patterns. Smaller designs interspersed with larger motifs for variety will emphasize the artless hand-printed effect.

In larger rooms, pencilled or chalked guidelines are necessary as small errors have a way of becoming magnified over a large area.

Materials for rubber stamping

Rubber stamps: a small sheet of glass with taped edges; artists' acrylic colours plus acrylic medium, or printers' tube colours; a small lino-cutters' roller [brayer]; solvent; sponge; chalk; plumbline; ruler and straight-edge; waste paper; white spirit [mineral spirit].

Preparation

Walls should be reasonably smooth and freshly painted in matt or mid-sheen paint.

For a regular grid pattern, measure and mark out the wall area, using a plumbline to secure verticals and a T-square or spirit level to get horizontals lined up, with 90° angles at intersections. A chalked line (see page 132) is a handy way of marking lines of any length and can be rubbed off again later. If you are using two stamps of different sizes, you will find they look best staggered – a small one equidistant from two larger ones, for example, so that a triangular pattern is formed.

Method

Prepare colour in a saucer before transferring it onto the glass sheet. Mix 1 to 1½ tablespoons of acrylic colour with ½ tablespoon of water and ½ tablespoon of acrylic medium. Making a larger quantity of acrylic colour is usually counter-productive, as it tends to harden off within an hour even if retardant is added in the form of acrylic medium and water. Special wet palettes can be obtained that keep acrylic colour soft and usable for days, but these are quite expensive. It is simpler and far cheaper to make a note of what colours were used, in which proportions, and to make up the colour and re-mix as and when necessary.

Once you are satisfied with the colour, transfer a spoonful or two to the glass sheet and roll it out smoothly with the roller. Press the stamp firmly into the rolled-out colour and try it out on a sheet of paper. If the print looks clear and crisp, you have got the right amount of colour on the stamp. Stamp the design on the wall surface in the usual way, replenishing the colour when necessary. You will almost certainly find some prints come out cleaner and brighter than others. Extremely blurry or splodgy prints can be wiped off again carefully, using a sponge moistened in water for acrylics, or solvent for printing inks. On the whole, a certain variation in tone and clarity is a bonus, adding to the hand-printed look.

To neaten up the overall effect, the edges of wall surfaces can be outlined with a painted ribbon or stripe, an inch or so wide, in the same colour as the motifs. This can be painted on by hand using a fine brush for the edges and a thicker one to fill in. Alternatively, masking tape can be used to delineate the painted stripe, and then peeled off later.

Another idea, especially attractive in an attic room with interesting sloping ceilings, is to mass the stamp motifs together closely and regularly to make an outside border of solid patterns. This will need setting off from the rest of the wall with a narrower painted stripe. You can also make a feature of cupboard doors by stamping them closely so that they stand out as a dense patch of colour in a more loosely patterned room.

It is worth giving stamped walls a coat or two of alkyd varnish or emulsion glaze to seal them and allow for wiping down from time to time.

Note: Don't think of decorative rubber stamps as a one-off investment. You can print off matching curtains or blinds, use the motif singly on lampshades, or even (as rubber stamps are meant to be used) for heading your own writing paper.

Wall painting

Wall paintings have an imaginative freedom that even the most beautiful stencilling cannot match. But it must be some lingering inhibition associated with scribbling on nice clean walls, plus a genuine diffidence about tackling a creative job without training, that accounts for the rarity of this form of decorative work. And yet, really, it is not so difficult. All sorts of untrained people quite unselfconsciously produce vigorous and charming murals. While I admire the sophisticated vistas and colonnaded loggias that artists have conjured up for their rich patrons, I often find these less memorable and pleasing than technically more modest efforts done with greater conviction.

Those who cannot manage freehand copying will find that the most faithful scaled-up representations can be achieved quite mechanically by using a grid, as shown on page 72. Once you have chalked the outlines on

Left Leafy arabesques and flowers painted freehand make a rococo background for regularly spaced but by no means strictly vertical columns. Droll painted figures such as these are often found, brandishing a stick, at the entrance to the 'party rooms' in old Scandinavian houses. This appealing interior demonstrates that rural decoration does not have to reach any great artistic height to be entirely captivating.

Above Vividly coloured woodwork balanced by a bold painted dado treatment provides all the visual interest in this sparsely furnished Pennsylvanian farmstead. The bare pine floors are of superb quality. One unusual, but practical, feature here is the black skirtings [baseboards], which are carried on right across doors and architraves.

the walls, all that remains is to reproduce the original colours, and the advice given in this book on mixing colours and producing decorative effects such as stippling or sponging should be of help here.

Designs   Be realistic in your choice of design – flat, two-dimensional treatments that rely on shape and colour rather than modelling and perspective for their effect are easiest to bring off. You need not choose to paint anything strictly representative – think also in terms of pattern. Look at the classical murals, Egyptian, Cretan, Etruscan and Pompeiian, at tapestries, at the paintings of Uccello, Matisse, Le Douanier Rousseau, at Moghul painting and Japanese prints, lacquer screens, Delft tiles, Jacobean crewel work, at samplers and at decorative borders in children's books – these last often prove a mine of ideas. Most inspiring and helpful of all perhaps is folk art in its many manifestations – embroidery, carving, ceramics, painted furniture and, of course, murals. Folk art is living proof of how a feeling for colour and a strong decorative impulse can transcend technical limitations. Some of my favourite wall paintings are those done by the journeyman stencillers and housepainters in eighteenth- and nineteenth-century New England homes. These charming rural scenes, with little hills, winding streams, clumps of sponged-in trees, have a charm and directness that have nothing to do with technique, only a certain sensitivity to colour and design.

Preparation and paints   If a mural is born of sudden impulse, by all means use whatever materials are to hand. Odds and ends of paints left over from jobs around the house, felt-tip pens and crayons can all be pressed into use, provided the surface you are painting on is sound and reasonably smooth. Flaky, cracked plaster, overpainted lining or wallpaper that has started to peel, old or greasy emulsion [latex] finish, will all reduce the life of your work. If you are planning a fairly elaborate, lengthy sort of mural, it would be worthwhile providing yourself with a durable, non-absorbent base coat such as the standard mid-sheen oil-based paint advocated for most of the decorative finishes, and the same paint, tinted with universal stainers [tinting colours] or artists' oils for the decorative painting. Or, if you object to a slight sheen, use flat paint or standard undercoat (which dries perfectly flat) for both ground and painting, tinted as before with stainers (see pages 216–17). On a new, sound emulsion base you could paint with emulsion paint tinted with stainers, artists' gouache, or artists' acrylic colours. Used neat, but extended with acrylic medium or water, they give glowing, fast-drying colours, useful for detail but expensive over large areas.

Brushes and other materials You will need brushes in various sizes: small artists' brushes for details and ordinary 12 or 25 mm [½ or 1 in] decorators' brushes (or artists' oil brushes if you can afford them) for brushing in larger areas; a wider, 75 or 100 mm [3 or 4 in] brush might be helpful for filling in sweeps of background colour such as blue sky or green hills.

Equipment for stippling, sponging or stencilling may be required (see appropriate sections). Chalk or charcoal for drawing in rough outlines; white spirit [mineral spirit]; jars with screwtop lids to hold surplus mixed paint colours; saucers to use as palettes, one for each colour; a paint kettle or bucket for larger amounts; stepladder; plumbline; rags and newspapers.

The design A simple project, such as painting orange trees on either side of a door, will give an idea of different ways of using materials and techniques for varying effects. In this example it is decorative shape and colour we are after, not botanical realism. So the trees should be stylized like those in a sampler, mop heads or pyramids or espalier shapes, studded with bright fruit (a stencil might be used to do these) and standing in decoratively shaped and textured containers – baskets or Versailles tubs. Sketch various shapes and arrangements first, on squared paper in coloured pens, until you find one you like. Copy this on one side of the door with chalk, scaling it up as shown on page 72, keeping to the proportions of your sketch. You can use the first tree to measure up the second.

Method

Painting a make-believe door with an enticing view beyond is a witty idea for a plain interior wall. Use grisaille for the doorway itself. Painted orange trees and tubs make charming additions to a doorway, real or trompe l'oeil.

81

Above A paintbrush has been busy on all the surfaces shown here. The woodwork is loosely sponged to give a marbled effect. Glass panes are stencilled to look like etched glass, but the real deception is the frieze of bold William de Morgan style tiles on the wall which are in fact trompe l'oeil paintings. Tiles are not too difficult to imitate in paint, using the same technique as trompe l'oeil panelling to suggest three dimensions.

Right This charming detail shows how little is needed in the way of shading and draping to suggest fringed swags of spotted muslin caught up by gilt pins. The elaborate cornice above is a trompe illusion too, probably a combination of stencilling and freehand work on highlights and shading. Ceiling borders like this are an early nineteenth century fashion that seems overdue for a revival – a delightful way to transform a plain box of a room and suggest a touch of glory.

Colour and relief Now for the colour – decide whether you want the colour simple and flat, which emphasizes shape and colour contrast, or enriched by glaze and surface treatments. If you can't immediately decide, play safe by painting different parts in flat, pale colour – grey trunk, sap-green leaves, pale orange fruit, yellow basket. The surface interest can then be added, if required, using darker tinted glazes – thinned versions of the paint you are using – brown for the trunk, bright green sponged on for foliage, vermilion stippled on the fruit, burnt umber dragged crisscross over the yellow to suggest basketwork. Glazes – see page 223 for how to thin and tint paint to make them – give depth of colour, and in this case a suggestion of relief or modelling. Stipple highlights on the fruit, by dabbing the bristle tips in off-white glaze, or paler areas of foliage, using yellow-green. Likewise, the basketwork can be given more prominence by shading and highlighting the wicker strands. But it is always as well to pause before elaborating a mural treatment too much and ask yourself whether you want your tree or whatever to stand out in greater relief. For while the eye happily accepts incongruities, like trees in tubs floating above the skirting board or baseboard when the treatment is flat and purely decorative, greater realism in the handling might make this sort of thing disturbingly surreal. Trompe l'oeil (see below) which is a sort of of visual joke, exploits such incongruities. Otherwise, it is an accepted mural convention that flat two-dimensional shapes work best unless the mural is actually intended to open up walls by suggesting landscapes seen in depth, framed by columns, perhaps, or fantastic topiary, or a vine-festooned pergola. Even here, though, keep the effects stylized, merely pinching a few tricks for suggesting distance, such as shading the sky from sky blue at the top to the merest wash of blue on the horizon, and using grey-mauve or grey-blue for distant hills.

Varnish Any mural that you are pleased with should be varnished with clear matt alkyd varnish, because walls are inevitably subject to wear and knocks and may need occasional wiping down; it would be sad to watch your masterpiece fading like Leonardo da Vinci's *Last Supper*.

Trompe l'oeil

Trompe l'oeil means 'to deceive the eye'. In terms of decorative painting this involves using the traditional resources of a skilled artist to suggest three dimensions where there are only two, so that for just a fraction of a moment one believes a painted object to be real. Trompe l'oeil is chiefly used as a witty solution to an architectural, or perhaps a decorative, problem. For example, a room is unbalanced by having a prettily domed alcove on one side of the mantelpiece, but not on the other. Rather than knocking back walls and commissioning expensive carpentry, a trompe l'oeil artist paints in a matching alcove, achieving symmetry and a talking point all at once. The charm of trompe l'oeil, of course, is that you can conjure up just about anything your imagination can create, and your technique can cope with.

Apart from its usefulness in disguising architectural defects, I like the jokiness, the element of surprise that never fails to get childish 'oohs' and 'aahs' as the deception is unmasked. One trompe l'oeil painting I found particularly appealing was a recessed alcove with shelves on a blank bathroom wall, holding a collection of the sort of thing one might not normally associate with bathrooms – some pretty old books with gilt tooled bindings, a vase of sweet williams, some china ornaments. As well as filling up the blank wall nicely it gave this most utilitarian room a civilized air.

There is no use pretending trompe l'oeil is easy, like stencilling or even simple mural painting. On the other hand, I think it is worth mentioning in a book for amateur painters and decorators because it is not beyond the reach of anyone clever and patient enough to copy exactly. In other words it is imitative rather than creative. And there are relatively simple, light-hearted trompe l'oeil effects which make for intriguing experiments; you could paint a trompe l'oeil carpet down the middle of a bare wooden staircase or cover a wall with mock Delft tiles, or liven up a room by painting mock panels on the walls, similar to the technique for doors described on pages 96–100. Another attractive idea is to simulate stone by painting lines on the wall to divide it into blocks.

Architectural trompe l'oeil effects are done in a technique reminiscent of 'grisaille', which is a decorative development of the old art student's exercise in monochrome painting, or suggesting solid form, perspective and so on, with different shades of one colour only – lightened with white or darkened with black.

Trompe l'oeil painting makes great use of shading to suggest three-dimensional realism. An amateur's best approach to realistic trompe l'oeil is undoubtedly to paint from a model – vase of flowers, blue-and-white china, a pile of old leather-bound volumes, or whatever – or from a good colour print. It is unlikely that an inexperienced artist would be able to achieve anything near the juicy realism of an old Dutch still life, but if you choose subjects that are decorative in shape and colour, the result can still be very attractive and a slight stiffness in execution can look quaintly primitive.

Some useful tips Don't be afraid of combining stencils with freehand work where the subject seems to admit it, for formalized forest trees, say, or sheep in a landscape, or bunches of grapes. The effect can be both pretty and witty. Using a stippled finish over any large coloured area can be effective, too, giving a pointillist effect. Sponging is always the quickest way to suggest foliage, as I have already suggested. Adding personal details is a sure way to enliven any mural – try putting familiar buildings into a landscape, or family portraits into scenes with figures, not detailed close-ups so much as characteristic outlines. Finally, over-brilliant colour effects can be toned down most easily by applying a cream glaze (white paint tinted with a little ochre and raw umber) over the whole work. Thin the glaze to make it a very fine, pale film.

Woodwork

The woodwork in a room – doors, windows, architraves, skirting or baseboard, dado – has something of the same relationship to the walls as a frame has to a picture. It acts as a boundary, creating a useful visual break between horizontal and vertical surfaces, indoors and outdoors. Chair and picture rails, as well as serving practical functions (to protect walls from chair backs and as an anchor for pictures respectively), are also architectural devices for breaking up flat planes and improving a room's proportions. In the days when wood and labour were cheaper, all such details were generously scaled, with handsome mouldings, both solid and structural looking. Doors were panelled, architraves of a dignified width, skirtings or baseboards of a depth and thickness that balanced ceiling height and cornices. Woodwork like this adds greatly to the appearance of a room and is worth making into a decorative feature. Painting it all shiny whiter-than-white makes it compete with the wall surfaces instead of framing them and you might like to consider other ways of treating it.

Making good and preparation

It always pays off to take special pains in preparing woodwork for painting. These surfaces get a lot of handling and if the paint is full of craters and cracks it will collect dirt that is hard to wipe off. The degree of making good required depends on the state of the old paintwork. If it is reasonably smooth and level it usually needs no more than washing down with weak sugar soap solution to remove grime, plus a little filling and sanding down to hide any cracks or nail holes.

Stripping down

Up to a point, badly scarred, chipped woodwork can be salvaged by extensive filling and making good. No one would needlessly undertake the job of burning off paint. But if the paintwork is really dilapidated, or if it is the sort of finish that is apt to discolour, or 'bleed' into the paint layers on top, you will save time in the long run by removing it.

Burning off with a blowlamp or heat stripper [heat gun] and combination shave hook is the quickest method: it is worth getting yourself a good-sized gas blowlamp or heat stripper, which will do the job properly. Start at the bottom of the area you are stripping – heat rises and will soften the paint just ahead of your scraper as you work upwards – and put a metal container on the floor to catch the hot, melted fragments. Move the blowlamp or heat stripper to and fro, following it with the scraper. Strip mouldings first, then panels and then flat surfaces such as skirtings or baseboards; strip with the grain of the wood.

Paint stripper is a slower method of getting back to the wood. Follow the maker's instructions, but allow time for the stripper to soak into the paint and soften it before you start to scrape – wear rubber gloves to protect your hands. Use a flat scraper for flat areas and a shave hook for working round windows, doors and mouldings. After stripping, wipe the wood surface with water and a little vinegar to neutralize the chemical. Wetting the wood raises the grain, so smooth with sandpaper when dry.

Previous page A wooden fire surround lavishly transformed by marbling.

To make a quick, neat job of filling hairline cracks along skirting or baseboard, round door panels, or where built-in units meet walls or ceiling, mix all-purpose filler [spackle] and water to a creamy consistency, and brush this into the cracks with an ordinary decorators' brush. This fills the cracks and levels off the filler so that little or no sanding is required. If you have extensive filling to do, buying a caulking gun could save time in the long run. For larger cracks, use all-purpose filler mixed to a soft paste, and put a dab of undercoat or primer in the cracks first to encourage the filler to grip, and discourage it from shrinking. Fill with a table knife, or artists' palette knife, and then level off while it is still malleable by wiping with a damp rag firmly over the top. Use special wood filler [wood putty] for window frames; it is designed to expand and contract with the wood, and is applied like other fillers.

Touch in knots with patent knotting [knot sealer] – use 1 coat on stripped, seasoned old wood, 2 or 3 on new. This is important, because otherwise resin from knots will seep up as a yellow stain through subsequent paint layers.

Cracks and knots

Give new or stripped woodwork a coat of primer – the first coat in a paint system – and then an undercoat [American readers will probably use an enamel undercoat only], which you can tint to match the top finish. Rub these down lightly with fine sandpaper when dry and hard to give a superfine base for the top coat. Ideally to give body there should be 2 coats of undercoat – the first being thinned with white spirit [mineral spirit], the second used straight from the tin.

Previously painted woodwork won't need a primer, but sand down old gloss [enamel] paint after cleaning to provide tooth for the undercoat.

Always leave paint plenty of time to dry out between coats.

Primer and undercoat

Most of the woodwork finishes described here are based on a lean, matt look, achieved with a flat oil-based paint, see page 210. This is the effect most decorators prefer, as being elegantly unobtrusive. Mid-sheen oil-based paint, see page 212, can be used if you prefer a slight sheen, but don't use semigloss, gloss or enamel unless you intend to get a lacquer effect. If you do want a high shine, and a greater depth of colour than gloss paint could provide, use a tinted glaze followed by gloss varnish, or just tinted varnish, as for lacquering walls, see pages 64–5.

The classic painters' routine for painting woodwork was door first, then windows, fireplaces, chair rails, and finally skirting or baseboard. This is because when painting the skirting one's brush may pick up stray dust from the floor, which will get into the paint and mar the surface.

Top coat

Narrow decorators' brushes, 50 or 75 mm [2 or 3 in], plus an even smaller one 12 or 25 mm [½ or 1 in] for fiddly 'cutting in'; a paint kettle or tin; white spirit [mineral spirit]; fine and medium grade sandpaper; newspaper; clean rags; a stepladder. See pages 92–3 for how to paint windows and for the sequence to observe in painting panelled doors.

Equipment

Simple
Treatments

Decorators often use a palette of 'dirty' or off-whites to emphasize panels on cupboards and doors, shutters, and other decorative details. This sophisticated treatment discreetly brings out their three-dimensional modelling while retaining a feeling of lightness and airiness. Equal discretion is shown in the choice of paint texture, usually flat or matt, occasionally with a sheen, never glossy. There is nothing precious or arbitrary about this, it just looks better, especially in old houses where it gives the effect of the old lead paints that changed colour with time.

Three shades of off-white are used: darkest for panels, a shade lighter for the mouldings round them, and the lightest of all for the surrounds – which would also include linking woodwork areas such as architrave, skirting or baseboard, chair rail and so forth. Some decorators reverse the sequence, using the palest shade for the panels and the darkest for surrounds. The degree of contrast between the three shades will depend on how elaborate the rest of the room scheme is, and therefore how subtle or interesting you want the woodwork to be.

Sequence of painting To paint all the woodwork in a small room you will need approximately 1 litre [2 US pints] of paint. Begin with the light areas, the surrounds. This may not be orthodox, but makes sense from the point of view of not wasting paint. Paint them in the lightest shade, just perceptibly off-white. To make it, mix a dollop of raw umber and a dot each of black and yellow ochre artists' oil colours into a flat or mid-sheen white oil-based paint to take the glare off the white.

Next tint some of the remaining paint a shade darker by adding a little more raw umber (very little, since the quantities are much reduced) and another speck of black and yellow. Try the effect before painting all the mouldings – it should be just perceptibly darker. Finally, repeat the tinting process again to get the darkest shade for the panels themselves. The paint by now will be a warm grey, with a slightly greenish cast, a most attractive colour that looks right with almost any wall colour.

Shades of white

Exciting colour contrasts on the architectural elements – floor, stairs, bannisters – are balanced by walls painted in various cool tones of off-white in an Arts and Crafts house. The bannisters and rails are finished with rustic dragging over a green eggshell base while the tongue and groove boarding is painted in a cream over white eggshell.

Matching colours

Colouring woodwork to match the walls is another approach effectively used in many old American houses. It looks particularly fine when there is a lot of woodwork to begin with – shutters, panelling, dado, as well as the usual doors and skirtings or baseboards. When all these are painted to match in one of the gentle but positive colours of the Colonial period –

Painting plain doors
For a good even surface, a large flat area, such as a flush door, is best painted in sections. Start at the top and work down, going quickly so that the paint doesn't dry before you have completed the routine of laying on, cross-brushing, smoothing out and laying off.

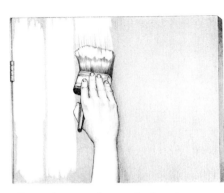

1 Lay paint on, using vertical strokes

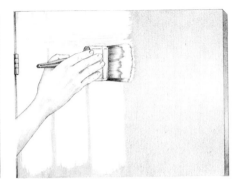

2 Without recharging bristles, cross-brush

3 Lay on and cross-brush a second section

4 Smooth out both sections

5 Lay off, moving away from the wet edge

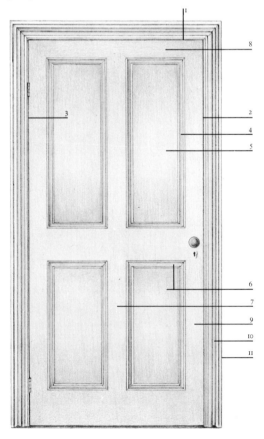

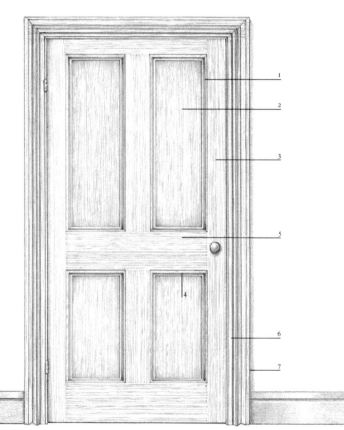

Painting panelled doors

Painting the different parts of a panelled door in a specific order (below, far left) is a proven logical saver of time, mess and effort.

If the door opens towards you, begin by painting (1) the rebates and (2) opening edge. If it opens away, paint the rebates and (3) hinged edge. Paint (4) the mouldings of the top panels next, then (5) the panels themselves – brush the paint well into decorative mouldings, but not so thickly that it spills over into 'runs'. Paint (6) the lower panels in the same way. Next paint (7) the central vertical section, then (8) the horizontal sections, or rails – top, middle and bottom in that order – and lastly, (9) the outer vertical sections, or stiles. Finally, paint (10) the door frame and (11) architrave. Leave the door wedged firmly ajar until dry.

Direction of dragging

The direction in which you drag the paint on doors and other panelled woodwork (see page 96 for dragging woodwork) usually echoes their construction – that is, the brushwork goes with the grain. Thus (below, left) dragging is vertical on (1) vertical mouldings, (2) panels and (3) stiles, and horizontal on (4) horizontal mouldings and (5) rails. Similarly, on (6) frame and (7) architrave, drag up the sides and across the top. An exception to this rule is a door with three or more crosswise panels – here the grain of the panels usually runs horizontally, and they should therefore be dragged in the same direction.

Painting windows

Like doors, windows should be painted in the correct sequence, which depends upon their construction. Use a metal shield or masking tape to keep paint from getting onto the glass.

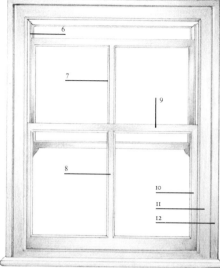

To paint a sash window, raise the lower sash and pull the upper sash down, so that you can paint (1) the meeting rail, including its rebate (where the pane meets the wood) and bottom edge. Then paint what you can of (2) the bars and stiles on the upper sash, (3) the bottom edge of the lower sash, (4) the soffit, (5) about 50 mm [2 in] down the outside runners.

Then close the window almost completely and paint (6) 50 mm [2 in] down the inside runners. Now paint all the (7) rebates, (8) the cross-bars, (9) the remaining cross-rails, (10) the stiles, (11) the window frame and (12) the architrave. Make sure you don't get paint on the sash-cords. There is no need to paint the whole length of the runners.

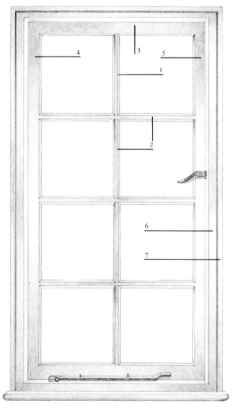

Paint a casement window in similar order, beginning with (1) the rebates, then (2) the cross-bars, (3) the cross-rails, (4) the hanging-stile, (5) the meeting stile, and finally, (6) and (7) the window frame and architrave.

93

blueberry, cinnamon, or that especially romantic blue-green that is formed by yellowing varnish over faded blue paint – the effect is extraordinarily reposeful, with a rigorous simplicity that gives added value to rich colours in pictures, rugs and furnishings. Again, the paint should be lean-textured, flat and non-reflective. (An all-over gloss [enamel] colour finish can be effective too, but in a quite different way, sleek and sophisticated, not atmospheric.) Both walls and woodwork can be dragged discreetly in a darker tone of the same colour for added texture and to soften and blend everything together.

This one-colour treatment is also useful where skirtings or baseboards and architraves are meagre and skimpy. In this case it is a mistake to call attention to them and painting them to match the walls is a good way to fade them out.

An unexpected combination of colours gives a typically Scandinavian lyricism to this interior of a Swedish house. Scandinavian painters often use the device shown here of a painted dado rail, allowing contrasting colours to be used above and below, so lowering the apparent ceiling height. Note how a plank wall is painted just as if it were plaster, right across the cracks.

Contrasting colours

Contrasting colour in woodwork can look rich or architectural. I remember a room with faded red walls and grey-blue woodwork, and another, more eccentric combination of tawny orange walls and pea green woodwork, which worked very well as a background to opulent Moorish pieces and vivid embroideries and rugs. Colours usually look best when they have a similar tonal value – that is, colours that would register identically grey in a black-and-white photograph. Soft reds and blues, or greens, can look very good together. Often these contrast colour treatments on walls and woodwork are given a dragged finish, in a glaze a tone or two darker, to soften them becomingly. An attractive variant of dragging is to give the tinted glaze a fanciful graining treatment, combing it to suggest some fantasy material between wood and marble. Latterly, the use of dark colours on woodwork, (including black) against strongly coloured walls, has become fashionable with younger decorators influenced by the Arts and Crafts movement.

Picking out mouldings

Picking out decorative mouldings, cornices and so on in colour is a favourite technique with decorators who want to give a crisply finished look to a room. It is also a good way to break up large expanses of woodwork, such as fitted cupboards. As the surfaces of new cupboards tend to be flat these days, you may need to add mouldings yourself first, mitring them at the corners and tacking or glueing them in place. One idea is to paint the prominent parts of the moulding or cornice in a strong colour, filling in the recessed space between them in a softer tone of the same colour. Choose your colour to reinforce one already in the room scheme – either a straight match or a tone lighter or darker.

Apply the colour in the form of a watery-thin glaze, made from flat [alkyd flat] or mid-sheen paint since it should look matt when dry. Try it out on a test area first, to check that it is intense enough to register. Use a soft, narrow brush – a 12 mm [½ in] paintbrush or artists' brush – then neaten up the edges with a fine sable one.

95

Dragging

Most of the decorative finishes described for use on wall surfaces – stippling, sponging, ragging – can be adapted to flatter beautiful woodwork or to make the best of the flat, usually meagre, fittings prevalent in so many modern houses. Dragging, particularly, is often employed with painted woodwork, using a thin tinted paint glaze to soften outlines and give a delicate patina of colour.

Off-white Dragging can be used very attractively in the three-shades-of-white treatment described above. To do this, first paint the woodwork surfaces with flat or mid-sheen white oil- or water-based eggshell paint and allow to dry hard. Then mix up a thin glaze, and drag on the three shades of off-white, tinting the glaze as already described with raw umber, black and yellow ochre oil colours.

Colour Woodwork painted to match the walls (see page 91) is sometimes dragged in a darker or lighter tone of the same colour to add texture. If a wall with a distressed finish has woodwork painted in a contrasting colour, it is a useful technique to drag the latter in a darker or lighter tone, since two distressed colours provide a softer contrast than two plain ones. If the contrast between walls and woodwork is very harsh, a glaze tinted with raw umber is an ideal choice as it softens any colour attractively.

Method Follow the instructions for dragging walls (see pages 45–9) using transparent oil glaze [glazing liquid] or thinned oil-based paint (see pages 223–4) tinted with stainers or oil colours, over a flat [alkyd flat] or mid-sheen base paint. The one difference is that dragging woodwork presents a directional problem, on panelled doors especially. I have seen these dragged entirely vertically, but the usual method is to drag in the direction of the wood grain beneath. Thus the brushstrokes are vertical on the panels, vertical timbers, and on both sides of the architrave or door frame, and horizontal on cross timbers and along the top of the frame. The same holds good for window frames and shutters. Skirting boards or baseboards, chair rails and other horizontal pieces of woodwork are dragged horizontally.

Varnish Apply 1 or 2 coats of clear, matt polyurethane varnish to protect dragged woodwork. It is especially important to varnish doors, since they do get a tremendous amount of wear, handling, slamming and so on.

Trompe l'oeil panelling

Flush doors are a legacy of the 1960s which can look rather dull, but a simple trompe l'oeil device intended to suggest recessed panelling and mouldings is a very effective way of breaking up the flat surface. The same trick of chiaroscuro can also be used to add interest to large, flat expanses of built-in cupboards fronted with blockboard and other recent builder's work.

Flush doors tend to be narrow for their height, so a two panel arrangement with the larger panel on top helps to make the door look better proportioned. French doors are traditionally panelled in this way, and the instructions given below are for a two panel arrangement. On doors of different proportions, another system of panels may look more convincing. See page 100 for examples. The convention is to paint trompe l'oeil effects of this kind in monochrome, that is shades of one colour, usually the 'dirty' whites, which may range from near-white to a tint that is almost grey.

Preparation

The ideal way to work is to take the door off its hinges and lay it flat, though of course this is not always possible. Surfaces should be clean, smooth, filled, and well sanded. After undercoating, give the door at least one coat of white mid-sheen oil- or water-based paint.

Materials

White eggshell paint; transparent oil glaze [glazing liquid]; white spirit [mineral spirit], artists' tube oil colour in raw umber and black; a soft bushy brush for stippling; a standard 35 mm [1½ in] brush for dragging plus a 25 mm [1 in] brush for dragging the trompe l'oeil mouldings; masking tape, rags, a pencil and ruler; bowls or small paint kettles for mixing the glazes.

Method

Pencil in panel shapes lightly to create squares or rectangles enclosed by mouldings. The dimensions you choose for both panels and mouldings may vary depending on the size of the door, and the arrangement of the panels. Looking at existing panelled doors will help you gain a sense of the right proportions. Masking tape makes a useful temporary moulding if you want to experiment with alternative arrangements. The traditional system used for trompe l'oeil panelling was to paint from the lightest element, on two sides of the mouldings, to the darkest, leaving each section to dry in between. This took longer, of course, but made plain sailing of such hazards as smudging new glaze. After the light mouldings were dry, the surround was dragged in a paint a couple of tones darker, then the panel was stippled in tones slightly darker than the surround. Finally the two dark or 'shadowed' mouldings were painted in. The same glaze was used each time, darkened in stages by adding a little more of the tinting colours.

Begin by mixing up a barely tinted glaze, using a little white eggshell, some transparent oil glaze [glazing liquid] plus a cautious addition of raw umber and a dot of black dissolved in white spirit [mineral spirit]. The glaze will register as palest greeny-grey on the white door paint. Use masking tape to mark the mitred corners of one pale section of 'moulding', so that pale and darker glazes do not overlap. Then paint the pale glaze between pencilled lines, using a narrow brush. Leave the glaze flat, or drag it lightly as shown on page 93. Let dry. Replace the masking tape to mark the mitred corners of the other light moulding adjacent. Paint as before and let dry.

The technique of painting trompe l'oeil panels can be used in many situations. Here, the mouldings have been painted in, and the surround dragged. The shadows and highlights should always be dictated by the fall of natural light.

97

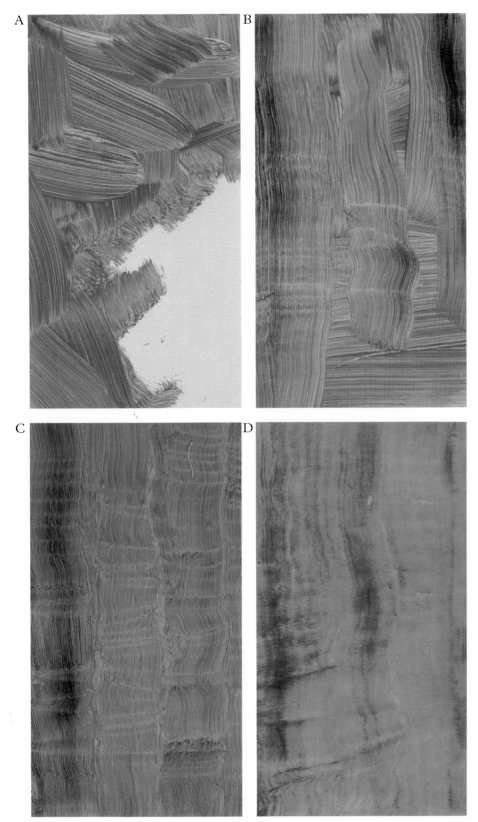

Bois clair or blonde wood graining

1 Paint the surface with an off-white eggshell paint, oil or water-based.

2 Mix up a tawny but cool tinted oil glaze with artists' oil colours in raw umber, raw sienna plus a little white to soften the shade. Thin in the usual way with white spirit [mineral spirit]. The glaze should be about the consistency of single cream. Tip some of this into a separate bowl, or paint kettle, and make a slightly darker version using more raw umber.

3 Paint the lighter glaze loosely every whichway over the surface with a standard 35–50 mm [1½–2 in] decorating brush (A).

4 With a glider streak darker colour onto the surface here and there as shown (B).

5 Wipe the glider on a rag, and then drag it with a wobbly stroke to create continuous grain, aiming to introduce the odd rippling streak of darker colour (C).

6 Soften lightly with a soft dusting brush (D). Let dry. Rather than polyurethane varnish, finish with one or two coats of eggshell or matt alkyd varnish which will not yellow or darken — this matters with pale wood-graining.

E

F

Mahogany graining

This technique uses the same basic steps as blonde wood graining (*opposite*), though of course the colours are different. The first and last stages are shown on the left.

Paint the base a golden shade of either oil or water-based eggshell for golden mahogany, or a pinky-red for red mahogany. Mix up a rich red-brown glaze using a little transparent oil glaze mixed with artists' oil (burnt umber and burnt sienna) colours and thinned with white spirit [mineral spirit] till it flows on easily but is not so thin it trickles and drips. Brush this on fast and loosely in all directions with a standard 35–40 mm [1½–2 in] decorating brush (E). Add more burnt umber to the first glaze in a separate dish, and use this with a glider or flogger to apply darker streaks here and there. Wipe the brush, then draw it through the glaze, wobbling the bristles to create ripples here and there. Flog patches of glaze for texture. Work over the whole area, aiming for a satiny flow of red-brown grain with darker streaks. Soften to diffuse these streaks, and to blur over-pronounced brushmarks (F). Let dry. Varnish with at least one coat of a mid-sheen polyurethane or alkyd varnish.

Above Blonde wood and mahogany graining techniques have been used to create trompe l'oeil panels in this elegant Biedemeier-style bathroom. Fake mouldings have been painted in black to simulate ebony. Several coats of clear matt or mid-sheen alkyd varnish should be used in a bathroom to protect the finish from splashes and condensation.

99

Trompe l'oeil panels can transform plain flush doors. Some possible combinations are shown below. For an alternative flourish, try painting a trompe l'oeil fanlight in grisaille above the door.

Add a squeeze more of both colours to the glaze, using much less black than raw umber. With this glaze you now paint, then drag, the outside frame to the panels, doing the horizontals first, then the verticals. If you work fast any slight excess glaze or ragged edges at each end of the horizontal strips will be tidied into neat right-angled joins as you paint and drag the vertical strips. Another way of cleaning up excess glaze is to wipe it off with a clean lint-free cloth dipped in a little solvent.

While the dragged frames are drying you can stipple the recessed panels, using the same glaze again darkened a tone or two with more raw umber and a very little black. To stipple, first brush the glaze over a panel, then with a soft, bushy brush 'pounce' the glaze with bristle tips to create a fine, powdery layer of colour. Repeat on the remaining panels, and let dry overnight.

Finish by painting the shadowed mouldings, which, to look realistic, should be those further from the main source of light in the room. Darken the remaining glaze by adding a little more colour than previously. Using masking tape again to mark the mitred corners, first fill in one side, let dry, then paint the second dark moulding as before. When completely dry give the whole door one or two coats of mid-sheen alkyd varnish for durability, or extra flat alkyd for matt elegance.

This approach to painting trompe l'oeil panelling is slow but foolproof, and is often used by professional painters who are able to slot the steps in between doing other jobs. If slick mitring matters less to you than getting the job finished, you could stipple the centre panels, drag the 'frame' and only add the dark and light mouldings separately when the rest is dry.

Fantasy Finishes

Grainers and marblers have always been considered the élite of the decorative painting fraternity, working in a tradition reaching back to Classical times (the Romans used both techniques) and beyond. It takes skill, judgment and taste to imitate marble and wood in paint, plus real knowledge of the materials themselves. For sheer technical virtuosity it would be hard to improve on the work of nineteenth-century marblers and grainers like Thomas Kershaw, whose sample boards can be seen at the Victoria and Albert Museum in London. My own personal preference, though, is for the bold exaggerations of the earlier Baroque painters, whose work can be seen at Ham House in Surrey, Belton House in Lincolnshire and Blenheim Palace, Oxfordshire, and whose influence I detect in the spirited style of much early American marbling and graining.

Graining

Graining can be pale, as in the 'bois clair' style, warm and ruddy, as seen in mahogany grained Victorian pubs, or dark like Jacobean oak panelling. One attraction of grained finishes is that they are an ideal disguise for joinery which uses a mix of cheap timber and wood-substitutes like medium density fibreboard. A run of new bookcases, for instance, grained to match existing woodwork, immediately gains a long-established air.

Graining can be a highly sophisticated and labour intensive process, involving skilful play with specialist brushes and tools. But it is surprising how easily a warm, woody effect can be arrived at by amateurs using a few brushes and a little tinted oil-based glaze [glazing liquid]. Though professionals favour water-based media for graining (like flat beer, see page 108), I think beginners are better off working with oil-based glazes. These are easier to manipulate and 'soften' and the slower drying time means you can have second thoughts, or even, if need be, rub the whole lot off with a rag dipped in solvent. Simply 'flogging' a wet glaze lightly with the appropriate brush (see page 232) immediately gives a grainy, fibrous texture which is attractive just left as it is.

'Softening', however, is the key process in most of the graining and marbling techniques dealt with in this section. Beginners usually have to force themselves to soften a careful piece of work; at first this feels too much like mussing it up. But persevere, and you will soon find that the final subtle flicks with the softener (a small badger softener is a justifiable investment, but any soft brush will do) make all the difference, blurring hard lines and blending colours into each other.

Burr walnut graining

1 Mix up a warm mid-brown glaze by adding raw sienna and a little of both raw and burnt umber artists' oil colours to a transparent oil glaze [glazing liquid]. Thin with white spirit [mineral spirit] as appropriate.

2 Brush this glaze rapidly every whichway with a 35–50 mm [1½–2 in] decorating brush onto a base of pale toffee-coloured eggshell (A).

3 Rag lightly with a soft piece of cotton. Add more burnt umber to the first glaze in a separate dish, and use this darker glaze to add squiggles and splodges here and there (B).

4 Fold a soft cotton rag into a squarish pad and use this to roll and swirl the wet glaze, blending the darker patches in with the rest. Use a No 3 artists' watercolour brush and the darkened glaze to add little dark dots randomly (C).

5 With a clean glider or varnishing brush, gently soften the graining here and there, or use the bristle tips to stipple areas of glaze (D). Or you might lightly flog the surface, using the standard decorating brush or, if you have one, a flogger, to create texture. But don't do all these things on the same patch – aim for a variety of flowing texture. When completely dry varnish with one or two coats of mid-sheen alkyd or polyurethane varnish.

Left This fine 18th-century wainscot has been beautifully walnut-grained, with panels of 'oyster' figuring in black mouldings. The effect is warm, rich and spirited.

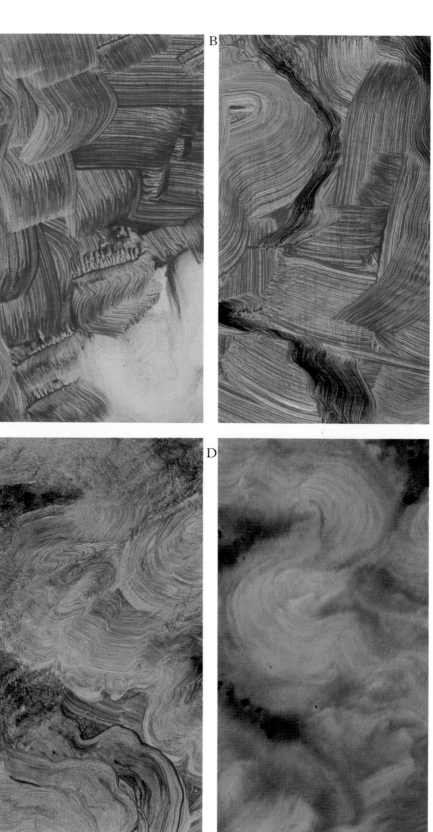

Oak graining

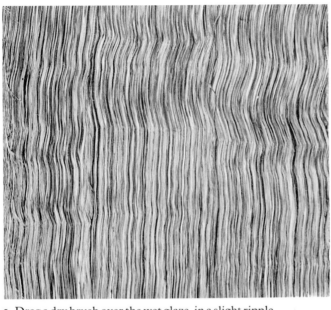

1 Drag a dry brush over the wet glaze, in a slight ripple.

2 Blur the lines very gently with a soft, clean brush.

3 Using the sharp edge of a cork, draw heartwood lines into the wet glaze, running very roughly parallel.

4 Sketch in a knot with the cork edge, then draw in grain lines so they part around it, but do not cross each other.

A smooth ground of mid-sheen oil-based paint is the usual choice, though water-based eggshell is becoming more popular, and at a pinch vinyl silk emulsion (available in UK) can be substituted. Eggshell or mid-sheen paint encourages the glaze to stay 'open' or workable for longer. The base colour will obviously vary from wood to wood. A cream or buff base suits most of the paler woods, golden mahogany needs a yellowish base, while red Cuban mahogany is frequently grained over a dull pink or red. The exact shade of the base colour is not critical, however, as it can be modified by altering the graining glaze itself.

Preparation

Glaze Glazes are made up of transparent oil glaze (home-made, see page 224, or proprietary) thinned with white spirit [mineral spirit] and tinted with artists' tube oil colours. Provide yourself with a card or board painted in your chosen base colour to experiment on, checking the glaze colour, or practising particular effects like 'wobbly' brushwork.

Materials

Brushes and tools Professional grainers work with a selection of brushes designed to create certain effects quickly and reliably. These may include overgrainers, sword liners and stipplers as well as a clutch of steel or rubber combs, and rockers to simulate knots and heartwood. There is no point in buying the whole shop to start with, but a 'glider' or varnishing brush, a 'flogger' and a 'rocker' (see section on brushes, pages 229–232) plus one or two fine sable watercolour brushes (No 2 and 3) will give you plenty of scope for experiment. As you become more expert you may decide to invest in a badger softener. A 'knot' tool can be whittled from a cork, or by cutting out the middle of a small stiff stencil brush to make a stamp. A chamois leather is useful for ragging but rags will do just as well.

Study a cleanly figured piece of wood and memorize some of the pleasant vagaries – knots, like islands parting the flow of the grain, heartwood like mountains on contour maps, highlights that ripple like stretch marks across the graining, zigzaggy or wobbly swerves in the basically parallel grain markings. It doesn't matter too much what type of wood you are studying, though the grainier ones – oak, mahogany, walnut, pine – are obviously more stimulating. The point to keep firmly in mind is that nature, most fertile of patternmakers, is never monotonous.

Method

As with all the more strongly marked finishes, it makes things easier to treat your painted surface as a series of panels – abstract pictures as it were, in which the various decorative elements are differently combined each time. Some conventions should be observed: for instance, the grain should flow the way it would if you were using real wood. Too many knots, unless you want a knotty bird's-eye maple or deal effect, look spotty. A preponderance of smoothly flowing, curving grain, broken only here and there by jagged heartwood or knots, is the effect to aim at.

Begin by brushing a thin glaze of colour over your surface. Then, using the glider, draw the bristle tips over the wet glaze to make fine stripes – like dragged painting – suggesting the general grain flow. Wobble your wrist

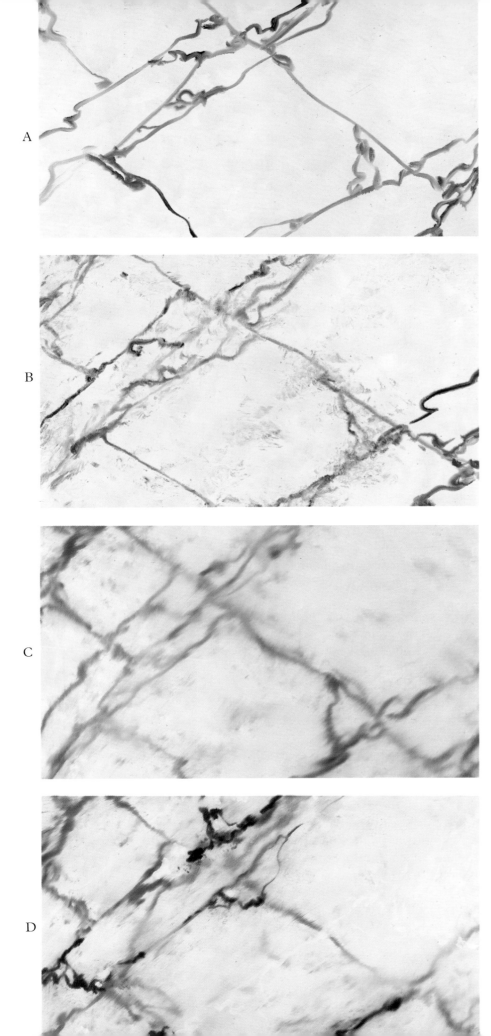

Grey marbling

1 For pale, greyish marbling, start with a dry ground of white mid-sheen oil-based paint, lightly sanded. Mix up a glaze of 2 parts flat or mid-sheen white oil-based paint to 1 part white spirit [mineral spirit], tinted with a squeeze of raw umber artists' oil colour and a dash of black. Brush this over the surface and gently sponge it.

2 Mix a little black oil colour into some raw umber to produce grey-brown. With a small brush and a fidgety brushstroke apply veins to the wet glazed surface. They should wander across it diagonally, branching off to left and right, and should have a beginning and end – genuine marble veining does not start or peter out in the middle of nowhere.

3 Sponge the veins lightly to remove excess paint. Take a dry paintbrush and gently draw it back and forth across the veining in one diagonal direction (say, bottom left to top right) and then the other, (bottom right to top left) – this softens the harsh lines. Mix up more black with less umber to get a dark grey, and take some up on your little brush. Fidget in some smaller veins, connecting them to the large ones. Like them, they should mostly run diagonally (A).

4 Use a sponge or paper tissue to soak up the excess paint from the little veins (B). You can then dab this on again in the plain areas, to imitate the variegations of real marble.

5 Now thoroughly soften the whole surface (C) drawing your dry paintbrush gently back and forth along each diagonal. Go over each diagonal at least 3 times.

6 When the surface is quite dry – after a few hours – fidget in extra veins in thinned white paint. Add dabs of the same colour to form pebble shapes (D). After 24 hours, varnish with matt or semigloss polyurethane or alkyd varnish – when this is almost dry, sprinkle it with French chalk or household flour, then polish it with a soft cloth. This reproduces the sheen of real marble.

Green marbling

1 Start with a dry ground of black oil-based paint. Mix up a glaze of white spirit [mineral spirit] and a little oil glaze tinted with a touch of viridian and a very little Van Dyke brown. Brush this glaze over the surface, creating cloudy areas and gently soften it, keeping it subtle. Make up a glaze with a tiny dab of yellow ochre, to create different tones, and repeat the same process (A).

2 Now using more viridian and a touch of emerald green and yellow ochre, with the point of a small artists' brush, apply veins to the wet glazed surface to form 'stones' of different sizes. Do not create stones everywhere, however – keep some areas bare of them. Vary the shades of green here and there, softening as you go, preferably with a badger hair softener (B).

3 Keep adding more colour and veins, softening as you go; and add more small stones. With a drier brush put in some smaller veins in a lighter colour, and link them with the existing ones (C).

4 When the surface is dry, add in some white veins and a few white pebble shapes (D). When the surface is dry, varnish it with a semigloss polyurethane varnish, preferably two coats to give a better finish.

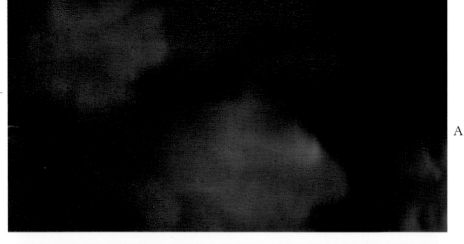

A

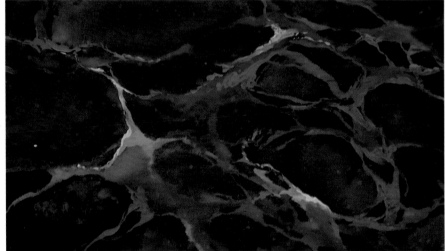

B

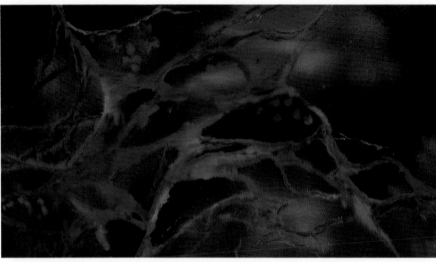

C

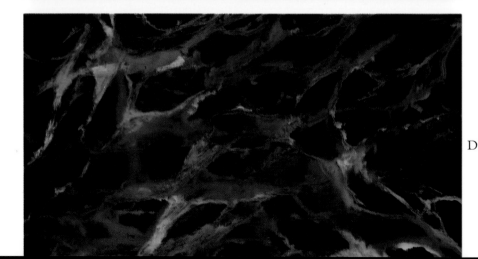

D

just a little in mid stroke to give a woody swerve. With the flogger, whip the stripes gently all over to blur them and give a flecked, almost hairy appearance. You now have the basic grain of the wood, a canvas with characteristic woody texture to which you can add highlights, heartwood and knots as desired. See illustration on page 104 for how to do this.

When you have blocked in your graining picture – with discretion, don't overdo it – a very gentle softening with the soft brush, bristle tips only, in the direction of the grain usually helps to pull it all together. But do go gently – a big blur is not what you want. If you think part of the surface looks too busy, wipe it out while the glaze is still wet. Try not to smudge the rest of the work. Leave the finished graining to dry hard.

Instructions for graining 'bois clair' (blonde woods), mahogany and burr walnut are given on pages 98, 99 and 103.

Beer or vinegar glazes Traditional grainers often worked with water-based glazes using flat beer or vinegar, preferring their special transparency and speedy drying. The vinegar or beer mixture described on page 188 is easier to manipulate than plain watercolour, as its sugar content makes it slightly sticky. Try this if you want a more delicate look.

Varnish Oil glazes are best varnished for durability. Use clear matt alkyd or semi-sheen alkyd varnish, depending on whether you want a quiet or shiny look. Vinegar or ale graining must have a thorough final varnishing to fix and protect it.

Marbling

Marbling falls into two categories: the highly skilled, closely imitative, technique, aiming to deceive the eye into accepting it as real, and then a much faster, impressionistic, tongue-in-cheek technique that is content merely to suggest the rich colours and endlessly varied patterning of marble, going for a 'fantasy' effect rather than an identifiable stone. The latter approach is lighter and less demanding, and for our purposes far more easily assimilated and successfully executed by amateurs. Having mastered the impressionistic style, there is nothing to prevent anyone getting hold of an example of the marble of their choice – working from life is the best training – and experimenting with coloured glazes, brushwork and feathering to get a closer imitation of the real thing. Since there are at least nine categories of marble – brecciated, serpentine, travertine, crinoidal, variegated, unicoloured, laminated, statuary, alabaster - and endless sub-sections, the subject is not one that can be compressed into a few pages. Fantasy marbling, however, is quick and fun and allows a great deal of scope.

A wooden fireplace surround looks impressive given the fantasy-marble treatment – you might perhaps continue the marbling on skirting board (baseboard) and dado. Alternatively, a bathroom is a good place to practise one's skills – starting with the bath surround, and extending over woodwork, walls and floors for a coherent effect.

It is probably a good idea to begin on something small, but if you are marbling a large surface, 'block' it out into separate rectangles, to be tackled one by one. This is easier and gives a more realistic effect, since natural marble tends to be supplied in smallish sheets. This way there is less chance of your marble pattern getting too fixed and unvarying, which is monotonous over a large area. Work quickly and decisively and don't be afraid of making mistakes; they probably won't show, and if they do, wipe them off and start again.

Preparation

The ground coat should be white mid-sheen oil-based paint, quite dry, and lightly rubbed down so that it is smooth and free from brushmarks.

Materials

White oil- or water-based eggshell paint or undercoat; artists' oil colours in raw umber and black; a 50 mm [2 in] decorators' brush; a badger softener – a No 2 badger mop or a 50 mm [2 in] flat badger are cheaper – for softening veins; a small, pointed artists' brush for details; a marine sponge; white spirit [mineral spirit]; jam jar; saucer; rags.

Method

The steps described here will give you a pale, grey-green marbled finish. Mix up a thin glaze in a jam jar with roughly 2 parts paint to 1 part white spirit. Add a good squeeze of raw umber and a little black, to give a greenish-grey tint that should be pale, but strong enough to contrast with the white ground. With the decorators' brush apply the glaze over your area or 'block', then sponge it lightly all over to break up the surface.

Veining Put a squirt of raw umber and a squirt of black on the saucer. Mix a little black into the umber for a darker shade of grey. With the small brush, pick up some of this colour and put in large veining across the wet glazed surface, using a fidgety brushstroke, not smooth straight lines. Marble veins tend to meander diagonally, forking off to left and right. But all veining lines should have an end and a beginning, not start in the middle of nothing and fade out again – think of them linking up like roads on a map. Gently sponge the painted veins to remove excess paint, then wipe your paintbrush dry on a rag and brush the veining lightly and diagonally, in one direction and then the other, to soften and blur. Now, with the small brush, take up a darker mix of black and umber, and fidget in smaller veins here and there, linking up the large ones, like secondary roads cutting across between major ones. Sponge lightly again, and soften with the dry brush. The brush softening has a magical effect – suddenly the crude squiggles begin to look like real marble. Stand back and study your handiwork. It may need a bit more veining somewhere, or perhaps a space enclosed by veining could be broken up into large and small pebble shapes, lightly drawn in with the small brush. But don't overwork it; half the battle with marbling is knowing when to stop. When the surface is dry (in a few hours), fidget some veins across the surface in plain white, to freshen, and 'lift' the marbling. Pebble shapes can be highlighted with a little white too. See the photographs on page 106.

To paint veins, hold the brush loosely and apply them with a fidgety stroke.

Left, above Dark grained woodwork enriched by a small leafy stencil makes a strong frame to the vivid blue glazework and gold leaf used on a panelled archway. Straight brushed glazework is balanced by mists of fantasy marbling in the same range of blues.

Left, below A fairly standard London fireplace adopts an ethnic air with a strong tortoiseshell finish that handsomely picks up the colouring of a carved gourd and a clutch of interestingly shaped pots. Black, white and tawny neutrals always look handsome together.

Tortoiseshelling

1 The ground must be bright yellow mid-sheen oil-based paint, dry and sanded. Using a large decorators' brush, cover it quickly with dark oak gloss varnish stain (A). Don't worry if this bubbles.

2 With the brush, fidget the wet varnish into diagonal stripes of zigzags about 5 cm [2 in] wide. These will begin to run into one another almost immediately. Dab walnut-sized splodges of varnish along the diagonal bands, at random but at least 6 or 7 cm [3 in] apart (B).

3 Squeeze a blob of burnt umber on to a saucer. Dip a small artists' brush in it and apply curly squiggles along the diagonals, say 2 or 3 cm [1 in] under the previous splodges (C).

4 Dip another small brush into black oil colour and place small groups of tadpole shapes in the spaces between the other markings (D). There should be fewer black marks than umber ones.

5 Take a clean, dry brush and very softly stroke it across the wet varnish, following the direction of the diagonal bands – in the photograph these run from left up to right. Stroke back even more gently the other way – here, from right down to left. Now repeat this 2-way stroking on the other diagonal, from right up to left, and from left down to right (E).

6 Finally, stroke once more back and forth along the first diagonal (F). You will find that the individual marks have been smoothed out into the subtle patterning of genuine tortoiseshell.

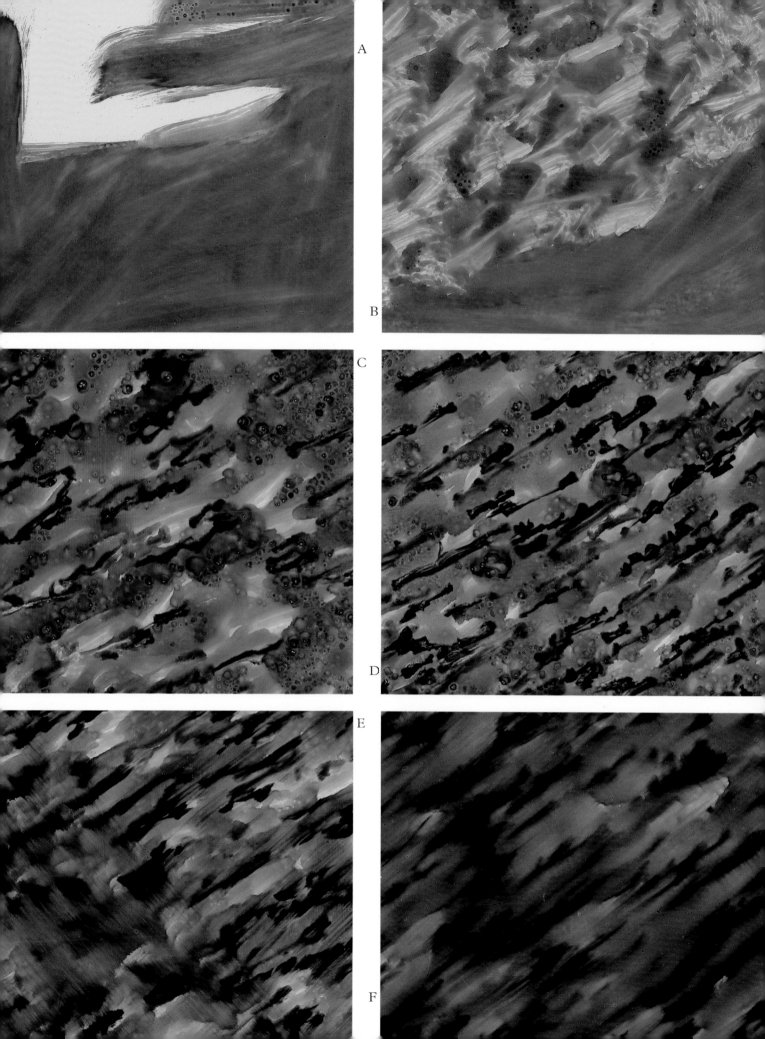

A

B

C

D

E

F

Varnish Leave for 24 hours before varnishing with matt or semigloss polyurethane or alkyd varnish. When almost dry, sprinkle the varnish with French chalk or household flour and polish it with a soft cloth for a marble-like sheen.

Some tips Study examples of real marble whenever you get a chance, to see the way the surface is broken up. Don't be timid – make your veining bold, thick enough to stand out, and rhythmic. Over a large surface it should change direction fairly often, whereas on a small area it needs to be more balanced.

   If you want more colour in your marble or a richer effect, you can repeat the marbling process using a different-coloured glaze – yellow, green, red-brown – on top of the first. The first layer of marbling will show through the second, creating a look of depth, as in the real stone.

Tortoise-shelling

The technique of painting woodwork, or even walls, to look like tortoiseshell is a beautiful example of the intelligent manipulation of paints and varnish to create a desired effect. Confronted by a spectacular tortoiseshell stretch, rippling with tawny yellow, chestnut brown and shiny black, I doubt whether anyone but an expert in paint behaviour would be able to figure out how it was achieved. Yet, once you grasp the technique, it is possible for the amateur to do, and goes fast enough to cover largish areas at a time. The secret is that the colours are laid into wet varnish, and the resultant 'spreading' is controlled by lightly brushing diagonally in two directions with a dry brush, creating the characteristic tortoiseshell markings almost automatically. This is not to say that you should tackle it mechanically, letting the paints do the work for you and repeating the same procedure unvaryingly across a surface. Monotony is always lifeless. Study examples of real or painted tortoiseshell before embarking on this finish, and observe the variety of figuring in the natural material or in the work of a skilled imitator. There are blonde tortoiseshells, leopard-spotted in translucent browns on an amber ground; red tortoiseshells, with a great deal of red-brown background; and darker ones inclining to black and dark browns, like the brown tortoiseshell described here. While the real thing comes only in small sizes, an expanse of tortoiseshell can look superb, but it takes a lot of living up to. The finish looks best in small, confined spaces – tiny front halls, with a lot of doors, small studies, a bathroom or cloakroom.

Preparation

The ground for brown tortoiseshell should be a smooth bright yellow, mid-sheen oil- or water-based paint. A light, sharp yellow is best, tinted with chrome yellow and raw sienna artists' oil colours, because the subsequent layers of colour will darken the ground considerably.

Materials

Medium oak varnish stain; burnt umber and black artists' oil colours; 2 standard decorators' brushes 50 mm [2 in] wide and 2 small, flat artists'

112

brushes about 12 mm [½ in] wide – one of each will do, but it means more wiping and cleaning; white spirit [mineral spirit]; clean rags; saucer.

Method

Using one of the large brushes, cover the surface with the oak varnish stain, working speedily and not too carefully. The varnish will probably bubble, but don't worry about this. When the area is covered, use the brush to fidget the wet varnish into diagonal bands of zigzags, roughly 5 cm [2 in] wide. The varnish will go on 'moving' after you have done this, so that the bands will run into each other creating an overall impression of movement. Dab some extra splodges of varnish – about the size of a walnut – along the diagonal rows. Position these fairly quickly and randomly, but not less than about 6 or 7 cm [3 in] apart. Now take the burnt umber and squeeze a blob onto a saucer. Dip one of the small brushes in it and make lively squiggles, like Arabic writing, maybe 2 or 3 cm [1 in] under the previous splodges. Keep working on the same diagonal, and again don't join up the squiggles or make them too regular. Then dip the second small brush into the black oil colour and dab small tadpole shapes in clusters here and there in the blank spaces between the other markings. You should have fewer black squiggles than brown ones.

Stroking Now comes the exciting part. Take up the dry large brush and, following the direction of the diagonals, very gently stroke it across the wet surface to make streaky graph-like peaks as the varnish and paints flow into each other; and then stroke even more gently back in the opposite direction. Repeat this two-way stroking operation on the other diagonal. Finally stroke a second time on the original diagonal – gently in one direction and then lightly back. In all, you will have brushed across the surface six times (you can soften more than this if you want), and as you do so, you'll see the blobs and streaks magically opening out into the subtle, transparent markings of tortoiseshell. The colours will continue moving gently for a while after you have finished – until the varnish 'goes off' – and will dry glossy, as tortoiseshell should be.

Blonde tortoiseshell For 'blonde' tortoiseshell, use a light oak varnish stain, or medium oak thinned with white spirit [mineral spirit] over the same yellow base colour; burnt umber – which thins to a rich red-brown when stroked – for the squiggles; and a very little black, or omit it altogether.

Panels

A tortoiseshell door, mantelpiece, or whatever, has to be completed in one go so that you don't end up with demarcation lines – unless it is conveniently divided into panels and surrounds that you can treat separately. If you have a large area to cover – a wall for instance – you will need two people on the job. The convention is to divide the surface into tortoise-sized rectangles, outlined in white or black and worked separately, varying the flow of the markings. Masking tape helps to keep a straight edge. Make sure a panel is completely dry before you start on the one next to it.

Floors

Floors always present a special problem when decorating. They are rarely good enough to leave exposed just as they are, with no more than an occasional waxing to keep them in shape. Covering them is expensive, especially if one has to deal with stairs, passages and landings as well as main rooms. One alternative to carpet, matting, tiles and vinyl that people are beginning to take seriously, since it can be as decorative as it is cheap, is to colour the boards with paint – opaque or transparent depending on the state of the wood – or with stains or varnish stains, which now come in a wide range of non-wood colours as well as the more traditional shades.

Fashion is on the side of the DIY decorator here. Instead of the elaborate designs and high-glossed finishes of a decade ago, the trend is increasingly towards simple effects, painted chequers, bold stencilled borders, or a cool wash which gives the bleached look of driftwood. The fashion for 'distressed' paint has influenced the treatment of floors too, encouraging people to see that it does not matter if paint wears down gradually and allows the wood texture to show through – that in fact this adds homeliness and atmosphere. Pictures of Scandinavian interiors have demonstrated convincingly that diagonally set black and white chequers look excellent when painted in matt, chalky water-based paint which has worn thin here and there to give a semi-transparent effect. Where the Scandinavians used distemper, we would probably choose a matt emulsion [latex]. Either way the saving in time and effort, when compared with a serious traditional paint system, is considerable, as these paints are applied directly to the bare wood and varnished with a matt alkyd varnish which goes on and dries more quickly. Transparent finishes which retain the natural wood texture and warmth are those based on stains, which can be used to create marquetry style effects, or the new varnish stains, which add a noticeable depth of colour and of course need no further sealing.

But there are floors in such poor shape, one way or another, that the best treatment is to paint them out, using opaque paint. Where boards have been crudely patched, stained black round the perimeter, or are noticeably battered, the easiest disguise is a sensible dark colour overall – navy, red oxide, dark green or black – to which light relief may be added by way of stencils, rugs or a floorcloth (see page 137). Dark colours will need a dark undercoat, and should be sealed with a suitably tough varnish. The new water-based eggshell paints could be a good choice, as they are odourless and fast drying and to save still more time they can be applied with a roller.

Light coloured paint calls attention to defects, but if you crave the brightening effect of a pale floor in a dark room, you could achieve this by priming the boards with acrylic primer, then painting over with a roller and a matt emulsion [latex] colour, and finally sealing with two coats of matt alkyd varnish. It is chiefly the varnishing which gives painted floors durability, but a matt finish is less demanding than a glossy one.

Intricately patterned floors can look wonderful, but the decks will need to be cleared for action, most of which takes place on hands and knees.

Previous page The simplest floor treatment can be the most effective. Big painted squares of alternating light and dark colour cut across existing floorboards, cracks and all, creating a strong architectural presence and an exciting perspective. Here the squares have been lightly marbled to soften the contrast of such large chequers and also to suggest the marble pavement from which the idea derives.

Stencils are a help when executing any repetitive pattern (see page 129).

Paint is a useful way of dealing with stairs. You could wash them over in a driftwood colour to go with Scandinavian style chequers on the hall floor. Or try painting and stencilling a stair carpet. Another idea is to scrub the steps and leave them bare, but stencil the risers in a tile motif to create a bank of colour when viewed from below.

Plain paint, without trimmings, looks good when the colour is imaginative – try mixing your own. A glossy cadet blue or a sunflower yellow makes a practical and cheerful finish in a child's playroom, while matt, weathered-looking earth shades like raw sienna or Venetian red look warm and friendly on a sitting-room floor, scattered with rugs. No one would paint fine parquet, or wide old oak boards, but as a finish for the average scarred, beat-up softwood planking, paint is hard to beat.

Making good and preparation

Unlike furniture, a floor does not need to provide an ultra-smooth foundation for a painted finish. In fact, one advantage of using paint on a floor is that it will cover a multitude of sins, provided that it is finished off with enough coats of varnish to build up a smooth, tough surface. Nevertheless, some filling and sanding down may be necessary to level the surface and disguise the worst blemishes.

Nails and tacks Nail down any loose boards and remove any protruding nails or tacks left over from previous floor coverings. Use pliers, a tack lifter or the forked end of a standard claw hammer. Obstinate nails can be punched down below the surface, using a 7 mm [¼ in] punch.

Stripping down

You may need to remove dark, gummy varnish stain before you can put a finish on a floor. This tenacious substance contains black-coloured preservatives that seep into the wood beneath. Small patches can be removed by scrubbing with methylated spirit [denatured alcohol], but the only way to deal with large areas is by deep sanding (see below), to remove the stained layer of wood. This can be very hard work, and time-consuming. If you have a floor that has been partially or wholly finished with varnish stain, your best move is probably to sand it to clean up the surface, and then paint it over completely.

Old paint usually responds to softening with a blowlamp or heat stripper [heat gun], scraping off the softened paint with a straight-ended paint scraper and a shave hook for tricky corners.

Homemade caustic stripper There are many chemical strippers available but you can make the strongest (and cheapest) kind yourself. Mix one can of caustic soda with 1 litre [1 US quart] of water, and thicken with flour or cornflour [cornstarch]. This must be used with great care: follow the maker's instructions precisely. Open all the windows and try not to breathe in fumes more than necessary. Wear protective clothing: heavy duty gloves, goggles and a rubber apron. Caustic burns skin, hair and

117

Right Combining elegance with simplicity, this Swedish 18th-century interior has all the ingredients that make the Gustavian style so appealing: delicately textured walls in faded ochre and blue, with trompe l'oeil panelling; bleached floor; 'sky' ceiling; painted chairs with simple red and white checks.

Left Sanded deal floorboards have been transformed by the imposition of a striking marquetry design in two colours, the palest tone being supplied by the wood itself. Designs like these can be carried out in coloured wood stains or paints sufficiently thinned to allow the wood grain to show through.

Left Faux marquetry can also be highly complex, involving multi-layer stencilling and painstaking brushwork. But notice how this elaborate design gains from the woody texture of the floorboards.

clothes, so if any lands on you wash it off at once with clean water. Apply it to the floor a small patch at a time, getting as far back as you conveniently can. It softens paint messily but thoroughly in anything from 10 minutes to a few hours. Do not allow it to dry out, but add more water now and then, and scrub hard with a brush to loosen the softened paint. Rinse thoroughly, first with clean water then with water plus a dash of vinegar to neutralize the caustic. Caustic leaves wood roughened and whiskery so, when dry, sand the whole surface thoroughly, working from coarse to fine sandpaper. Caustic is best used for small, controllable areas like stair treads, rather than for stripping a whole floor, where you should use a heat stripper [heat gun].

Levelling up A painted or stained floor will look better if larger cracks and craters in the wood are filled. For a transparent finish, such as a stain or dye, use one of the proprietary fillers designed for woodwork [wood putty], since they expand and contract with the wood, and are thus less likely to shrink and drop out. Tint the filler to match the bare wood roughly, using water-based colours or universal stainers [tinting colours]. Alternatively, tint it with the dye or stain you are going to use on the floor. When the filler has dried, sand it smooth. Under an opaque, painted surface you can use putty for filling. The crack or hole must first be roughened and given a dab of primer or undercoat, to prevent the putty from shrinking and 'lifting'. Do not attempt to fill every crack and knothole, just the worst scars.

Sanding If a floor is to be left *au naturel* and sealed, or given a transparent finish, it should first be sanded down, to remove accretions of dirt, varnish, paint or stain and to present a nice, clean blotting-paper surface. Power sanding machines do the job infinitely quicker than any small domestic sanding appliance, and can be hired from most do-it-yourself shops. The shop will advise you on how to operate them. Use a large sander for the main floor area and a small edge sander for borders and corners.

Sand down the floor before you do any other decorating. Clear the room of everything moveable and keep it sealed, since wood dust clings. Sanders produce a lot of dust, so wear a face mask or scarf over your nose and mouth. Keep the machine on the move, so that you don't scar the wood. Starting from one corner, sand the floor in diagonal strips, each strip overlapping its neighbour by about 7 cm [3 in]. When you have been over the entire floor, sand along the other diagonal in the same way. Lastly, fit a finer abrasive and sand the floor following the direction of the woodgrain. Vacuum up the dust as you go along, and finish the floor off by scrubbing with water and a little bleach. Allow to dry out thoroughly.

Failing a sanding machine the best course is to give boards a thorough scrub. I find a strong cream cleaner and a scrubbing brush does a good job. Rinse over with a mop and hot water and let dry thoroughly.

Sandpaper will rub away the odd scar or stain – wrap it round a sanding block for greater efficiency. Sand in the direction of the grain with long, smooth strokes, using coarse or medium, then fine, sandpaper.

Transparent Finishes

Dyes

Standard fabric, carpet and leather dyes work quite well on bare wood floors, provided that any wax or grease on the surface is first removed. This should be done by sanding, scrubbing and finally wiping over with rags dipped in white spirit [mineral spirit] or vinegar and water. Remember to allow for the natural tone of the wood when choosing your colour and visualizing the effect. Greens, blues and maroons look good.

Mix up a strong dye solution, following the maker's instructions, but using about half as much water. Try out a little on a patch of wood, and let it dry to gauge the effect. If you are satisfied with it, use a wad of clean, lint-free rags to swab the rest quickly, and as evenly as possible, over the entire floor. Two or three successive applications may be needed to alter the wood colour appreciably. The result is likely to be streaky, since waterborne colour permeates wood patchily according to the amount of resin the wood contains, but it looks none the less attractive for that.

The dyed floor should be left to dry, and sanded lightly with medium sandpaper to smooth the water-roughened grain, before being coated with varnish. See page 122 on varnishing.

Stains

See the chart on page 214. Stains penetrate deeper into wood than dyes. They usually come in woody colours, but ranges of stains in fantasy, non-wood colours are also available.

The various types of stain use different media to help the pigment to penetrate the wood – water, spirit, oil and varnish. The water-based ones are the easiest to apply, but tend to dry patchily. Oil-based stains are best if you require a very even colour, since they dry more slowly. Spirit stains dry very fast, so that you have to take care not to go over the same patch too often, or it will become darker than the rest. Modern varnish stains are quick and easy to apply and available in a good colour range but tend to be very shiny when dry.

All stains should be applied over clean, bare wood – sanded, scrubbed, and rubbed with white spirit [mineral spirit]. Follow the manufacturer's instructions. The one exception is wax stain, which needs a coat of floor seal beneath it. Make this stain by melting beeswax or paraffin wax with artists' oils in a double boiler. Let it cool to a soft paste, rub it hard into the boards with a brush or cloth, then polish for a rich shine. The surface will need frequent rubbing, however, to keep it burnished, and the wax stain must be removed completely before another finish is applied.

Stains and stencils

One interesting decorative possibility is to use a dark wood stain to stencil an overall design on a light-stained floor. This gives a warm marquetry effect that allows the grain of the wood to show through.

Method

Apply the first stain over the entire floor, and leave it to dry completely. See pages 129–134 for stencilling techniques. Use simple geometric stencils. Dab the darker stain through the stencil holes with a lint-free rag or a brush. Do not take up too much stain at a time, or it may creep under the stencil and ruin the outline. This can be prevented by first pencilling in the stencil and coating the adjacent areas with shellac. When the stain is dry, wipe away the shellac – plus seepage – with a cloth dipped in methylated spirit [denatured alcohol]. The marquetry effect may be heightened further by carefully scoring round the designs with a sharp knife, or by outlining them with black felt-tip pen or paint, to imitate ebony inlay. Finish off by varnishing (see below).

Varnish

Polyurethane/alkyd varnishes (see page 214) are tough and easy to apply. They can be applied straight over a sanded wooden floor, as long as the wood is well seasoned. Any filling should be done with a compatible filler

Grey underfoot arrives at a completely different result from that shown on page 126 when the colour is semi-transparent but finished with enough layers of polyurethane varnish to arrive at a watery gleam. The boards are of good quality; they were bleached, then rubbed with grey paint and finally sealed with a gloss varnish.

A board floor painted in brisk chequers of grey and white is a clever choice for this small hallway with its eclectic mix of furnishings, from austere antiques to startling contemporary pieces.

first. Choose matt, semigloss or gloss, depending on the degree of shine you want. Gloss varnish is slower-drying and harder. It is easier to apply smoothly when thinned. If too shiny, it can be toned down by rubbing gently when quite dry and hard with medium steel wool. Varnish comes in tinted and clear finishes, all of which darken and yellow a little, though much less than they used to. Acrylic varnishes do not yellow, and some are now tough enough for floors.

Method

The room should be as clean and dust-free as possible. Apply varnish with a clean brush reserved for the purpose, laying the first coat across the grain, then levelling it off with the grain. When dry, sand it down before applying the next coat. Polyurethane varnish is touch-dry in 6 to 8 hours, but is best left overnight before recoating. From the second coat on, it can be thinned with a little white spirit [mineral spirit]: 3 parts varnish to 1 part solvent. The thinned varnish can be poured into a container, and if preferred, swabbed on with a soft pad made from a wad of cotton wool [absorbent cotton] wrapped in a clean, lint-free cloth.

The more thin coats of varnish you give the floor, the better it will wear – 3 is the minimum, but allow for 5 on a floor that takes a fair amount of traffic. It will need another coat every year or two. Before recoating it, make sure that the surface is clean, dry and free from grease.

A final thin coat of wax improves the look and durability of the varnish. But bear in mind that it will have to be taken off again before the floor can be revarnished.

Proprietary floor seal

Floor seal is a conveniently easy finish to apply, thin enough to be swabbed on with a soft cloth. Not as tough as polyurethane varnish, and slower-drying, it requires 2 or 3 coats to build up a surface that will withstand much wear.

The first coat should be rubbed into the wood across the grain, and the succeeding ones rubbed with the grain. Sand lightly between coats.

Like varnish, floor seal can be re-applied if it is wearing thin, but all wax and grease should be removed first by rubbing with solvent soaked rags or scrubbing with a mild sugar soap solution.

Wax

Wax smells agreeable, gives an incomparable shine and enriches the natural wood colour in a sympathetic way. But there is no getting away from the fact that it involves hard work.

Do not apply wax directly onto bare wood, particularly a softwood like pine, since it may allow dirt to become embedded in the fibres of the wood. Coat the surface first with floor seal. This will prevent the wax sinking in too far and will make raising a shine much easier. Swab the seal well into the woodgrain, and sand it down with fine sandpaper in the direction of the grain when it is dry.

The oldest, simplest form of waxing, using nothing more than beeswax and turpentine, is still to my mind the most pleasing, because of its delicious smell and its beautifully rich honey colour. It is now expensive for use on a large scale, and has always been a devil to apply and burnish, but for people who would like to try it out – especially on stripped pine, for which it is ideal – here is the formula. Beeswax can be bought from chemists [druggists] or craft shops.

Beeswax polish To make beeswax polish, melt a chunk of wax with some pure turpentine, in roughly equal proportions, in a double boiler or an old can placed in a saucepan of water. Take care that neither the wax nor the turpentine comes near direct heat, since both are highly inflammable. Leave the mixture to cool a little, and while it is still soft (but not liquid), scrub it thinly but thoroughly into the surface with an old soft brush or a lint-free cloth pad. Leave it for several hours to harden completely, then

124

rub it up to a shine with a clean soft brush – a shoe-cleaning brush will do. This is harder and slower than it sounds, and you will need to clean the brush often or swap it for another as it clogs up. The reward is a sweet-smelling finish with a soft depth of colour and a rich gleam.

Modern waxes are considerably easier to apply, and contain silicones to make them tougher, and driers to speed hardening. Use a soft cloth to spread the wax thinly, and after a few hours' drying, a soft brush to buff up the surface. End by polishing with a soft cloth.

Lightening

This technique for toning down natural wood colour is particularly helpful on knotty deal, or on any pine, which tends to go a hot orange colour if sealed or varnished after sanding.

Tinted white paint is brushed onto the wood and then rubbed off again, so that a residue is deposited in the cracks and pores. Use a flat white oil-based undercoat softened with a squirt of raw umber and dashes of ochre and black artists' oil colour or a greyish matt emulsion [latex]. With a stiff brush scrub this liberally over a small section of the wood, leave it for a few minutes, test to see if it is adhering, then rub it off with a rag. Rub against the grain quite firmly but not so hard that you remove all the paint, which should leave a distinct film of pale colour. Repeat this treatment over the entire floor.

If you want the paint to act as a grain filler as well, add a little wood filler [wood putty] or all-purpose filler [spackle] to thicken it up. This may need rubbing down with a medium sandpaper, wrapped round a cork block, to level up the surface again.

Bleaching

The smooth floors of bone-coloured wooden planks, which are such an attractive and distinctive feature in old Swedish houses, are the result of decades, if not centuries, of regular scrubbing and scouring with green soap and sometimes wet silver sand. Softwood, subjected to regular scrubbing, gradually whitens and leaves the harder sapwood slightly upstanding. There is no shortcut to attaining this weathered and worn effect, but a reasonable approximation can be achieved on a standard plank floor of pine or deal by rubbing in a tinted greyish white undercoat or emulsion [latex] paint as above.

Diluted emulsion [latex] colours can be brushed on and wiped off with a squeegee mop for driftwood effects. Choose cool off-white to grey shades with a grey-green cast to counteract any yellowness in the floor boards. For the chalkiest, the driest and most powdery looking finish, however, a water-based paint with a high proportion of plastery filler gives the best results, and here I must admit to an interest, having devised a paint of this type, called Woodwash (see list of suppliers). It can be diluted with water to give the desired degree of transparency, yet it has sufficient pigmentation to alter the overall shade and even out knots and other blemishes in the surface colour.

Painted Finishes

A priming coat is needed for an opaque finish as it helps paint go over wood smoothly, to cover better and to last longer. Give wooden floors, old or new, 2 coats of acrylic primer, which both primes and undercoats. If the top coat is to be a rich or dark colour, follow with a dark toned – but not matching – undercoat. This will show up any 'skips' in the top coat so that they can be quickly painted out before the paint has time to dry. One coat of the top colour should be enough for a plain paint finish, or as a ground for further decoration, although 2 may be needed in some instances.

Paint Most types of paint can be used successfully on floors, because a good varnish finish (polyurethane or alkyd) will prevent even soft-textured paints from being rubbed off. Matt emulsion [latex] paints are suitable, provided they are well varnished. I find their dry powdery surface an excellent base for decoration. The degree of shine in the paint is not really important, since the finish will be provided by the type of varnish you choose – matt, semigloss, or gloss. Undercoats or flat white oil paints have more opacity than gloss [enamel] paints, and are particularly suitable for painting floors. Professional decorators like flat white oil-based paint, tinted with universal stainers [tinting colours] or artists' oils, because of its pleasant brushing qualities and velvety texture, but frequently substitute standard undercoat these days. An eggshell paint is still best for designs, like those imitating tiles or china, where a hard, poreless ground is an advantage.

The room should be cleared, cleaned and sealed off as far as possible while you are working – but keep one window open to let out the paint smells.

Like walls, floors should be painted a section at a time, using roller or brush. Choose a brush wide enough to help, but not so wide that it cannot be handled comfortably. The chief thing to remember is to plan your floor painting so that you end up at the exit, not boxed up in a corner surrounded by sticky wet paint.

It makes a great difference to the final result if you sand lightly between coats, to smooth new paint surfaces and get rid of any grit, dust or fibres. Use medium sandpaper and vacuum away the dust.

When you have obtained the opacity of colour you want, leave the floor to dry out thoroughly. If you are not going to add any further decoration, all that is left is to varnish it – matt, semigloss or gloss, depending on the degree of shine required. See page 122 on varnishing.

Plain colour

Method

A smooth overall coat of pewter grey paint with a subtle graphite quality to it gives a cool slatey look to the board floor of an American country room. A shade or two darker grey has been used for the painted woodwork to give a feeling of continuity.

Chequers

Squares of alternating light and dark colour arranged on the diagonal (at a 45 degree angle to your boards) provide the most exhilarating and uncomplicated transformation for any painted floor, adding an unpretentious dignity and a sense of perspective which both strengthens a space and fits in with most decorating schemes. Which is why, of course, its noble progenitor, the chequered marble pavement, became *de rigeur* in so many grand houses, especially, though not exclusively, in hallways and formal rooms. I think the painted version sits well with much less ostentatious decors, from bathrooms to garden rooms. The delight of it, at least in my preferred chalky colours, is that it offers light (because of the pale squares) without glare, structure (because of the dark squares) without oppressiveness; it creates a trick of perspective which never fails to expand your given space and yet can be made flexible enough, given a simple dark border, to fit the most meandering, crooked or simply cussed architectural details.

Preparation

Scale is the first question to resolve. Huge checks which work beautifully in a ballroom or palatial foyer look overblown on a small irregular floor. But equally, small tile-sized squares may be too busy for visual repose, as well as being the devil to paint. A floor plan, carefully measured to scale, will help determine the best chequer size, although some people can more or less gauge this by eye. A floor plan helps to take account of unexpected factors such as walls which slope off on a diagonal, hallways which narrow suddenly, nooks and so on, which interrupt a precisely geometric plan. A

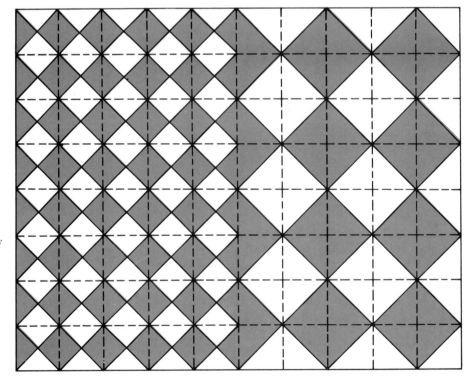

To mark out a chequered floor, first follow the instructions on pages 132–3 for squaring it off. Having chalked out your squares, draw in the diagonals, passing through every point where a horizontal and a vertical line cross. Start in a corner and work out across the room. For larger chequers for bigger floors, *right*, put in diagonals through alternate crossing-points only or measure off larger squares.

dark border, in the same colours as your dark chequer, can accommodate all these irregularities, narrowing or broadening to suit the case but remaining visually credible. In this context, think of your chequers as a geometrically exact carpet or rug, set at the correct angle to the doors, but with an unobtrusive border which can assimilate structural oddities.

When it comes to marking out I find the LP sleeve, if you are old enough to remember such things, a useful one for most situations – having an ingrained resistance to practising what I preach when it comes to serious measuring and graph paper, I have painted chequered floors successfully simply by tracing round one of these useful templates over and over again. The more sternly practical reader can invest in an automatic chalk line, obtained from builders' merchants and some specialist paint shops. This consists of thin string wound into a receptacle containing chalk dust, which becomes 'chalked' as it is released, depositing a chalk line when it is stretched between two points and plucked firmly.

Method

Marking out is the hard bit of the project. What you do now depends on the type of paint used and the desired finish. If you want opaque chequers, apply undercoat, followed by the topcoat of your chosen pale colour. If you are going for the semi-transparent look apply the pale topcoat directly onto the boards. Let the paint dry, then pencil or chalk in the main guidelines and fill in alternate squares with the dark shade, using a fat brush to fill in and a fine pointed watercolour brush (No 4 or 5) to give punctilious neat-edged lines. For a matt colourless seal the best varnish over any paint is an extra pale dead flat alkyd applied according to the maker's instructions. One or two coats will be sufficient.

Floor stencils

The most successful floor stencils I have seen kept quite close to effects created by more traditional types of flooring, using fairly dark and subdued colours and regular, repetitive designs. Apart from the practical consideration of not showing dirt and dust, there is an aesthetic or psychological point behind this preference. Visually, a room gains from being weighted at the bottom with a solid-looking floor – a delicate flowered porcelain effect on a pale ground may look pretty, but it can make one feel vaguely uneasy unless the other colours in the room have been chosen with care to balance the insubstantial-looking floor. Study the examples shown here, as well as traditional floorings and decide for yourself. Technically speaking, floors are stencilled in the same way as walls. See pages 69–72 on how to design, prepare and cut stencils.

Preparation

The floor surface must be fairly good for stencilling; it needs to be reasonably smooth if the stencils are to look crisp. Stencilled patterns look more dramatic and carpet-like over an opaquely painted ground, softer and less demanding over a semi-transparent finish. If you want an opaque ground, finish with a matt emulsion [latex] or undercoat plus a top coat of water-based eggshell paint. See page 127 for how to paint a floor.

129

Above Painted floors can be delightfully carefree and animated in their design. This pretty stencilled floor was given a coat of white paint to provide a cool background to sprays of blue flowers. A delicate border echoes – and may even be actively inspired by – a profusion of pattern in a nearby collection of blue and white porcelain.

Right The dazzling colours of a Swedish neoclassical interior are handsomely counterpointed by a stencilled floor scheme of dramatic simplicity. The brown octagons, which are the colour of the timber, and the black diamonds have been stencilled on a pale grey background. A matt varnish is best suited to a floor scheme like this.

Squaring off a floor
To square off a floor (whether for a
chequered or squared, stencilled design)
you will need a pencil, ruler and squared
paper; chalk, ball of string and/or a long
wooden batten; a set square for checking
angles. Two people will speed up this slow
and rather fiddly operation.

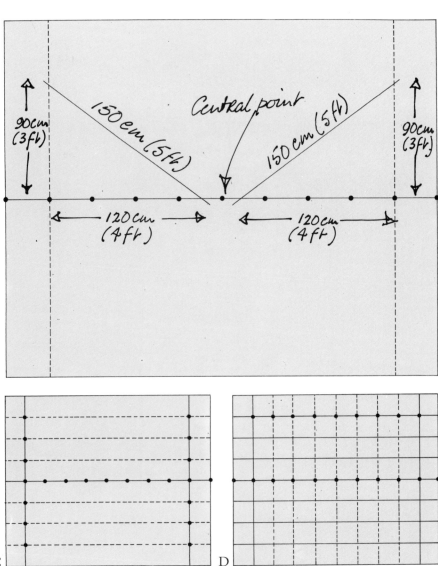

B

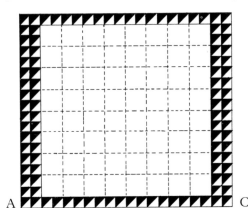

A

C

D

1 Measure the room or floor space and
draw it out to scale on a sheet of squared
paper. Having decided on the size of the
squares (or pattern blocks for stencils)
mark these off in pencil along the sides of
the floor plan, working outwards from the
central point of each wall. You may have to
adjust the size of the squares to suit the
floor space, because most simple patterns
look best if they complete a run. A border
(A) gives room for adjustment here.

2 Find and mark the centres of two
opposite walls. Using chalk and a long
batten, or a length of heavily chalked
string pulled taut across the floor and
snapped in the middle, mark a straight line
across the floor between these points. The
centre of this line is the centre of the room.

3 Working from the central point,
measure off the width of the squares in
both directions along the line you have
just drawn. Through the two outer points
draw two more lines, parallel to each other
and at right angles to the first line, running
the length of the room. Accuracy is
important in measuring a floor, as small
mistakes soon become large ones when the
lines drawn are very long. Check the right
angles with a set square, or better still by
the following simple method. Measure
90 cm [3 ft] along one parallel, 120 cm
[4 ft] along the central line, mark these

points and draw a line between them. This
third line should measure exactly 150 cm
[5 ft], if it doesn't the angle is not a right
angle (B).

4 Having drawn these lines with chalked
string or batten, mark off the squares
along them, as for line one. You are now in
a position to draw in all the lines in one
direction by joining up the points across
the floor as shown (C).

5 Choose one of the outer lines (parallel to
line one) and again mark off the width of
the squares from the centre outwards.
Complete the grid by joining the two sets
of points as before (D).

Paint The paints to choose for stencilling floors, as well as walls, are those that dry quickly, give maximum coverage and come in good colours. Most professional painters today use artists' acrylic tube colours for all stencilling purposes, because they dry almost instantly, can be diluted with water to the required transparency, and avoid the health hazards posed by using spray paint in a confined space. The joy of spray paint was its soft yet clear image, but I find this can be matched by using acrylic colours very sparingly on a rounded mop brush or stipple brush. American readers may prefer to use japan colours thinned with white spirit [mineral spirit]. These have the advantage that the stencils dry almost as you do them, so there is little risk of smudging as you move across the floor.

A flat paint, either undercoat or matt emulsion [latex], either gives good coverage for stencils.

Brushes A rounded mop brush or stippling brush, used in a round and round movement, gives the crispest definition, with a nice, textured look. If you are stencilling with more than one colour at a time, use a different brush for each colour.

Other equipment Squared paper; chalked string or chalk and straight-edge; the usual supply of rags for mopping up; saucers for mixing paints; stencils or stencil-making materials.

Before beginning to stencil, you will need to square off the floor so that you have one square for each stencil position. Measure out the floor and make a floor plan on squared paper. Mark out on the plan squares based on the size of your stencil (see instructions opposite). Use your plan to mark guidelines on the floor, using a chalked string or a straight-edge to help you place your stencils. For an all-over, regularly spaced pattern, square off the floor as shown opposite. To plan a border, divide the wall lengths by the size of the motifs to calculate how many repeats will fit in. Chalk a guideline the length of the floor at the required distance from the skirting, and mark off short lines along it at the central point of each motif. On each stencil again mark the centre of the motif and draw two lines at right angles through this point so that the stencil can be accurately positioned at each 'cross' on the guideline.

For instructions on how to mix colours, and place and paint stencils, see stencilling on walls, pages 69–76. Stencilling floors is a strain on the back muscles, so it is best not to try to cover too much ground in each session. Also, because of the heavier pressure one tends to exert on the brush in this position, there is more likelihood of smudges and blobs. Have a good supply of clean rags or tissues handy to wipe these away as you go along, and clean the back of the stencil frequently. Lift off the stencil carefully each time so as not to slide it over the wet paint. But a *bit* of sloppiness in the stencilling here and there is quite acceptable and will not show up too much when the floor is finished.

Materials for painting stencils

Method

133

Part of a remarkable painted floor, whose design was based on a seventeenth century carpet. A profusion of flowers, fruit and trees were applied straight onto the floor using stencils, car spray and acrylic paints.

Leave the completed floor for no fewer than 24 hours before varnishing. The paint must be perfectly dry. Give it at least 3 coats of matt, semigloss or gloss polyurethane varnish, or matt alkyd varnish.

Marbled floors

Painting a floor to look like marble adds a palatial air to any room. It is not as difficult as it sounds, because over a large surface the marbling can be done in a very loose and impressionistic way and still look convincing. You will find the technique easier to handle if you divide the floor into squares, to imitate paving slabs.

At the other end of the scale, marbling the floor in pale, cool colours adds a look of space and light to small, confined areas like hallways, landings and corridors. As long as it is given several protective coats of varnish, a painted marble floor stands up well to foot traffic.

Fossilstone marbling

The marbling technique described below is particularly effective. It is suitable for any flat, horizontal surface – table top, picture frame – but do not try it on a vertical one because the colours will run off. Its fossilstone appearance is achieved by spattering wet glaze with solvent – easy and surprisingly convincing. It looks best using low-keyed pebble colours –

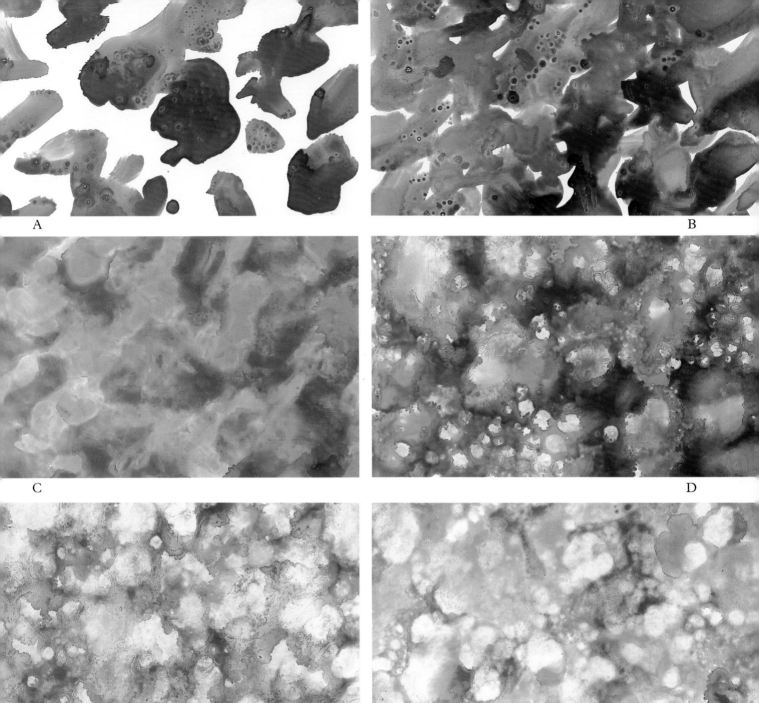

A

B

C

D

E

F

Fossilstone marbling

1 Apply a ground of white or off-white oil-based mid-sheen paint. When dry, sand it. With a soft cloth rub on a thin film of linseed oil. Mix up two paint glazes, from 1 part of the ground paint thinned with 2 parts white spirit [mineral spirit] and tinted with artists' oils or stainers [tinting colours]. Here, glaze 1 has been tinted with burnt sienna and yellow ochre, and glaze 2 with cobalt and raw umber. Dab on glaze 1 with a stiff brush (A).

2 Using the same brush, apply glaze 2 roughly in the spaces left by glaze 1 (B). Clean the brush.

3 Go lightly over the entire surface with a marine sponge or crumpled paper tissue to soak up excess glaze and give a softened effect (C).

4 Take up some white spirit [mineral spirit] on the brush. Flick the bristles with your thumb to spatter the glazed surface liberally. Little holes will open out where the solvent lands (D).

5 To add extra variety to the pattern (E), flick on drops of methylated spirit [denatured alcohol].

6 Soften again with a sponge or paper tissue (F). When the surface is quite dry, give it 3 to 5 coats of gloss polyurethane varnish, thinned 3 parts to 1 of white spirit. Lightly sand each coat except the first.

135

greeny-grey, dull blue and tawny brown – and is especially impressive on hardboard [particle board or masonite] tiles used as a floor covering.

Preparation　Cut hardboard into large tiles about 120 cm [4ft] square. Prime it with acrylic primer, standard undercoat or thinned emulsion [latex] paint.

Cover your working area with newspaper or sheets of plastic. Paint over the tiles with white or off-white oil-based mid-sheen paint. When the surface is dry, sand it smooth with medium sandpaper. The finish should be not only smooth, but also opaquely white, so it will probably need as many as 3 coats of paint, each one sanded down. Smoothness matters with this marbling technique, because brushmarks or bumps left on the paint surface interfere with the opening-out movement of the glaze that produces the fossil shapes. Rub over the surface with the thinnest smear of raw or boiled linseed oil, just enough to give a faint sheen. This will stop the moving glaze from spreading uncontrollably.

Filling woodgrain If you plan to marble a table top and the wood is coarse textured and open grained, you will get much better results by filling the wood grain before painting. Use proprietary wood filler [wood putty], all-purpose filler [spackle] or synthetic gesso, applying as many coats as necessary to level up the grain. Rub the surface smooth with sandpaper, then undercoat it and paint it with oil-based mid-sheen paint for a hard, fine-textured surface. Table tops undergo closer inspection than floors, so it is worth taking extra trouble to get a first-rate finish.

Materials　Two paint glazes, made by mixing 1 part white flat or mid-sheen oil-based paint with 2 parts white spirit [mineral spirit], and tinting with artists' oil colours or universal stainers [tinting colours]. The glazes should be as thin as milk, and dark enough to show up well on the white ground – test them on a corner of a hardboard tile.

You will also need a 75 mm [3 in] brush; a stiff stencil brush; white spirit [mineral spirit]; methylated spirit [denatured alcohol]; a marine sponge or some crumpled paper tissue.

Method　Work on one tile at a time, laying it flat, face-up, on your protected work area. Dip your brush into one of the glazes, and with it dab a roughly chequered pattern over the surface. Then dip the brush into the other glaze and use it to fill in the gaps, not worrying too much about keeping the sections apart. Go over the whole surface with the sponge or paper tissue to remove some of the heaviest glaze and produce a crumpled-looking, slightly blended effect.

Now take up some white spirit on the stiff stencil brush, and flick this with your thumb, to spatter the wet glazed surface quite thickly. In seconds, the glaze will start 'cissing' – little holes opening up and radiating outwards to suggest round fossil shapes. For more variety you can flick on some methylated spirit at this stage – it also cisses, but produces rather different shapes. Small drops of water will leave neat little rings. If you spatter on any extra large blobs that threaten to ciss rampageously, mop up the excess liquid quickly with a corner of paper tissue. See the photographs on pages 135 and 178 for an idea of the effect.

This is a technique to have fun with – the difficulty is knowing when to stop. Do not overwork the effect. When you are quite satisfied with it, leave the tile to dry perfectly flat.

Varnishing Once the marbled tiles are completely dry, varnish them with up to 5 coats of clear gloss polyurethane varnish – thinned 3 parts varnish to 1 part solvent. Rub lightly with sandpaper after every coat except the first. When the tiles are finished, scrub a little water into the back and leave them overnight to adjust to the conditions of the room before laying.

This finish can of course be used on furniture as well as floors. For a superbly smooth finish on a table top, do not sand the last coat of varnish, but rub it over with powdered pumice, rottenstone or household scouring powder and a little baby oil or salad oil. Apply this goo with a piece of felt or with a soft flannel cloth, using long strokes and following the direction of the grain underneath. Wipe it off with a damp cloth, and when dry, polish the surface with a soft, clean one.

Marbled floorboards

You can also marble directly onto the floorboards, provided that the cracks are not too noticeable and the surfaces are reasonably smooth. See pages 117–120 for how to get them that way. New wood should be primed; over 1 or 2 undercoats, paint the ground colour in oil-based mid-sheen paint, which gives the best surface for marbling. Use the marbling method described on pages 108–112, but divide the floor area into large squares – see pages 132–3 for squaring off a floor. Mark these out carefully on the surface with ruler and black felt-tip pen, since they become part of the design. Marble one square at a time; this breaks the job up into manageable units and it will look better too, since you can vary the direction of the veining from square to square in a naturalistic way. Finish with 3 to 5 coats of thinned clear gloss varnish (3 parts varnish to 1 part solvent) for protection.

Floorcloths

Floorcloths, 'painted carpets' of primed, painted and varnished canvas, were popular during the eighteenth and nineteenth centuries before being largely replaced by linoleum. In view of modern scepticism about the wearing qualities of paint underfoot, it is worth noting that in their day floorcloths were valued because they were both hard-wearing and easy to clean. In darker colours, painted to suggest marble pavement or patterned tiles, sometimes stencilled in imitation of straw matting or even Turkey carpet, these floor coverings were thought especially suitable for hallways, dining rooms, corridors, and the upper servants' rooms in country houses, all areas which might expect hard wear. A seamless floorcloth was often made to fit a given space and the requirement for extra-wide canvas

Right Pale painted marble paving cleverly picks up – without precisely copying – a warm and sunny melon-coloured paint on the walls, bringing still more light and a formal elegance to a handsome hallway. The use of colour is instructive: two soft colours for the Siena and Carrara style squares stand out against a dirty white ground, but it is the small brown lozenges that sharpen the design, marrying with strong dark accents like the polished handrail, black lantern and dark painting and plinth.

Opposite A floorcloth in a teasing 'stepped' design, is an interesting feature of this early American house.

led to many floorcloth factories starting up near sail-making centres in sea ports and docklands.

Today the chief appeal of a floorcloth is surely aesthetic; it surpasses mass-produced vinyl floor covering by virtue of being hand painted and retaining something of the pleasant texture of the canvas base. The design and colouring can be adapted to suit every decorating scheme. But it remains a practical proposition too – with periodic revarnishing, a floorcloth will last many years. (The durability of a floorcloth does in fact depend more on the varnishing than on the type of paint used.) Modern primer, paints and varnishes make the creation of a floorcloth a

comparatively speedy process, as each stage is quick to dry, and if you tackle the job yourself the cost, when set against any commercial product of comparable style, is negligible.

The critical factor in deciding the size of a floorcloth is the amount of space you have available in which to work. A small floorcloth, say the size of a bedside mat, can be done on the kitchen table, as long as you have somewhere it can be laid out to dry between coats. A room-sized cloth is best painted *in situ*, which of course puts the room in question out of bounds until the project is completed. The intermediate sizes are probably the biggest problem because the cloth should be stretched during priming and drying. One solution is to pin the cloth out on a reasonably flat stretch of lawn during a spell of fine weather.

Designs These can be as traditional or as fanciful as you please. Geometric designs forming a regular grid are probably the easiest to execute and look handsome underfoot. Or you could cut down the work by stencilling a wide border and a central medallion against a plain coloured or spatter painted background (porphyry looks excellent – see page 182.) Look through magazines for inspiration: chequered stone or marble, marquetry inlay, Roman mosaics, medieval tiles, flooring designs by architects like Robert Adam and William Chambers – all these sources could provide ideas and may be interpreted with stencils and paint. For colour and gaiety underfoot, copy blue and white Spanish tiles, or the motifs appliquéd on an old quilt. One of the most helpful design source books I have come across is a slim volume called *Country House Floors* (see reading list for further details).

Materials You will need canvas or cotton duck which comes in widths up to 9.5 metres (10⅓ yards) – suppliers will advise here. When measuring up, allow for shrinkage of approximately 75 mm per metre [1 in per linear foot], also for a turnback all round of 40–80 mm [1½–3 in, depending on the overall size]. PVA adhesive in tub size; heavy duty craft knife plus packet of spare blades; acrylic primer in 2½ or 5 litre size [5 to 10 US pints] according to the scale of the project; stencil card; carbon paper; hard lead pencils; 1 litre [1¾ US pints] emulsion [latex] paint in your chosen base colour; assorted acrylic tube colours plus rounded stippling brush (see page 232) for applying decoration; abrasive papers in medium to fine grades; steel or plastic rule, or a length of moulding, for marking off and ruling lines; standard 2.5 cm [1 in] decorating brush for filling in; No 3 watercolour brush for fine detail; your chosen varnish – see page 145 for more about choosing an appropriate varnish for your floorcloth. (A standard roller as sold for applying emulsion [latex] paint enormously speeds up priming and base coating though the surface will need rubbing down to smooth it between coats.)

Optional extras The easiest way to keep canvas stretched in the early priming stage is to staple it to a wooden floor, or table top, depending on how large it is. To do this use a heavy duty staple gun and $\frac{1}{2}$ in [12 mm] staples, or drawing pins [thumbtacks]. A preliminary sizing of the canvas or duck with rabbit's skin size, (see page 37) applied warm, makes the primer go further and adds flexibility. Alternatively coat the surface with diluted PVA.

Preparation

Staple or tack down your square or rectangle of canvas or cotton duck, pulling it taut, and keeping the staples (or tacks) within the turnback allowance. Be generous, as too few staples will lead to wavy edges. If you are using size, dilute this in a *bain marie* or double boiler to a thin fluid consistency and apply it first with a large brush, letting it dry overnight. Otherwise start straight in with the acrylic primer, using a mohair roller and working it well into the fabric so that to some extent it fills in the weave. Allow up to 2 hours drying time. When dry, repeat the priming. Two coats is the minimum requirement. Perfectionists may turn the cloth over (using a tack lifter or screwdriver to loosen the staples or tacks) and give the back one coat too. This gives more 'body' and distributes the shrinkage evenly. When thoroughly dry, use medium grade abrasive paper to smooth off the primer coats.

Now check the outer measurements of your cloth and pencil them in with a ruler, checking that corners are right-angled. Apply PVA adhesive to both turnback and the surface it will fold back on, let the adhesive dry for the required time, then fold back neatly along the pencilled guideline and press the surfaces down firmly to bond. With a large cloth this is more easily done with an extra pair of helping hands.

What you do next depends on the style chosen for your cloth, and on its colour scheme. If you are using coloured motifs on a pale ground, the whole cloth should be given one or two coats of base colour, using a roller. When dry your canvas will now be ready for marking out and decoration.

Marking out the pattern and painting

Use coloured chalk or tiny pencil dots to plot the design on the floorcloth. Regular repeat motifs, such as appliqué blocks or tile patterns, can be positioned by chalking in the centre line of the cloth both ways and working outwards from the middle. Designs relying on templates should be drawn in all over before you start. These can then either be painted in by hand, or, if this seems too longwinded and the pattern is suitable, you can make a stencil of the main part of the design in acetate, register it over each of your drawn shapes and paint it in.

It is probably a matter of temperament how long you spend over getting your design mathematically aligned on the floorcloth. Some people will want to mark in the position of each stencil block or pattern before painting, others will position them by eye as they go along – quicker, but it does lead to errors. However, if you allow a generous margin for a border all the way round, any major slip-ups can be corrected later by reducing the size or style of the border.

With strongly contrasting schemes using predominantly dark base colours it is obviously easier to cover a pale colour with dark than vice

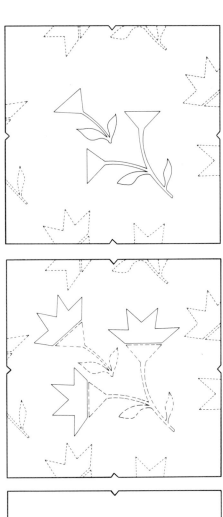

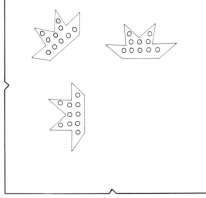

Above One example of a repeat design is this floorcloth using the hearty red and green and the crisp, formalized motifs of an old appliqué quilt.

Left Make a separate stencil for each colour in a motif: registration marks on the acetate mean that you can align each one accurately over the previous ones.

Right above Porphyry spattering is the ideal foil for neoclassical ornament in terracotta, black and white on this painted and varnished canvas floorcloth.

Right below Stencilling on a woven sisal mat gives an astonishingly close approximation to antique needlework. While the basic scroll designs have been stencilled, the shading and detail have been added freehand.

versa. So mark out your pattern on the unpainted canvas and paint the light areas first in your chosen colour, let dry, then fill in the dark surrounding areas. Alternatively, a light or vivid design on a dark base can be whited out before you start to paint it in. Suppose you wished to paint pink roses on a black ground, you would first apply the black base, let it dry, then stencil or paint in your motifs freehand in white primer, or white acrylic tube colour. When this is dry and opaque, brush in the flowers in colours as transparent and soft as you please.

With spattered backgrounds some spatter colours will inevitably stray past their limits, over the border or a central medallion, so it is best to complete the spatter sequence (see page 177 for method) and let it dry before adding a paler colour and medallion colour, which will obliterate unwanted spots.

Another way to add interest to a floorcloth is to use a thin tinted wash of colour over the background colour. For the floorcloth shown on page 142, we used Smoke Woodwash, much diluted, over white matt emulsion [latex] for a creamy colour like the calico that might have been used in a real quilt. A marine sponge is the simplest tool with which to apply a thin wash. Don't make it too wet, and use a brush and rag to soften and even out the effect further if you wish.

Stencilled patterns

Stencilling makes repetitive decoration so much faster and more controlled that the extra time given up to designing, drawing and cutting stencils is well worthwhile. If you want clear but even colour and crisp shapes a bushy stippling brush used with the barest minimum of colour gives better results with less fuss than any other method. Or for a painterly texture experiment with a foam pad or a marine sponge. Take up the minimum of wet colour and first practise applying it through the stencil onto waste paper. Inexperienced painters always use too much colour to start with, so that it seeps under the stencil edges and smudges when the stencil is lifted off. If this happens, simply paint out the smudge with the base colour. But a little error is not serious; a hand-painted floorcloth should not look like machine-printed vinyl.

A more detailed account of stencilling, from transferring to cutting and registering overlays is given on pages 69–76; here I will simply mention points especially relevant to decorating floorcloths. Use a photocopier to enlarge or shrink designs to fit your grid – if you make a few extra copies you can lay them out to get a sense of the finished effect. You may find a motif needs simplifying to strengthen its impact as a repeat. Or it may be that colours need adjusting to make them 'lie down'; colours which jump out at you are an unhappy choice for floors. Try dirtying bright colours with raw umber, and in the main use subdued colours of similar intensity with light or bright accents. If your ideas have been taken from rugs or carpets remember that the texture and pile of these softens and diffuses colours, and a design will therefore look rather different on the flat shiny surface of a floorcloth. A final wash with diluted raw umber acrylic will blend most colours.

The lasting qualities of a painted finish underfoot are largely dependent on adequate final varnishing. In my experience the protection provided by thorough varnishing operates as effectively over standard water-based emulsions as over the inherently tougher oil-based paints. So, on balance it makes sense to go for fast-drying acrylics and emulsion [latex] for the basic painting and decorating, relying on the tough protective film provided by the varnish to keep the work in good shape. There are many varnishes to choose from, and when deciding which to use you should be guided by considerations such as yellowing, drying time and ease of application.

Varnishing

Acrylic varnish is far the quickest drying, useful if you are desperate to complete a job fast. It is also non-yellowing, which makes it a good choice over pale colours. On the other hand it is a little 'sullen' in application, brushing out less readily than traditional varnish, and the film, though tough, is less flexible so your floorcloth will not take kindly to being bundled about or rolled up. It is also more expensive.

Of the oil-based varnishes, very pale, flat alkyd finish is the least prone to yellowing, giving an almost 'water white' seal with reasonable resistance to wear. It is, however, matt in appearance, which suits some floorcloth designs better than others.

The standard polyurethane varnishes, described as 'clear', come in finishes from matt to gloss. Cheap and easy to apply, they give good protection but will darken and yellow noticeably over a period of time, due to oxidation caused by exposure to light. If your colours allow for this modification, there is no problem, but if you plan to stand furniture on the floorcloth you may find you are left with noticeably different colours once it is moved.

Yacht or spar varnish, devised to provide lasting protection under extreme conditions, is probably the toughest and best finish available, at least if the flexibility of the floor cloth is a consideration. The colours will yellow a fair bit, but in the case of an initially dark-toned cloth this would hardly matter, and the yellowing can add a certain attractive patina. Normally full gloss, these varnishes rapidly become less shiny with wear and tear underfoot.

Whichever varnish you choose, try to give your floorcloth a minimum of three coats. Tedious as this finishing process seems, the immediate reward is a deepening and enrichment of your painted work, bringing up unsuspected subtleties of colour and texture, while the long-term pay-off is simply that the piece stands up better to daily traffic.

If possible, varnish under a strong enough light source to ensure no bits are 'skipped'. The final surface is markedly improved if you refine and smooth the second, third and any subsequent coats with fine wet-or-dry sandpaper or aluminium oxide paper to remove any 'nibs', grit, dust and hairs which a drying varnish attracts.

Furniture

Furniture has been painted since earliest times, usually to add surface colour and texture, sometimes to protect or conceal inferior wood, or to disguise crude workmanship. Each creative historical period has added some particular refinement of technique or decorative flourish.

There has never been a more beautiful plain finish than the old lacquer that the Chinese made from the sap of the lac tree. The 'japanning' techniques used by later European craftsmen to simulate lacquer are flimsy by comparison, although they do have a witty sophistication.

No painted furniture is more poetic in its fantastic decoration and tender colouring than that produced by the Venetians from the time of the Renaissance onwards, yet their very refinement of the gesso and tempera finish served the more prosaic purpose of disguising inferior woods and joinery. For elegance of a highly strung sort, French and English furniture of the late eighteenth century is unrivalled, the colours and decoration applied with taste, discretion and consummate technique. Regency craftsmen added the spice of wit, sparkling colours and a great deal of gilt to shapes that are a lively spoof of the Gothic and the Chinese. Later in the nineteenth century, painted furniture entered a brief new phase in England under the inspiration of William Morris.

Such painted furniture belonged to the world of rich patrons, but alongside it evolved a democratic form – usually now called folk, rustic or provincial furniture. The workmanship is solid rather than refined, the shapes often clumsy, while the painted decoration itself tends to be bold and uninhibitedly colourful. It is often spirited, and like the decoration on Delft tiles or Staffordshire figures, skilful for all its apparent slapdashedness. Its brash colouring softened by time and use, much of this folk-style furniture is highly endearing, and perfectly at ease in modern homes.

Unless one is very lucky, the chances of picking up an attractive old piece cheaply are getting smaller all the time. The only really inexpensive items around seem to be the boarding-house and office furniture of thirty years or more ago, often solidly made, usually of oak, but with a treacly varnished finish that looks unhappy anywhere. Painting them in the ordinary way makes them inconspicuous, but decorative finishes can transform them into really attractive, colourful pieces.

Painting furniture is tempting to try, because the preparation and work can be done in a small space without making too much mess or disrupting the household. In most cases the materials are cheap and easily available – filler, paint, stainers or artists' colours, varnish.

There is a decorative finish to enhance any type of piece and emphasize its attractive features while camouflaging its worst points. Ugly, coarse-grained wood texture is easily hidden by priming with the modern equivalent of the old Venetian gesso, to build up a hard, poreless surface for paint. Large, looming wardrobes, sideboards or chests of drawers undergo a visual shrinking process when given a simple distressed finish in quiet colours that match or tone with the wall colour. Such outsize pieces are always improved by a matt or at most a semigloss finish because

Previous page Old Delft tiles, with spirited scenes in cobalt blue, are the theme for this attractive piece of trompe l'oeil painting. These 'tiles' were used to decorate a chimney board, but the same idea would work on a table top or door panels.

non-shiny surfaces seem to look smaller than glossy, reflecting ones.

Two big changes in the field of furniture painting over the past few years have been the steady rise in popularity of water-based paints and varnishes as against the older oil-based ones and, in tandem, a marked preference for paint surfaces which have been crazed, crackled, nibbled at, rubbed away and otherwise 'heavily distressed'.

Mostly acrylic based, water-based products dry in a twinkling compared with their oil-bound relations. They are also healthier, being free from solvents like white spirit [mineral spirit]. The practical gains in terms of speed of application, odourlessness and being easier to clean are countered by an aesthetic loss: there is a certain flatness and stodginess of texture about standard emulsion [latex] water-based paints. There are, however, ways of handling and finishing them which give back some richness and texture, and this is where 'heavy distressing' plays such an important role (see page 164).

Whatever materials or paint effects you have in mind, however, start by looking for items in good working order: drawers that slide, hinges in place, doors that fit, chairs that do not wobble. Choose a simple shape, an air of solidity, sensible proportions – in other words a piece with recognizable kinship to the classic models. Superfluous twiddly bits or gimcrack detail such as nasty handles can simply be removed, while some more stylish ornament can be made a feature of, with a suitable finish. Furniture with built-in decoration – relief carving on panels, turned knobs or curlicues – can be painted, too. A fantastic Gothic-style piece responds to a folk approach using strong, contrasting colours, but keeping the finish quite matt to resemble the powdery texture of old paint. Offbeat colours are best: dull reds, maroon, pea green, murky yellows, faded indigo, bistre, all of which can be achieved by mixing raw umber into a basic tint. In total contrast, furniture with shallow relief carving, the sort that looks more pressed than carved and usually goes with thirties shapes, looks surprisingly urbane and attractive if given a finish of that period – ultra-sleek creamy 'lacquered' paint achieved by patient rubbing down and varnishing. Good colours are cream, black and vermilion red.

Odd dining chairs can be given a visual link by painting them all in the same way. Spattering (see page 177) is a good finish, a technique so simple that a child could tackle it quite effectively. Paint cane-seated chairs of almost any style in soft, matt blues and greens, with the caning itself painted in a trellis pattern. Use the same colours and patterns to give a French provincial charm to the most ordinary, battered kitchen units – useful again if you want to link up pieces with disparate finishes.

Furniture does not, of course, have to be hideous or in a hideous condition to qualify for decorative painting. But no one would be rash enough to paint anything made of rare or expensive hardwood, or wood with attractive figuring. As a general rule, the best articles to paint are those of wood that looks better covered up, and these are usually of recent make. Sometimes an old piece may need painting to conceal unsightly repairs in wood that does not match, or to replace an old finish that has

What looks like an antique cupboard packed with blue and white china is a complete fraud; the cupboard was made yesterday, of medium density fibreboard and deal, but has been given a lightly distressed paint finish and gilded to suggest age and class. The china collection is make-believe, painted in trompe l'oeil on the door panels which have then had chicken wire stretched across them to strengthen the illusion.

worn off – though be careful here, since old paintwork in tolerable condition adds to the value of a good item. If you do repaint, make sure the technique and finish are appropriate to the piece.

Small wooden items, such as picture frames, boxes, trays or hanging shelves are great fun to decorate and one can afford to lavish more pains over a small thing that takes only a few minutes for each step. Marbled picture frames look immensely chic, as do blonde tortoiseshell painted boxes. Trays and table tops look elegant covered with neat, formal stencil patterns. Fossilstone marbling makes an easy and convincing finish for table tops. See pages 134–137, and 135 for examples.

Preparing furniture for painting

Decorative finishes of the sort discussed in this section are wasted effort unless the surface beneath is prepared to a high standard. Any surface imperfections, such as rough grain and unfilled scars or screw-holes, will show through the finish you put on top, and detract from the overall effect. Although giving a first-class finish to an old item of furniture usually involves painstaking preparation, extra time and trouble taken at this stage are well worthwhile since the result is an elegant piece that looks as though it comes from a professional studio.

Stripping down

The most important step is to take off the old finish and get back to clean, bare wood. Occasionally old paint is in good enough condition to paint over. Paint that has gone thin and chalky with time makes an excellent undercoat and small chips and cracks can be filled in with all-purpose filler [spackle]. But more often the old paint has been badly applied, sometimes straight over varnish, and is flaky, blistered and wrinkled. If you sand it down, wear a paper mask (as bought from a chemist [druggist]) or a scarf tied over nose and mouth, because old paints can contain lead, the dust of which should not be inhaled. Varnish should always be stripped or sanded down, to provide a good finish for painting. It is easily dissolved either with proprietary paint or varnish stripper or, in the case of a shellac finish like French polish, with methylated spirit [denatured alcohol]. It is often difficult to tell what the finish is, so try a little methylated spirit on the piece first, and if that fails to soften the finish quickly, progress to paint stripper. In any case, use proprietary stripper for smaller pieces, especially those with fine detail such as carving, fretwork and turned ornament, or on pieces that may prove to be made of superior wood. Unscrew hinged doors and remove drawer pulls and other metal attachments. Cover the surrounding floor with sheets of plastic, wear gloves, and apply the stripper with an old paintbrush, following the maker's instructions. When the top layers of paint have softened, which usually takes 10 minutes or so, scrape the sticky paste off large surfaces with a flat scraper, taking care not to scratch and scar the wood. Then clean up tricky surfaces with coarse, then finer, steel wool. It can take several applications of paint remover to work through many old paint layers. Small pointed knives or nail files, as well as matchsticks and toothbrushes, are handy for digging paint out of cracks or carving.

The rugged look of 'bush' furniture has been cleverly evoked in a DIY dresser made from reclaimed (and much nailed) timber beams. Thinned grey emulsion [latex] paint was rubbed into the bare timber and wiped back with a damp cloth. This was followed by an application of liming wax, which was lightly buffed with a rag to polish it. The door panels are cut from sheet tin.

Caustic Large pieces, covered with numerous layers of paint, are best cleaned with a strong caustic solution, see page 117 for the recipe. This should be done out of doors, using rubber gloves and applying the mixture with the type of spatula sold for putting on oven cleaner. Loosen the paint layers with an old scrubbing brush. A hose is handy for rinsing off the sludgy dissolved paint. Removing layers of paint may take several successive applications, and the mess is considerable, but over a large area it is infinitely cheaper to use caustic than proprietary stripper. To make things easier for yourself, lay as many sections as possible flat before rubbing it on. This will concentrate its action, since it tends to run off vertical surfaces. Caustic leaves wood fuzzy and discoloured, but patient, gentle sanding down with finer and finer grades of sandpaper will restore a smooth finish. Some firms advertize a paint-stripping service using tubs of caustic – useful if you live in an apartment block.

Primer As the name suggests, primer is the first coat of paint in a system. Experts insist that it should always be used if you are painting new wood, as it protects the wood by counteracting its natural porosity, so that subsequent coats of paint do not sink in. Of the various types available, the toughest is the traditional pink or white oil-based primer, sold for use on wood alone; it should be thinned 3 parts primer to 1 part white spirit [mineral spirit], applied liberally and brushed well into the wood. White universal primer can be used on wood or plaster, while aluminium primer goes over any highly resinous woods or varnished surfaces. Acrylic primer, for use on wood, acts as a combined primer and undercoat. Metal has its own primers.

The knots in pine and deal must be sealed with patent knotting [knot sealer] before priming. Do not skip this; knots continue to exude resin for years, and unsealed ones will cause surface paint to crack and discolour. Use it according to the maker's directions, applying 2 coats – more if the wood is really raw – over each knot. Dabbing it on with a rag goes faster than brushing.

Filler Coarse woodgrain, cracks and scars should be filled to present an even surface for painting. Use a proprietary woodwork filler [wood putty] or standard all-purpose filler [spackle]. Mix it to a creamy consistency and apply it with a brush. Apply the first layer with the grain; allow it to dry and then, if necessary, apply a second layer against the grain. When it is dry rub it down firmly, with the grain, using medium sandpaper. Coarse-grained woods like oak may need 2 applications to level them up.

Larger holes, dents or chips should be filled with a stiffer mix of filler, applied with a palette knife, left proud (above wood level) and sanded flat when dry. Really bad holes should be filled with a harder substance such as plastic wood – follow the manufacturer's instructions.

Sand down the primed and filled surface until smooth before going on to the undercoat stage. It is a good idea to apply a coat of shellac to any extra special piece, or one that will get a lot of handling, now – it really does improve the look and feel of the paint finish, giving a fine surface for paint. Thin it with 1 part methylated spirit [denatured alcohol] to 2 of shellac. See pages 159–60 on applying shellac.

Undercoat More highly pigmented than most paints, undercoat does a good cover-up job on furniture, as well as providing the ideal flat, 'hungry' surface for subsequent paints. Undercoat should be brushed out well to give even coverage and laid off lightly with the bristle tips to flatten out brushmarks. Apply 1 or 2 coats (thin it with a little white spirit [mineral spirit] if you are applying 2), depending on the state of the surface beneath. American readers can use an enamel undercoater, which doubles as a primer as well. Under pale colours, white undercoat is fine, but under dark ones it will need tinting to something near the final colour.

Rub it down firmly when dry with medium then fine sandpaper. On large surfaces begin rubbing in a circular motion, and end by rubbing in the direction of the grain beneath; on smaller pieces, rub with the grain throughout. For a supersmooth finish, use a special quick-drying fine filler, which comes ready mixed, to level up any little remaining blemishes. Keep the lid on this, since it hardens quickly if exposed to the air.

The routine of primer, filler and undercoat can be replaced by the application of gesso or two coats of acrylic primer (see page 152), which fulfils all requirements and takes less time.

Gesso

Gesso consists of whiting, a very fine chalky powder, mixed with water and bound with rabbit-skin glue. Kept warm in a double boiler, this mixture remains fluid enough to apply to different surfaces with a brush. Many layers of applied gesso build up a surface which can be rubbed down with abrasive paper to create a surface as fine, flawless and hard as porcelain; it is cheap to make, and versatile. Traditionally, it was used to prime wooden surfaces for painting or gilding, as well as for priming artists' canvases. It not only provides an immaculate and 'thirsty' surface for paint, but, as cabinetmakers were quick to discover, helpfully disguises coarse-textured wood and hasty workmanship. During the vogue for 'japanning' in the eighteenth and nineteenth centuries, gesso was used to build up the raised figures and other elements which, carved and gilded, are such as attractive feature of the style.

Framers, gilders, restorers and the like still swear by traditionally made gesso as a primer and base, especially for water gilding. Though it takes a little practice to get the hang of making and applying gesso, it is worth the effort for anyone aiming to achieve a high standard.

Watercolour in the form of gouache in gum arabic can be painted directly onto gesso. A coat of diluted orange shellac gives it the colour of old ivory, an excellent base for penwork. Tinted red, gesso makes the traditional base for water gilding. Or it can simply be treated as a superlatively smooth and strong primer/filler/undercoat for an oil-based paint system, in which case it is usual to seal it first with shellac.

Materials for making gesso

You need rabbit-skin glue granules and whiting, both obtainable from artists' suppliers; a bowl for soaking the glue size granules; a conical sieve; wooden spoon and some sort of double boiler on a hot plate.

Method

Soak half a cup of granules overnight in cold water to cover. They will swell and soften. Put this mixture into the top of a double boiler, over water which is just simmering, and add $\frac{1}{2}$–$\frac{3}{4}$ litre [1–1$\frac{1}{2}$ US pints] of water. Heat slowly, stirring to dissolve the glue, and when hot start adding whiting, sifted in through a conical sieve, stirring to blend and break up any lumps. The whiting should amount to between $\frac{1}{3}-\frac{1}{2}$ of the total volume of the gesso, and the gesso should have the consistency of thin cream. The traditional test of consistency is to pinch a little between finger and thumb; if the mixture is just perceptibly 'sticky' as you separate finger and thumb, it is strong enough. If not, add more dissolved glue granules. On the other hand if the mixture shows up transparent rather than whiteish when painted on a piece of wood, it is short of whiting, and you should add more, stirring as before. Apply warm with a soft brush, avoiding brushmarks as far as possible, though these can be smoothed off with sandpaper when dry. A coat takes roughly two hours to dry depending on climate and heating. One coat must be absolutely dry before applying the next, which should be brushed on at right angles to the previous coat. Rubbing down between coats smooths and compacts the gesso.

Acrylic gesso/acrylic primer

People with less exacting requirements may prefer to substitute one of the modern, acrylic-based products which are sold ready prepared and dry much more quickly, though the final surface will not be as hard and fine-textured as traditional gesso. Acrylic gesso, sold by artists' suppliers, is convenient but expensive and many decorative painters use ordinary acrylic primer instead because it has many of the same properties when

Above This newly painted chest shows how a striking design can be painted in quick-drying water soluble paint and muted colours on a distressed background to give something of the effect of faded watercolour on gesso.

Right The mellow look of old paint shows to advantage on an antique armoire. The light and dark green colours are picked out simply and effectively with their complementary shade of red.

154

A simple but stylish stencil inspired by eighteenth century marquetry borders dresses up recent joiners' work. Shelving of timber and medium density fibreboard have been grained in a blonde wood finish and stencilled in off-white.

built up in layers and well rubbed down between coats. Acrylic gesso and primers are delightfully easy to use. The piece of furniture does not even need to be stripped of paint or varnish first, although gesso adheres better and builds more rapidly if the surfaces are well sanded first to provide tooth. Depending on the state of the original finish, sand it first with coarse, then medium sandpaper. Fill in cracks and chipped veneer with wood filler [wood putty] or all-purpose filler [spackle], and sand it level when dry. Wipe over the whole piece with a rag dipped in white spirit [mineral spirit] to remove grease and dust.

Using an old brush – these plastery substances are hard on brushes – paint a thin coat of acrylic gesso or primer over the entire piece. Do not bother with the insides and unseen parts of furniture, but paint over all the previously finished surfaces, which usually include the edges of doors and tops of drawers.

The first coat takes about an hour to dry, subsequent ones somewhat less. Rub over the gesso or primer with folded medium sandpaper in the direction of the woodgrain, using firm pressure and long, level strokes. Dust off with a rag, and recoat, repeating the whole routine several times until you have built up a smooth, white, level surface over the whole piece.

Rub the gesso or primer down harder on door and drawer edges or they may not fit properly. If you are rubbing down correctly the finish will be so fine and compacted that the original finish will just show through on sharp edges. Beginners tend to go too gently from a natural reluctance to remove too much of what they have just laboriously put on – the ideal result is a thin, level and very smooth surface.

The number of coats needed varies with the type and condition of the wood and its previous finish. For example, open-grained wood will require 4 or 5 coats, previously painted wood only 2 or 3. Pieces that get a lot of handling, like chairs, should have several coats, and these should be rubbed down harder in between. You will need at least 5 coats of gesso if you are going to put transparent watercolour on top, to build up a white, shadow-free surface.

All-purpose filler [*spackle*] It is worthwhile using traditional or acrylic gesso or primer for special pieces. For less important items use all-purpose filler [spackle] thinned with water to a creamy, brushable consistency. Apply and rub it down in exactly the same way as acrylic gesso, although you will find that each stage takes longer.

Sanding down Sanding between layers of filler, undercoat, gesso, paint and varnish smooths the surface, while providing tooth for the next coat. Scrupulous sanding makes a difference to the final look and feel of a painted piece out of all proportion to the time involved. Professional work is *always* sanded, at every stage.

What we tend to call 'sandpaper' is, strictly speaking, abrasive paper, which may be coated with one of a number of substances such as glass, aluminium oxide or silicon carbide. These papers come in grades between coarse and fine, which are split into progressively finer subdivisions. The routine is to begin with a coarse paper and work down to a fine one. The finer you want your finish to be, the finer the grade of paper you must end up with.

When sanding a flat surface wrap your paper round a sanding block. This distributes your hand pressure evenly. Use firm pressure, and long, smooth strokes. Rub backwards and forwards in the general direction of the grain beneath, going gently over sharp edges, relief carving and turned detail. To sand a narrow, rounded surface, such as a chair arm or leg, wrap a small piece of sandpaper round it, like a scratchy collar.

Wet-or-dry (silicon carbide) paper, as its name suggests, can be used in either condition. Use it dry over bare wood. For rubbing down paint and varnish, it should be used with soapy water to soften the abrasive action and prevent scratching. Mix pure soap flakes with water and pat the sudsy solution over the surface. Rub the paper smoothly with long strokes from edge to edge of the surface, following the direction of the grain and going easy on projecting areas. Test the surface with your fingertips for smoothness from time to time, and wipe off the soapy mixture to check your progress. When you have gone over the whole piece, wipe it dry with a clean, damp rag.

As an alternative to wet-or-dry paper you can use steel wool, also with soapy water, but throw away the pads after use, since they rust up quickly. Like abrasive paper, steel wool comes in coarse to fine grades.

Painting Furniture

To produce a high-class paint finish requires patience – you need to linger longer over each stage. The aim is to achieve a sleek, level paint surface, thin enough not to obscure any carved or turned detail, flat and smooth enough for any decorative finish to glide into place. The more thoroughly you do the base painting, the better the final finish will look and the more gracefully it will age.

Paint

Mix your colours by hand, tinting you own paint as in the instructions on pages 216–221. This not only allows for much finer colour adjustments, but is also more convenient, since one can of paint plus the various tints takes up less room than an equivalent range of cans of bought colours.

Gloss [enamel] paints are not used in good quality furniture painting. Shiny paint does not provide enough tooth for subsequent decoration, and it looks wrong, especially on old pieces. Any shine required is added later by means of clear or tinted varnish coats, rubbed and polished.

Flat white oil-based paint, tinted with artists' oil colours, is the one commonly used for most furniture painting by professional decorators and restorers. Being relatively soft-textured, it needs several coats of varnish as protection against use and handling. Flat paint protected with matt varnish is the ideal finish for large, vividly decorated country-style pieces that look brash given a gloss finish. A cheaper, quicker-drying alternative to these is standard oil-based undercoat, which dries with an attractive chalkiness and can be tinted in the same way. Being soft-textured, it too will need adequate varnishing. Mid-sheen, or eggshell, paint is also used in furniture painting, especially under glaze work. It is somewhat more durable than flat oil or undercoat, and gives a nice smooth surface for lining, stencilling and other applied decorations. Recently a water-based eggshell paint has been introduced which has the added advantages of drying speedily and being low-odour.

Emulsion [latex] paint and acrylic colours are widely available, easy to use and quick-drying, giving a pleasantly chalky texture very close to that of the aged lead paint found on many old country pieces. Use matt emulsion to paint any piece that would look best with a simple, rustic finish, and acrylic colours for any decorative painting on top. This gives a quick and passable imitation of the old gouache over gesso decoration. Varnish renders an emulsion finish as durable as any other. Use 2 coats of clear matt varnish to give protection while retaining the flat, lean look.

Brushes Use a standard paintbrush on large pieces. On small, delicately detailed ones, a brush with soft, fine bristles, such as a glider brush, helps the paint to flow on so that it needs less rubbing down afterwards. Use a pointed sable watercolour brush (No 3, 4 or 5) for fine decorative work and a swordliner or lining brush for 'lining'.

Method *Applying oil-based paint* After tinting, mix the paint thoroughly with white spirit [mineral spirit] to a thin cream consistency – about 1 part white spirit to about 4 of paint. Leave each paint coat plenty of time – say overnight – to dry hard, before applying the next. Most of the troubles that arise in painting come from applying paint before the surface beneath is hard and dry. You will need between 2 and 5 coats of coloured paint to provide a good finish, or a ground for subsequent decoration. More but

Tiny floral motifs, on a background of muted Gustavian blue, soften the lines of this pine cabinet – typically Scandinavian in design. The mouldings have been deliberately rubbed down to give a convincing weathered and worn effect.

thinner coats give a professional appearance, and rubbing down is crucial. Use medium-grade sandpaper for the first coat, fine wet-or-dry paper with soap and water for the following ones.

Applying emulsion [latex] paint Although emulsion can be applied directly to bare wood, it tends to sink in and raise the grain. It is better to apply primer first, rubbed smooth when dry. You will need 2 or 3 coats of emulsion paint over primer, 3 or 4 over bare wood, each sanded down with medium sandpaper.

To capitalize on the inherently dry texture of this finish, apply further decoration in acrylics straight on to the emulsion ground. Be warned, however, that once a colour is brushed on to the emulsion surface, it is pretty permanent. You can apply a barrier coat of clear matt varnish, but this means some loss of texture. However, you can always paint out a real disaster area with a couple more coats of emulsion and start again.

Glazes and washes For how to make and apply these, see pages 223–228. Although tinted glazes are traditionally used in furniture decoration, their slow drying time means that they are often rejected in favour of quicker-drying tinted varnish.

The little gentleman surrounded by admiring birds – a detail from a 19th-century Danish cupboard – epitomizes the innocent style of early folk decoration. Try painting a portrait of one of the family. Mix raw umber into your basic paints to imitate these beautiful colours.

Transparent paint

For a special richness, an inimitable depth and glow unmodified by white pigment, you can make a sort of transparent paint, or tinted varnish, by combining a varnish finish with a tinting agent. Discreetly used, this is an easy way to give depth of colour to a painted wall or piece of furniture; it can also create the effect of an aged patina of dusty colour. It is essential that both varnish and tinting agent are of the same composition – oil being mixed with oil, water with water. Dissolve the tinting agent in the appropriate solvent, then mix it thoroughly with some decanted varnish, and test on paper before use. Raw umber, burnt umber, and burnt sienna are all colours which age a piece effectively. Layering varnishes tinted with slightly different tones of the base colour – orange-red, brown-red or crimson-red over red-red for example – creates a complexity of tone which can be very pleasing.

Application

Wipe the surface with a rag moistened in white spirit [mineral spirit] or in vinegar. Brush on the transparent paint like varnish (see page 162) thinly and rapidly.

Shellac

A spirit varnish, soluble only in methylated spirit [denatured alcohol], shellac comes in various colours ranging from orange (also called button polish) to clear white. It is most frequently used in French polishing, but because of its imperviousness to most solvents and its quick drying time – an hour for 1 coat, a little longer for 2 – it is often used in furniture restoration and painting as a barrier between different stages in the work.

159

It is also used in high-class work to seal surfaces after priming and filling and before undercoating. At a later stage, it can be added after painting in the body colour but before glazing or decorating, so that the glaze or applied decoration can be rubbed down, or even wiped off altogether, without fear of disturbing the coat beneath. In effects involving media and colours of possibly conflicting ingredients, a coat of shellac is a useful insurance against what the textbooks sinisterly describe as a 'breakdown' of the paint system.

Do not buy too much shellac at a time since it does not keep well. For this reason, try to buy it from a shop that has a quick turnover of stock.

Brushes   Reserve a special brush for shellac – it need not be large, but it should be soft-bristled. After use, wash it out in methylated spirit [denatured alcohol], and then in warm water with a little ammonia added, *not* soap or detergent. If the bristles harden, they can be softened before use by dipping again into methylated spirit.

Application   Manufacturers often recommend shaking shellac before it is applied, but this creates bubbles that show up on the finish. It is better to tip it into a saucer, add 1 part methylated spirit to 2 of shellac, and stir gently. This thins and blends it nicely. Shellac should be used in a dry, warm atmosphere – if applied in damp, draughty conditions a white bloom appears on the surface, although this usually fades as the shellac dries. If the weather is damp, close the windows and heat the room up slightly.

Shellac can be awkward to brush on, drying so fast that one brushstroke is half-dry before the next overlaps with it, which creates build-ups of colour and a patchy look. Charge the bristles quite generously with shellac, press out the surplus against the inner sides of the can. Lay it on in the middle of the surface and with quick strokes draw it out toward the outer edges, trying not to overlap. Smooth it out by brushing from edge to edge, lightly and fast. A little patchiness in the final result is not too serious – correct the worst mistakes by rubbing down gently with fine steel wool and a little soapy water.

Varnish as a barrier coat   In place of shellac, you can use a coat of clear acrylic or alkyd varnish to seal off a surface or finish. Although this is much tougher – shellac is not water- or alcohol-proof – it has the disadvantage of being slower drying.

Varnish

Recent years have seen such a proliferation of new types of varnish that even professional decorators are confused, let alone those of us wanting to select the appropriate protective seal for anything from a painted wardrobe to a little penworked box. Here I give a resumé of the main categories of varnish currently on offer, but if your particular case or problem is not covered, I suggest you talk to a trade supplier who will be well placed to give comprehensive information based not only on manufacturers' updates but also on customer feedback.

Most painted surfaces look better and last longer when treated to between 1 and 3 coats of an appropriate varnish. Broadly, varnishes can be divided into four main types, oil-based, resin-based, alkyd and acrylic. Oil-based varnishes are the most traditional and are slow-drying – 12–24 hours. By far the most familiar to DIY painters are the resin-based varnishes, comprising the polyurethane group, which come in matt, mid-sheen and gloss finishes. These are the workhorse varnishes, tough, fairly slow-drying (4 to 5 hours) with a tendency to darken and yellow over time due to their resin content. Professionals recommend them for surfaces which can expect hard wear, such as painted floors, children's toys and furniture, table tops, garden furniture. The alkyd and uralkyd varnishes are more refined, giving a more sensitive patina, and are as near to colourless as a traditionally formulated varnish can be while still affording reasonable protection. The most popular of these are matt (absolutely no-shine) and eggshell versions with drying times of 2 to 4 hours. These are the products professional painters choose for finishing fine-painted furniture, woodwork and in some cases walls, where time is not the most pressing concern. See pages 214 and 233 for product details and suppliers – in the last few years these excellent varnishes have become much more widely available.

Newest of all are the acrylic varnishes, water-based, low-odour, colourless and extra fast-drying (1 to 1½ hours). They dry rapidly and do not yellow. They do, however, have some disadvantages. The varnish is as yet only available in gloss and mid-sheen, both with a distinct shine; they are a little awkward to brush out smoothly, though the manufacturers have brought out a special nylon brush to make them easier to apply, and they are still more expensive. They do not take to burnishing and smoothing as readily as the polyurethanes and the alkyds, but they are useful for rapid finishing of woodwork and furniture.

Preparation

The basic drill to follow for best results remains much the same with all types of varnish. Surfaces to be varnished should be dry, well dusted, clean and free of fingermarks. Get rid of these by wiping the surface with a rag moistened with white spirit [mineral spirit]. Sandpaper leaves fine particles - dust these off with a brush. The ideal conditions for varnishing are as warm, airy and dust-free as possible. Any adhering dust, grit and hairs can later be smoothed off with abrasive paper, but prevention, where possible, is better than cure. When varnishing large areas such as woodwork, roll back the carpet, take down curtains and blinds and mass furniture under a dust sheet. Large single pieces should be tackled in a garage or garden room, standing on a dust sheet. For small items, where a perfect finish matters most, it should be possible to rig up a temporary plastic tent to make an ideal micro-climate for drying varnish.

Brushes

Special varnish brushes have fine bristles which help to brush most varnishes out smoothly, with fewer brushmarks (see page 232). Some painters find rubber applicators help in applying varnish smoothly and quickly over larger areas. For smaller items soft artists' oxhair brushes are useful. If you are working in different media, it saves time to provide one brush for each, clearly marked. This also keeps brushes in better shape – a mixture of different solvents and cleaning processes beats the life out of a brush. Brushes can be stored overnight by slotting through a cardboard lid into a jar of the appropriate solvent.

Applying varnish

Varnishes are usually applied with a more loaded brush than one would use when painting, with the varnish applied copiously to the middle of a surface and brushed out smoothly in all directions. The aim is to avoid brushmarks and bubbles, the results of slapdash handling; varnishing should proceed calmly and gravely, under a good light if possible, to avoid 'skips'. With awkward pieces it pays to think through the procedure first. With a chair, for instance, turn it upside down and begin on the legs.

Check the drying time with the manufacturer's instructions. Several thin coats of varnish give better results than one or two thick ones. Two to three coats are usually needed, with more for special pieces or lacquer effects. It is customary to thin the first application with the appropriate solvent (20% or so) to float it on extra smoothly.

Rubbing down, an essential concomitant of effective varnishing, begins after the second coat is hard dry. Lightly rubbing down clears off surface imperfections and gradually creates a finish that is clear and silky. Fine wet-or-dry paper, used with a little water as lubrication, or aluminium oxide paper, is a popular choice. Some people swear by fine steel wool, but this deposits lots of tiny particles which must be dusted well before recoating. Gloss varnishes can take more rubbing down than the rest, and this can also usefully soften the hard shine they create. But all varnishing is improved by patient smoothing. In case this sounds tiresomely perfectionist, it might be worth mentioning that eighteenth-century japanned pieces customarily had 30 coats of varnish (or shellac) and oriental lacquer at least 40.

Multi-layered varnish finishes

Traditionally, some complex decorative paintwork, marbling and graining for example, was treated to a special sequence of varnishes; first gloss, for clarity and toughness, then eggshell for a more subdued sheen, or matt, if a flat effect was the aim. Sometimes this was finally waxed and polished with a soft cloth for a soft lustre.

Polishing or burnishing

It is traditional to give any varnished work a last going over with fine abrasive powders such as rottenstone, powdered pumice or French chalk to work up a texture of baby-skin delicacy, and the process is not difficult. Using a pad of firm but soft material, preferably felt or flannel, dip it into a light oil (salad oil or baby oil), then into the powder, and gently rub the surfaces in a round and round motion till all is silky, compact, immaculate. Rinse off with a damp sponge or cloth and when dry, rub briskly with a soft clean cloth for that superior final lustre.

Quick colour

There are going to be occasions when short cuts are not just a help but a necessity – you might want to decorate a box, tray or frame quickly to give away as a present. This is where modern superquick-drying paints come in useful. Acrylic colours dry so fast and immovably that you can complete the basic colouring of a piece in a few hours.

This is the routine for painting a piece in a tearing hurry. After basic filling and tidying of cracks and scars and rubbing down – a process that cannot be rushed – give the piece 2–3 coats of acrylic primer. This takes a couple of hours to apply and dry. Then paint a base coat of one of the water-based paints, matt emulsion [latex], artists' acrylic colour thinned with water or one of the excellent casein paints (see page 210) which have exceptional covering power. Decoration can be painted straight onto this base using artists' acrylic colours. When the decoration dries, give the piece whatever antiquing it may need by sponging a thin wash of acrylic colour over the whole surface. Then apply 2 coats of thinned alkyd or polyurethane varnish, matt, semigloss or gloss as required. If you are really pushed, use a fast-drying acrylic varnish. Rub the first down lightly with fine steel wool and polish the second with rottenstone or scouring powder (see page 162). Finally polish the piece with a soft cloth.

If you cannot spare the time for a second coat of varnish, try polishing over the first one with floor or furniture wax.

Above French sculptors make furniture shaped and painted to look like animals, and this notion is wittily exploited here for a hippopotamus toybox, lotus flowers decorating his fat sides.

Left Distressing on plank doors is commonplace, but distressing enamelled fridge freezer units to look like roughly daubed planks could be thought rather over the top, if not outlandish. Thick coats of acrylic gesso, combed to look woody and textured, provide the base. French blue and cerulean emulsion [latex], rubbed back here and there, provide the battered colours.

Paint Finishes & Decorative Flourishes

Distressing

The lead in the taste for distressed furniture seems to have come from the USA where people with an eye have been collecting old, battered, painted country-style pieces for many years now, and putting them together in modern as well as rural interiors where their well-worn surfaces and colours add a comfortingly human dimension to a room. In Australia the McAlpine Collection of bush furniture, toys and artefacts, simple yet vigorous, has led to a new appreciation of the resourcefulness of early settlers in the outback. Furniture manufacturers have picked up on this trend rapidly, introducing distressed finishes into their more avant-garde ranges of kitchen furniture and fittings, partly to make them look old and atmospheric, and partly too, no doubt, to hide the fact that a fair proportion of them are made not of timber but of one of the substitutes such as medium density fibreboard (MDF).

The appeal of distressed finishes to amateurs is that they are easy to do, fast and visually effective in a rugged, understated style that suits the way most people live today. Distressed surfaces are decorative just as they are, but they can also provide a foil for applied decoration, painted lines, stencils or designs painted on freehand or with transfers. They can be further 'antiqued' with coloured washes, tinted varnishes, or simply with dark boot polish. The simplest distressed finish is achieved by rubbing back, which creates a time-worn look.

Rubbing back

The rubbing back technique concentrates on the areas which would get the most handling, such as leading edges, doors, the area around drawer handles and door knobs. Remove all handles, knobs and fittings first, for easier access to the parts you want to concentrate on. On a wooden piece the usual approach is to apply the chosen base colour directly to clean, bare wood (all varnish, wax or lacquer must be removed for a good grip), brushing on sufficient coats to build up a dense colour – two are usually enough. When dry, the paint is rubbed back with fine wet-or-dry paper softened with soapy water, until the bare wood surfaces again here and there. Don't rub too fast or hard, or you may take off the top layer of wood too. When the effect satisfies you, let the piece dry then go over all the surfaces with a flat alkyd varnish. If the contrast between paint and exposed wood looks too raw, soften this by rubbing or brushing a suitably 'dirty' wash of thinned acrylic tube colour, in raw or burnt umber, over the whole piece. This can be done before or after varnishing. Use a rag to even it or lighten some areas. Alternatively, if the paint looks too matt and chalky, a rub over with boot polish will add depth, warmth of tone and a subdued shine when buffed with a soft cloth.

Over mixed surfaces, such as MDF panels framed in deal, the simplest solution is to apply two coats of matt emulsion [latex] in different colours to both surfaces, rubbing back the top coat carefully just before it is quite dry to reveal the colour beneath, rather than the underlying material. On the whole a dark base colour under a brighter top one looks best.

Rubbing back over wax

Wax can be used as a 'parting agent' to stop the second coat of paint from covering the whole of the first one. The effect is similar to the one described above, but easier to control. House Style Woodwash, a densely pigmented, water-based paint does a good job of this finish, but any water-based paint can be used. You will need an ordinary cheap wax candle, and pads of medium and fine steel wool.

Brush the base colour densely over clean, bare wood and let dry. Rub the candle over areas you want to show through the top colour, applying the wax thickly where you want streaks and gashes of contrast, or rubbing lengthwise across the whole surface for a light speckling of colour. Brush the second emulsion [latex] colour on top and let it dry. With the medium steel wool followed by the fine steel wool, rub firmly but not too forcefully across the waxed areas and you will find the base colour surfacing cleanly. This is a rustic finish, suited to simple shapes and strong, folk colours – red-brown, dark blue or green, ochre yellow. If you are planning further painted decoration, use artists' acrylic colours, and remember that these too should be rubbed back sensitively when dry to remain in keeping with the distressed finish.

Woodwash takes a pleasant burnish when rubbed down all over with steel wool, and this can substitute for varnishing, especially when the piece is waxed and buffed. But furniture which gets a lot of handling should be varnished with either flat or eggshell alkyd varnish.

Antiquing

Antiquing with paint, as distinct from the roughing up of furniture with bunches of keys, chains and dropped bricks that restorers use to match reproduction pieces to time-scarred antiques, is of interest to anyone who paints furniture, because it is a process that not only ages a piece in a trice but makes it look more convincing. Imitating the complex patina acquired over years of use is an effective way to restore character to a refinished old piece and to enrich the appearance of a newer one. It should be done with some understanding of the way in which wear and tear operate naturally on painted surfaces – abrading the finish on parts that get the most handling and along exposed sharp edges, while darkening and softening the parts that collect dust or grime. This is not to say that antiquing should

Below This somewhat geometrical style of decoration was popular in an area of Massachusetts in the early 18th century. The designs are easy to imitate, if you use a compass, but half of the charm lies in the scarred texture of the cream ground. Try painting on a strongly grained wood such as oak (not valuable old oak, of course), then rub it down to reveal the grain patchily, give it an umber antique glaze, and finish it with matt varnish.

Right Old or newly distressed? These days it is hard to tell, but it hardly matters when the final result looks like this attractive rustic dresser, whose original pine surfaces warmly emerge here and there from a much rubbed subtle green paint. Note the clever juxtaposition of formal objects with country pieces.

make a piece look merely dirty; if it appears grubby and smeary, the technique has been misjudged. Properly handled, it is more like subtle shading in half-tones, emphasizing structure and modelling, and delicately softening paint texture and colour. It is no exaggeration to say that any piece of furniture newly painted by a professional will have been 'aged', 'distressed', or 'dirtied down' by one means or another, not simply to counterfeit age and wear but to soften the raw, blank look of new paint. Antiquing gives painted finishes a 'lived-in' look.

A combination of techniques, sparingly applied, gives a more convincing effect of age and patina than any single one pushed to the limits. Shading with neutral, earth-coloured glazes distressed in some way is one method; a light spattering of brown or black dots another; or you can give varnish a final rub with rottenstone and leave some of the dusty powder behind in corners and carvings. Brash new gilding looks better rubbed back and dulled, and hard painted lines or stencils can look more appealing discreetly rubbed away here and there. An isolating coat of bleached shellac or alkyd varnish over the paint finish will allow you to experiment with various antiquing effects, and rub away the ones you do not like, without affecting the finish itself.

Antiquing glazes and washes For antiquing effects, glazes and washes are usually tinted with the duller earth colours, but grey or much-thinned black is sometimes used. A little of the ground colour of the piece can be added to the antiquing glaze to soften the contrast. Glazes are usually thinned to transparency, applied overall and then gently manipulated as they begin to set, to create a softly shaded effect.

Materials *Oil-based paint glazes* These give the most subtle and controlled patina. A glaze containing flat white oil-based paint (see pages 157, 224) will be slightly opaque: for a completely transparent one, blend artists' oil colour with a little linseed oil (see note, page 185) and a lot of white spirit [mineral spirit]. Artists' oil colour, rubbed on neat from the tube and then mostly rubbed off, can be sealed with shellac within 30 minutes.

Washes For instant antiquing on flat or well rubbed-down finishes, use watered-down acrylic colour or gouache (see page 226 for recipes). Washes allow less time for adjustment, softening – or second thoughts. So begin cautiously with a dilute mixture of colour, sponging or wiping it on with a rag, and softening at once where required by wiping off the wash again. Though a little tricky to control, the drying speed of such washes is a point strongly in their favour. Fix with shellac or a spray varnish.

Colours Tint the glaze or wash with earth colours – raw or burnt sienna, raw or burnt umber, plus a speck of black. Raw umber is the standard antiquing colour, because it ages and softens almost every other hue without muddying it. It is a safe standby when in doubt. Raw sienna adds a warmer tinge to glazes applied over cold colours. A speck of black with each intensifies their effect. A little rottenstone mixed with the glaze medium or with polyurethane varnish makes a very convincing, dust-coloured antiquing liquid. The tint of the glaze or wash should be a couple of tones darker than the base colour.

Other equipment Soft brush; rags or a marine sponge; fine steel wool. Optional: shellac; brush for shellac.

Method

Applying a glaze With a soft brush, cover all the surfaces of the piece thinly and evenly. The longer the glaze is left to dry before blending and rubbing down, the heavier the antiquing effect. Heavy antiquing looks better on rustic-looking pieces – for this effect, leave a glaze overnight. Light, urbane furniture needs a much gentler nuance of colour, achieved by leaving the glaze until just tacky, and then rubbing it down.

Rub the surfaces gently with a pad of fine steel wood so as to lift the glaze from the parts that would get most wear, while leaving it like a dark bloom over the rest. Rub down harder on places like chair arms and backs that get worn naturally. Rub away, too, over the centre of flat tops, sides and drawer fronts. Any prominent mouldings or raised carving should be rubbed down hard on the highest points, leaving the glaze darker in the recesses. The glaze should blend very gradually from highlight to dark, without streaks or smears or sudden transitions. Even where you have rubbed most of it away, just enough will remain embedded in the minuscule flaws of the paint finish. As you work, stand back from time to time to judge the overall effect. Go gently when rubbing over any applied painted decoration unless you want it to emerge slightly worn and tattered. If not, apply a coat of clear varnish or thinned shellac first.

Distressed antiquing glaze The glaze can be finely dragged, sponged or stippled over the paint finish to give more texture than the method described above (see pages 45–9, 57–61 and 49–53). Rub down a distressed glaze in the same way, when drying or dry, to soften it.

Applying a wash A wash should be sponged on with a rag or sponge, left to dry for a moment or two, then rubbed with lint-free rags bunched to make a soft pad, and finally blended with fine steel wool. It works best over a flat and slightly absorbent paint finish.

Varnishing

You should protect the finish with varnish, as described on page 162. Antiquing is usually done before the final protective coats of varnish. Over antiqued paint the most suitable varnish is matt or semigloss alkyd or polyurethane – if you use gloss you should rub it down well, to dull it. Use a clear varnish, unless you want to emphasize the antiquing tone further, in which case you can add a little of the same tint to the varnish.

On a special piece, use a rottenstone rub and polish for a very fine finish, (see page 162); allow a little of the dusty powder to remain in cracks and recesses.

Above Superficial crazing adds a mysterious dimension to painted decoration, especially when a dark colour is rubbed in to show up the craquelure effect. Crackle glaze and scraped back gesso together give this vignette a Pompeiian look.

Right A humble meat safe or food cupboard, with punched tin panels to admit air while repelling flies and ants, moves upmarket in the wake of the current passion for primitive country pieces. A little distress and a hint of natural 'crackle' enliven an authentically old plain grey paint.

Instant antiquing   For an immediate softening effect which works especially well over dry-looking matt emulsion [latex] or other water-based paints, there is nothing to beat old-fashioned boot polish, in light or dark tan or black, wiped on with a soft cloth, rubbed in, then briskly buffed up with a soft cloth to an agreeable gentle lustre. The one disadvantage is that the wax must be cleaned off with white spirit [mineral spirit] and soft steel wool, before repainting at a future date.

Crackle glaze

The varnish on old painted pieces owes its mellowness not only to the warm depth of colour the varnish acquires, but also to the fine network of crazing that develops as it ages. Paint often ages in the some same way, with a layer in a different colour showing through the crackled top coat. These time-worn effects can be created almost instantaneously with crackle glaze and craquelure (see page 172). Crackle glaze is a commercial product, colourless and somewhat sticky, which can be applied between contrasting colours of emulsion [latex] to create a strongly cracked surface that lets the base colour show through. It can be used over an entire piece, or on isolated patches in conjunction with the rubbing back effect (see page 164) for variety and texture.

Materials

Crackle glaze can be obtained from artists' suppliers and other specialist shops, in bulk, or in ½ litre [1 US pint] containers, enough to crackle an area of 7 sq m, [21 sq ft]. Apply with a standard 25 mm [1 in] brush between two coats of emulsion [latex].

Method

To produce a good crackle, the glaze itself should be brushed out thinly and evenly overall. Use random brushstrokes, radiating out every which-way; the cracks follow the brush and regular ones look monotonous and unnatural. When the glaze is dry the top coat of emulsion [latex] can be applied in the usual way. Once the water in the top coat activates the crackle glaze the top coat becomes volatile; this can make it awkward to control, particularly on a vertical surface. The solution is to apply the top coat on horizontal surfaces only, one facet of the piece at a time, laying it on thickly and quickly, but taking care not to rebrush once cracks start appearing, or the whole surface skids and smears.

On a large or fiddly-shaped piece this becomes a tedious business, compensated for, however, by the unfailing excitement of watching the crackle appear. Cracks continue to spread and open for some time, so

Above Craquelure, the two-tier system of a quick-drying varnish applied over slow-drying varnish, is a pretty finish for this simple mirror frame painted cream and decorated with découpage subjects tinted with watercolour.

Left A proprietary crackle glaze sandwiched between two strongly contrasted matt emulsion colours produces a dramatically fissured bark-like appearance. This is an attractive finish in itself, or it may be used in conjunction with other decoration and distressing techniques.

leave each facet to dry out thoroughly before moving the piece round to tackle a new one. The thicker the top coat, I find, the bolder the crackle. Firms using crackled finishes commercially spray on the top coat, thus cutting out a good bit of waiting. But this needs special equipment.

Obviously you can have fun playing off the two emulsion [latex] colours involved. Don't underestimate the subtle effectiveness of subdued browns, greys and creams, as well as the dramatic primaries.

Sealing Crackle glazed surfaces *must* be sealed, otherwise any water that gets to the surface will start it sliding and moving again. Use a flat or matt alkyd varnish over bleached shellac.

Fine crackling

An American correspondent suggests a different method of crackling top coats of matt emulsion [latex], which gives a finer and more even 'crazing', similar to the craquelure described below. Because she intends an antique effect she customarily base-coats a piece in a raw umber shade (sludgy green/brown) of emulsion. When dry she covers this with an even coat of animal glue size (preferably rabbit skin glue) dissolved thoroughly in hot water and kept warm in a *bain marie*. When this has dried she recoats the piece in her chosen final colour of emulsion [latex], which as it dries, becomes finely crazed in a random, natural-looking fashion.

Craquelure

Often confused with crackle glaze, this is in fact a two-tier varnish system, with a fast-drying varnish applied over a slower drying one, or water-based over oil-based. Marketed together, these varnishes can be found in most artists' suppliers; they are expensive, but they give the most reliable results, a nice fine, cobwebby craquelure which looks handsome when burnt umber tube oil colour is rubbed into it to bring up the effect (the craquelure remains invisible in the transparent varnish until this final step). For a home-made and cheaper two-tier craquelure system see 'Fine crackling', above.

Preparation The craquelure effect is set off to best advantage by pale base coats, cream, ivory, grey, or pastels. The varnish adds its own warm yellowish tone, so this should also be taken into account – white becomes cream, pale blue becomes duck egg. I find it a usefully flattering finish for any piece with applied decoration, because it helps to blend colours, soften contrasts and create a mellow finish.

Materials Craquelure varnishes; varnish brush; artists' oil colours in burnt or raw umber; shellac; alkyd varnish, for final sealing.

Method The two types of varnish are applied to a clean, painted surface, which should be smooth, dry and dusted. Follow the maker's instructions as to which varnish goes on first. Using a varnish brush cover the whole surface with 'Vernis à Viellir' (ageing varnish), checking the piece against the light to ensure there are no 'skips'. Set the piece aside for approximately 45–50 minutes. It will still feel sticky, but this is as it should be. Now recoat with the 'Vernis à Craqueler' (crackle varnish) again taking care to avoid missing out patches. Set aside for half an hour, or longer. You should begin to see fine, superficial cracks forming a network over the surface. You can now leave the piece to dry naturally, overnight, or give it a blast of hot air from a hairdryer or heat stripper [gun] – there is debate as to which works most satisfactorily. In my experience the varnishes can prove a touch temperamental, one craquelure coming up clear and even and another less so for no apparent reason. But one point needs emphasizing – the craquelure varnish must be allowed to dry hard before you go to the next stage, the rubbing in of dark oil colour. Once hard dry, it can be safely treated to an application of artists' oils in burnt umber or raw umber, straight from the tube, rubbed in gently with a soft rag. The colour can be applied quite freely, and rubbed back again till the dark craquelure seen against the rest of the surface has the degree of emphasis you like. Leave the piece to settle down, overnight. Then coat it all over with shellac. When this is dry, recoat with alkyd varnish, in flat or eggshell. Take care not to let the piece get wet before applying the varnish as the finish is not permanent until it is sealed.

Spatter antiquing

Spattering is an elegant way to antique a slender, shapely piece in light or medium colours, giving artful shading and emphasis that never looks crude, and one soon acquires the knack of producing an even shower of colour that does not go all over the room.

Another trick, often used in combination with a heavily rubbed, or dragged, glaze, is to use just a scattering of spots in a strongly contrasting colour – brown or black – to suggest an aged freckled look.

Method

Make up a thin antiquing glaze or wash as on page 168. Spatter it with a stiff brush, using the method suggested on page 180, practising first over a piece of paper. The spattering should not be too uniform. When it is dry, you can apply a second coat, concentrating on the parts that you want deeply shaded. When the whole surface is quite dry and the colour sufficiently softened, the spatter coats can be blended a little by very gently rubbing down with fine steel wool.

Freckles For a coarse, random spatter, use a little black or sepia drawing ink. If it is permanent ink, either use it over a barrier coat of varnish or shellac, or dilute it a little with water so that blobs and mistakes can be wiped off with rags. Diluted Indian ink, blotted as it falls, leaves faint grey rings that look most convincing on delicate pastel finishes. Take a little ink up on your brush, and knock it on a stick with a quick, jerky movement to direct the spatter where you want it. You can spatter (sparingly) anywhere on a previously antiqued piece, to add contrast and texture.

Above A cheap terracotta planter looks smart enough to move indoors when given the verdigris treatment. The base coat is applied direct to the clay. If the container is going to live outdoors it should be varnished with at least one coat of thinned matt alkyd.

Verdigris

1 Over a base coat of sludge-brown/green matt emulsion (think of old bronze) a coat of turquoise blue matt emulsion [latex] is stippled with a soft, but firm rounded fitch, using a light 'pouncing' movement and the least amount of colour worked up into the bristles. Some base colour 'ghosts' through the fine mist of blue stipple.

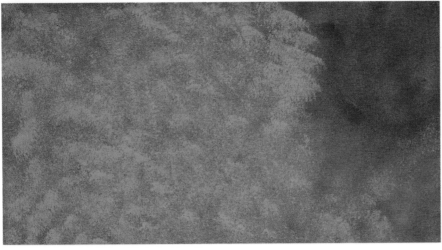

2 A second coat, this time of lime green emulsion, is stippled over the first in the same way but more sparingly, as a sort of highlight. This works particularly well on raised modelled surfaces.

Verdigris

One of the current darlings of the decorative effects trade is the painted imitation of verdigris, the vivid blue-green patination which occurs on copper and bronze when these metals are exposed to weathering. Verdigris is a flattering and undemanding finish for many materials, from wrought iron to wicker and wood, and for objects as varied as flower pots and fireplace surrounds. For all its undoubted elegance, it is gratifyingly quick and easy to apply and is best done in water-based paints. The method suggested below uses emulsion [latex] paints, but you could also use acrylics.

Materials

Depending on the size of the object, you will need a quantity of standard matt emulsion [latex] paint in a sludge or khaki colour for the base coat; small quantities of emulsion in blue and green for the stipple colours – a turquoise and sharp lime green work well together; a standard decorating brush to apply the base colour, and a rounded brush, such as a rounded fitch, for stippling; flat alkyd varnish if protection is needed.

Method

Coat the piece with one or two coats of base colour to give a solid cover and let dry. Tip some of the turquoise stipple colour into a saucer. Dip the stippling brush into the colour, then work the colour up into the bristles by pounding them onto waste paper (this also blots up surplus moisture). When the stippling on the paper gives a soft, clear impression, not a wet splat, the brush is ready. Using a light, jabbing movement, 'pounce' a fine dusting of colour over the entire surface, leaving a ghost of the base colour showing through. Pile the turquoise colour on more densely over any relief mouldings, and work it into crevices.

Next, with a rinsed dried brush repeat the process with the sharp lime green emulsion, covering some, but not all, of the turquoise colour. The green acts a sort of highlight, intensifying the effect. The whole secret of this finish is to use a drier brush than you think possible.

For a chalkier, crumbly look wash over the whole finish with thinned white emulsion [latex], brushing on and wiping off with a rag to leave white deposits. To even up a verdigris which looks patchy or blotchy, simply stipple over lightly with some of the base colour. Verdigris also gains from a discreet contrast of gold; gilt cream (see page 209) is easy to apply and looks well. Shine looks incongruous on this finish, so if you need to varnish, choose a pale flat alkyd.

Marbling

Traditionally, marbling would have been used on parts of a piece which might plausibly have been made of real marble – the top of a table or commode, for instance, or to fill in small recessed panels on the front of an armoire or cabinet. On such pieces, verisimilitude in marbling was the aim and a painter would often combine several different 'marbles' of contrasting colour and formation to enrich the overall effect.

A quite different and much freer approach to marbling grew up in the seventeenth and eighteenth centuries for decorating the sort of furniture which might loosely be classified as 'provincial'. The best examples of this cruder but more boldly decorative use of the technique come from northern Europe – Germany, Holland and Scandinavia in particular. Provincial painters were not fettered by precedent or anxious to be 'correct' and, lacking first rate examples to study at close quarters, they would often work from the copy of a copy, a process that inevitably tends to blur the original and leads to something more individual and – sometimes – more picturesque.

Latterly, marbling has become fashionable again as one of the painted finishes used to ennoble certain types of furniture which benefit from a highly decorative finish. When deciding which furniture to marble, consider its suitability, style and period. Painted finishes are a merciful disguise for plywood or blockboard, but it would be a folly to paint over precious woods such as mahogany or satinwood. Vigorous marbling, decorative swags and floral motifs look handsome on a nineteenth-century dresser but less convincing on a 1950s bedside table, which lacks the necessary weight and presence.

Preparation   The piece should have the usual sequence of undercoats – primer followed by 1 or 2 coats of undercoat and 1 or 2 coats of base colour. The base colour will set the tone of the finished piece so it should be chosen to fit in with the decorating scheme. An eggshell or mid-sheen paint is best, as it is both durable and smooth enough to give a good surface for marbling. All paint coats should be rubbed smooth when dry.

Materials   Transparent oil glaze; artists' oil colours; white spirit [mineral spirit]; whiting (optional, see page 37); boiled linseed oil (see note, page 185); paper, rag or polythene bag; painters' dusting brush for softening; artists' pointed sable or lining fitch for 'veining'.

Method   Brush over the area to be marbled with a transparent glaze – using 1 part oil glaze to 4 parts white spirit [mineral spirit] to give a surface with enough 'flow' to allow marks to be softened out realistically. If the glaze is drying too fast, add a teaspoon or less of boiled linseed oil. Some professionals add a little powdered whiting to the glaze to add body.

Fantasy marbling Dissolve artists' oil colour in white spirit [mineral spirit] in a flat saucer. Scrumple paper, rag or polythene, dip in colour and dab in a deliberately random fashion over the wet glazed surface. Go over these marks with the softening brush for a naturalistic and attractive effect, gently stroking the colour into the wet glaze, applying only a very light pressure, so that it blurs and softens a little. 'Softening' is the key to successful marbling effects, and can be practised first on a spare sample board. The aim is to give a slight cloudiness to the crumpled prints, resembling 'sedimentary veins' in real marble. Change direction of the softening brush as you go so the blurring does not get too uniform.

Imitation marbling For a closer imitation of 'real marble', you can add a second or third 'scrumpled' layer of colour, using varied tones (look at a real piece) to give depth and richness. Finish up by painting in 'veins' of a more distinct and positive sort, using a fine pointed brush or lining fitch, or a goose feather if you can get hold of one. If this is done before the wet glaze has dried hard, the veins, which should always 'go somewhere' and intersect as in the real stone, may not need softening. On a dry surface, however, softening will help to make them more convincing. Use the dusting brush again, gently brushing out the veins in all directions.

Varnishing Allow 24 to 48 hours for the piece to dry and then seal with 2 or 3 coats of clear semigloss varnish. For an ultra-smooth finish, gently smooth over the final varnish coat with fine grade wet-and-dry paper lubricated with soap and water. Alternatively, rub over gently with fine grade wire wool. A final light waxing can be an embellishment, giving the dull lustre of real stone.

Decorative spattering

Spattering – the name decorators use for showering a surface with flecks of coloured paint – is one of the easiest and most artful ways of distressing a painted surface. Since the colour is broken up into such tiny particles, it never looks heavy or clumsy, as can happen with brushed-on glazes.

Use it to give a rich flick of extra colour to a plain painted surface. A heavy spatter of bright green over turquoise, for instance, creates a vivid blue-green with far more depth and vivacity than if you had mixed the two colours together in the pot, or even brushed the green over the turquoise in the form of transparent glaze. A fine spatter of black over a red, mock-lacquer surface adds the merest suggestion of texture without obscuring the glossy colour beneath. Spattering in a neutralizing umber or black will tone down or simply add a texture to whatever is beneath.

Colours It is helpful to keep in mind the principle that complementary colours of the same intensity, viewed at a distance, neutralize each other. Thus, two spatter coats of roughly equal density, one of red and one of green (or orange and blue, or purple and yellow), will appear softened to an indeterminate neutral.

Preparation

The snag with spattering is that it makes a bit of a mess over a pretty wide area – especially if you are trying it for the first time. Ideally, take the piece into the garden, if it is a fine day. Indoors, cover the floor with newspaper, rigging some more up to form a protective screen behind.

The ground coat should be of flat [alkyd flat] paint, tinted with artists' oils, stainers [tinting colours] or, for American readers, japan colours.

Materials

Paint You can spatter with any kind of paint or glaze, as long as it is thinned to a watery, flickable consistency. If you are experimenting, the water-based colours – gouache or acrylic – are a good idea, since they can

177

Right Each fossilstone marble sample was produced with two glazes made of thinned oil paint tinted as indicated. These were then spattered with a variety of solvents while wet to give random but pleasing textures which look handsome as table tops, for bathroom cabinet finishes, with bath surrounds and so forth.

Glaze 1: burnt sienna, a little burnt umber, a little yellow ochre. Glaze 2: yellow ochre, raw umber.

Glaze 1: grey. Glaze 2: indigo. Spotted with red oxide.

Glaze 1: raw umber. Glaze 2: lots of cobalt, a little raw umber.

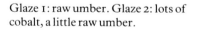

Left The base of what appears to be a fairly nondescript cupboard fitted with a new top becomes an imposing and useful hall chest after it has been smartened up with a variety of marbling techniques, including fossilstone.

be wiped off quickly with a damp sponge. Gouache is particularly good for spattering several coats one on top of the other, and can still be washed off. It will, however, need extra heavy protective varnishing.

Brush The best type to use is a long-handled stencil brush. A stiff, round hogshair brush or a fitch are good, too. You can also use an old artists' brush, with about half the bristle length sliced off to leave it stiff and straight-ended. Swedish painters used a bunch of small birch twigs.

Spattering is done by passing your finger or a metal blade (a knife, ruler or comb) over the painty bristles. You can get very even spattering by rubbing your paint-laden brush through a medium-mesh, round wire sieve. For spattering as fine as mist use a 'diffuser' [atomizer], which can be bought from artists' suppliers (see page 233). For a heavier spatter, a stencil brush can be scrubbed across a wide-toothed comb.

Other equipment The appropriate solvent for the paint; paper for practising on; rags; paper tissues; saucers for mixing colours.

Method Having made a watery thin paint, pick up a little on the bristle tips of your stiff brush. Then pass your finger steadily over them, releasing a few at a time. Experiment on sheets of white paper – with a little practice you will find that you can aim your coloured spray quite evenly and accurately from a short distance away. Avoid overloading the brush, as this gives a heavier spray, with some blobs that might start to run. If they do run, blot them up quickly with a corner of paper tissue.

Very fine spattering dries almost immediately, heavier coats should be left to dry before applying further colours. Finish off with varnish.

Spatter prints

Spattering can be used to completely different effect over templates to leave negative prints. This technique was a favourite in the heyday of hobbies, the mid-nineteenth century, when use was often made of the elegant lacy outlines of that beloved Victorian pot-plant, the common fern. Fern fronds, dried flat, still make ideal templates, arranged into patterns with plainer leaves as borders. You can also try cut paper, doilies or any other decorative shapes. Spattering for this technique is most easily done with a diffuser [atomizer].

Early examples imitated marquetry, using dark spatters over colours like red-brown or golden-brown. This looks pretty with fern patterns, which then appear in gentle relief against a dark ground. Another good combination is olive green over a light or golden brown ground. For a more imposing effect, suggestive of inlaid marble, try the spatter mixtures suggested for porphyry (see page 182) over templates fixed to a black or grey ground.

Materials You can make up the spatter paint with oil-based colours as for porphyry, but for a softer, mistier spray, use gouache colours in water. Other possibilities are acrylics or coloured drawing inks. You will also need a diffuser [atomizer]; leaves or other shapes to spatter round and a jam jar or similar container.

Whatever type of colour you use, it should be poured into a container and stirred well. Arrange your leaves, then place one end of the diffuser in the paint, and blow hard through the other, mouthpiece, end. Blowing creates a vacuum that forces the contents of the jar to rush up the tube. If you point the angle formed by the two sections toward the surface to be spattered, and puff, the paint will flow over it in a fine mist of colour. Practise on sheets of paper laid flat and propped up vertically, to get an idea of how to control the spray.

    A diffused spray of paint is too fine to run so you need not confine this spattering to horizontal surfaces. Tackle each surface separately, beginning at one end and working across to the other, and moving the piece as necessary. Let the spatter dry, remove the templates, and touch up any 'holidays' in the spatter by stippling in dots of the same paint with the tip of a small stiff brush. Use a fine sable artists' brush and the same paint to add further detail such as leaf veins or vine tendrils.

Method

For best results with spatter prints, use a diffuser [atomizer]. Place the end of the vertical tube in the paint container, direct the right-angled joint toward the template to be spattered, and blow through the mouthpiece.

181

Porphyry

1 For a Swedish porphyry finish, the piece is first covered with an opaque coat of bitter chocolate matt emulsion [latex]. When dry, this is spattered lightly with coral red emulsion or acrylic thinned with water. The colour is flicked onto the surface by running a finger briskly across a loaded (but not too charged) brush. Considerable base colour is left showing.

2 A second spatter coat of pale pink covers more of the brown base and lightens the whole effect. The spatter need not be even; indeed, it looks more convincing like this.

3 The last spatter coat is a pale grey, not too evenly flicked. This porphyry finish is a splendid foil to gilding and gains enormously from final varnishing – follow instructions for varnishing marble (see page 177).

Lapis lazuli

1 A base coat of vivid ultramarine emulsion [latex] is spattered lightly with a pale blue thinned emulsion or acrylic wash.

2 The second lapis spatter is a deep blue-black and covers more of the base colour.

3 A spatter of lemon yellow brings the ensemble to life. For fun, and to suggest the 'fool's gold' often found in lapis, the finish has also been flecked with gold metallic paint, done at the last stage. Like porphyry, this is a finish improved by careful varnishing and rubbing to create a smooth lustre.

Graphiting

This first appearance of a 'graphite' finish represents the climax to the search for a texture which combines the softness of a 4B pencil with the discreet elegance of antique Japanese lacquer, and gives a subdued metallic lustre to the surfaces of furniture, woodwork and walls. It can be achieved quite simply by incorporating a small quantity of graphite powder (available from artists' suppliers) into a varnish coat. Sophisticated, with a distinct pewtery sheen (which can be emphasized by buffing it with a soft cloth once the varnish has dried), a graphite finish is also very simple to apply and costs next to nothing.

By varying the colour of the base paint and the tint for the varnish, you can achieve a wide range of different tones and still retain the characteristic 'soft pencil' look of graphite. Mixed into a clear, semigloss polyurethane varnish and applied over a pale grey base paint, the effect will be pewtery grey, with a quiet lustre. Added to a deep-blue-tinted varnish and applied over a mid-grey paint, the resulting colour will be a softly metallic deep blue. The amount of graphite used will depend on the degree of lustre you are after – the more graphite, the more lustre.

Graphite is not lead and does not present a health hazard provided it is used sensibly and care is taken not to inhale the powder. Wear a mask.

Once you have the colour and lustre you desire, it is a good idea to apply another clear coat of semigloss varnish to prevent the graphite in the previous coat from being disturbed by hard rubbing or cleaning later on.

Preparation

Cover surfaces with a base of good quality flat or mid-sheen paint before applying a graphite finish. Any varnished finish tends to emphasize roughness or imperfections, so spend a little time beforehand getting a smooth, even finish on the wood. As usual, any patches of filler need to be rubbed down and touched out with extra care to prevent them showing through in the final finish.

Materials

170 to 225 g [6 to 8 oz] of powdered graphite should be ample; a good-sized tin of clear semigloss polyurethane varnish; artists' oil colours or universal stainers [tinting colours] for tinting the varnish; a long handled artists' brush for mixing; a 50 to 100 mm [2 to 4 in] wide flat varnishing brush for applying the varnish; rags; solvent; a spoon for adding the powder; a small container or paint kettle.

Method

Tip a little varnish into the container. If the varnish is to be tinted, add a little of the desired colour or colours, mix well and try out on a small section of the wood to judge the effect. When the right tone has been reached, spoon a little graphite powder into the tinted varnish, mix well and try it out again. Sample patches can easily be wiped off again with a rag and solvent. Once you have the effect you are after, use the same procedure to mix up a much larger quantity of the mixture. You may need to use a whole tin of the prepared varnish mixture if you are planning to cover the walls of an average sized room.

As with all varnishing, it is a good idea to give the room a good clean before starting work as dust and grit tend to settle on varnish while it is drying, and while they may not show up much, they do make the finished surface less pleasantly smooth to handle. The temperature in the room needs to be warm – 21°C [70°F] – for the varnish to handle well.

Apply the prepared mixture as you would a standard varnish, in light but even strokes, brushing out smoothly but quickly to avoid runs. Check carefully against the light as you go for 'skips' in the varnish coat. Leave to harden overnight in a warm room, preferably not heated by a gas or paraffin stove as these discharge moisture into the air and may sometimes cause 'blooming' and other problems in the drying varnish. Once dry, the graphite finish can be gently buffed up with a soft cloth to increase the sheen. A second coat of varnish can then be applied to seal the finish.

Rosewood graining

The quickest, simplest version of rosewood graining consists of dragging a thinned brownish black glaze over a rich brownish red ground. Well varnished, this looks fine over large areas, where it would be dauntingly slow to attempt really elaborate graining, or as a base for gold stencils. The other, more complicated version would be suited to something a bit special. It involves more preparation and final coats of transparent colour, and so takes longer to do, but the reward is a glowing intensity of colour, with something of the depth of natural wood. This longer method is described below.

Preparation

The finer the painted surface the more lustrous and convincing the finish. To imitate the dense, finegrained texture of rosewood, most cheap wood or veneered boards will need preliminary filling. Use proprietary wood filler [wood putty] or all-purpose filler [spackle], watered down to paint consistency, or else synthetic gesso (see pages 154–6). Two or 3 coats may be needed, depending on the wood texture and type of filler. Finish with 1 coat of standard undercoat, also sanded when dry.

Materials

Flat red paint Flat white oil-based paint tinted with 4 parts alizarin crimson, 2 parts burnt sienna and 1 part vermilion artists' oil colours mixed in white spirit [mineral spirit], with a teaspoon of liquid drier (optional). This will be a rich red brown, and fairly thin.

Transparent red paint The same artists' oil colours as above mixed into 3 parts clear gloss varnish thinned with 1 part white spirit.

Dark glaze 4 parts raw umber, 1 part burnt umber and 1 part black artists' oil colours, mixed in equal parts of gloss polyurethane varnish and white spirit [mineral spirit]. Add a little boiled linseed oil, about $\frac{1}{8}$ as much as the white spirit (measuring in tablespoons helps with these sums), also $\frac{1}{2}$ teaspoon of liquid drier. (NB: Linseed oil is sold either raw or boiled. Never attempt to boil it at home.)

185

Above A detail of a plain tool box given the rosewood graining treatment. Over this was added gilding, using stencils and metallic powder, in a pattern taken from an Ottoman textile.

Opposite No half measures about the way the painter of this early 19th-century American chest handled his effects: simple painting is combined with wild sponging, combed borders, and rosette patterns produced by pressing fans of crisply pleated cartridge paper into the wet paint. Vinegar paint is the ideal medium for these effects, but follow the example of this gifted craftsman and handle it boldly.

Other equipment Orange shellac; methylated spirit [denatured alcohol]; a brush for shellac; a 50 mm [2 in] decorators' brush for the red paint; a dragging brush or dusting brush (see page 232), or other paintbrush for streaking the glaze; wet-or-dry paper; very fine steel wool; a soft cloth dipped in solvent or vinegar, for removing grease.

Method

Red ground Apply 2 coats of flat red paint (see 'Materials' on page 185). A teaspoon of drier can be added to counteract the slow drying oils in the paint colours. Mix more paint than you need for 1 coat and store the remainder in a jar sealed with clingfilm [Saran wrap]. Follow the flat paint with 2 or 3 coats of the transparent red paint. As usual rub down all but the first 2 coats of paint using wet-or-dry paper and soapy water for the finest, smoothest surface. Now give 2 coats of orange shellac diluted half and half with methylated spirit [denatured alcohol]. This seals off the red body colour, allowing more play with the dark glaze.

Glaze Before streaking, wipe down the red surfaces with a cloth pad dipped in vinegar or white spirit to remove grease and fingermarks. Dip the brush bristle tips into the glaze and test on a piece of paper for colour and consistency. More burnt umber will make a warmer colour, but remember the red base is going to show through the dark streaks. Streak the glaze on by drawing the bristles firmly over the red ground to give even, dark, fairly parallel stripes. Cover the whole surface in this way. You will find the glaze easy to manipulate, drying slowly enough to allow bits to be gone over again until the graining effects looks right. Don't aim for a ruled regularity, which is hard to achieve anyway – a little build-up of glaze on corners, or where strokes overlap helps give a naturalistic effect. Leave the glaze to dry and harden for at least 24 hours, then smooth it in the direction of the graining with very fine steel wool and soapy water. This leaves a dulled, deliciously sleek surface.

Varnish Apply two coats of clear gloss varnish. Rub the second coat over with steel wool and soapy water and polish with a soft cloth when dry.

Quick method Fast rosewood graining for less precious pieces requires 3 coats of flat red paint, followed by the dark streaked glaze and 2 coats of varnish. Omit the transparent red and shellac stages altogether.

Vinegar painting or putty graining

This intriguingly named technique is one of many devised by busy country craftsmen of the nineteenth century to meet the increasing demand for 'fancy graining' on furniture and woodwork. Compared with the convincing wood effects produced by master grainers, vinegar painting was a wild parody, but it was quick and easy to do, and the materials were few, cheap and handy. The irony is that to modern eyes the early American pieces in this vigorous style, with their bold patterning,

often look more attractive than the expert work.

It remains a beguilingly simple method of decorating large, flat surfaces rapidly, and looks prettiest in purely decorative colour mixtures: dark over light red, dark over light blue, dark over light green, or any of these colours over off-white. It is a technique that one can really have fun with, since the vinegar medium takes clear, bold impressions of almost anything that comes to hand – a cork, a roll of modelling clay [modelling dough] or the putty traditionally used, crumpled paper or fingerprints. The more playful and bizarre the effects, the better they look, especially on large pieces like chests and dressers, where tight, repetitive patterns could look monotonous. For small things like trays, boxes or table-lampstands, elegant little patterns can easily be built up with close-printed impressions made with a cork or a blob of modelling clay.

There is plenty of time to experiment in the fifteen or so minutes before the colour dries, and if you do not like what you have done, you can easily wash it all off again. Vinegar-painted pieces, like all those finished in watercolour, need thorough varnishing as a final protection.

Preparation The piece to be vinegar-painted should be finished in flat oil-based paint, tinted to the required colour, and when dry rubbed smooth with fine wet-or-dry paper and soapy water. Mid-sheen oil-based paint can be used instead, but it should be rubbed down thoroughly to cut the sheen.

Materials Vinegar and sugar (the traditional grainer's alternative to vinegar and sugar was flat beer – by all means use that if you have it to hand); a squeeze of detergent; dry powder colour: if you cannot get artists' quality powder pigment, children's poster colours will do; 2 jam jars; standard decorators' brush; sundry objects with which to make patterns: for example, a cork, modelling clay [modelling dough] or putty, cardboard cut into comb shapes, a rag or crumpled paper.

Method Mix half a cupful of malt vinegar and a squeeze of detergent in one jam jar. Put some powder colour and a little sugar in the second. Add a little of the vinegar and blend it to a paste, then pour in the rest and mix the whole lot together thoroughly. Test the colour on a piece of paper. Hold it vertical for a minute or two – if the mixture runs in 'curtains', it is too thick – dilute with more vinegar and test again.

Before you get to work on your piece in earnest, spend a few minutes experimenting with different effects: brush a little mixture onto it and try stamping, combing and cross-combing (for a woven effect), dabbing with crumpled rag or paper or printing with a coiled roll of modelling clay to leave delicate whorls.

When you have hit on an effective combination, wipe the surface clean again with a rag moistened with plain vinegar. Then brush the vinegar mixture over a large area and begin making your patterns. Its slow drying-speed leaves enough time for patterning an area as large as a dresser door or the side of a chest, but if the colour begins to dry out and gets harder to work, simply brush more vinegar mixture over it, and start that bit afresh. The real problem is knowing when to stop, and being sufficiently disciplined to impose a coherent design over the whole piece. Brushed out finely, the vinegar solution makes a pleasant semi-transparent wash in itself, which can be used to create restful areas among the patterns.

When the vinegar paint is quite dry, in about an hour, varnish it overall with clear semigloss or gloss polyurethane varnish – 2 or 3 coats on a piece that will not get much handling, 4 or 5 on a piece that will. Rub down the last coat lightly with wet-or-dry paper lubricated with soapy water, followed, if you like, by a rub with rottenstone and oil (see page 162). Polish it with a soft cloth for a mellow shine.

Varnishing

Malachite

This is a bold and vivid finish which looks handsome as a table top, and gives a precious look to smaller objects such as lamps or obelisks.

The base colour is a clear pale greeny blue. It can be painted in 2 coats of oil- or water-based eggshell, or 3 of vinyl silk emulsion [latex].

Preparation

Transparent oil glaze; white spirit [mineral spirit]; artists' oil colours in viridian, oxide of chromium green, yellow ochre, white; a fan brush, from specialist suppliers, to create the distinctively contoured stripy curves; a fine sable (No 2 or 3) brush for fine detail; softening brush.

Materials

Mix up a light, vivid blue-green glaze with the two greens, using transparent oil glaze and white spirit, to a single cream consistency. Put blobs of all the oil colours on a plate. With the fan brush dipped into the glaze start drawing in scalloped curves, like chinoiserie 'clouds', as shown. Overlap these, irregularly, until the surface is covered. With the fine brush, mix a little of the various oil colours into the basic glaze and touch in patches or strips of more vivid green or paler blue green. These can be gone over again with the fan brush to blend them, or gently softened in all directions with the softening brush for a hint of blur – not too much because this is a clearly marked stone. Use the fine brush to 'tweak' the jags on the scallop shapes into little wispy peaks. Leave to dry for 24 hours. Varnish with 1 or 2 coats of mid-sheen alkyd.

Method

Tortoise-shelling

The tortoiseshell finish described on pages 112–13 is a stylized effect especially suited to large surfaces, with its strong directional flow and slightly exaggerated markings. For furniture the whole effect needs scaling down and simplifying if it is to be a background for further decoration. There are several traditional methods of achieving the rich tones and varied markings of the natural shell, in which varnish stain is a key ingredient. Other 'fantasy' tortoiseshell finishes can be achieved with oil glazes.

Malachite

Malachite is one of the most impressive looking decorative stones, with its vivid colouring and instantly recognizable markings. It was a favourite with the Czars, who had a soft spot for gilt consoles with malachite tops. The stone is rare and expensive, which has encouraged painters to develop a 'faux version'. Surprisingly perhaps, malachite is quite a simple finish to do; the most important thing is to have some visual references to consult – photographs of a large slab of stone – to get the hang of its markings. The stripy, interlocking curves need to be done boldly and decisively; there are no fuzzy or indeterminate areas in a piece of malachite.

1 Malachite comes in a range of greens and blue-greens. The glaze has been made up of viridian green, mixed into an oil glaze. The glaze is thicker than usual – 60–70% transparent oil glaze to 30–40% white spirit [mineral spirit]. The base colour used here was a pale turquoise vinyl silk emulsion [latex] from a commercial range.

2 The base colour is covered with the blue-green glaze, brushed on with a standard brush. Then with the special fan brush, the characteristic curving stripes are described in the wet glaze. Some painters use the torn edge of a piece of cardboard instead, pulling this through the wet glaze to make random stripes.

3 The finish looks more convincing if the malachite colour varies a little here and there. Make up variations on the basic glaze by mixing it with a little white or yellow. With a fine brush, add touches of these to some of the thicker stripes. Mix up a much darker version of the basic glaze by adding more viridian, and use this to darken some of the finer stripes. Soften lightly across the stripes, to make 'peaks'. Varnish with matt alkyd.

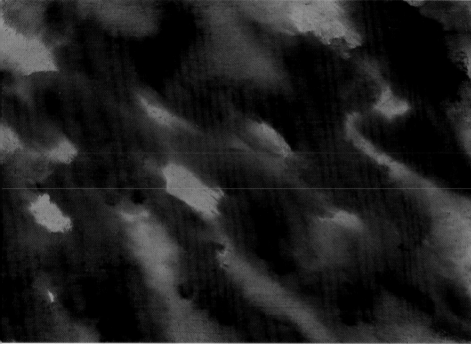

Above and top left Bold red and black tortoiseshell makes a striking finish for a plaster obelisk.

Centre left Shades of amber and brown have been dabbed onto a pea-green base to make 'islands', creating an elegant and unusual tortoiseshell veneer.

Below left Blonde tortoiseshell over metal leaf.

Tortoise-shelling with varnish stains

A bold and stunning finish, streaky black and red tortoiseshelling was often found on early American japanned pieces. It looks superb under gilt decoration, raised or flat, and is best used on furniture, not on walls, where it would be overpowering. The technique is based on the standard one for tortoiseshell. Where possible, paint a horizontal surface, laying cupboards and so forth on their backs or sides on the floor. It is possible to work on a vertical surface, but with less control and comfort. Paint one surface at a time and try to see each surface as part of a whole, so that the black and red streaks carry on parallel over drawer fronts and doors.

Use dark bronze powder for gilding on top of it, antiqued with earth-coloured glazes (see page 168), but reserve this finish for suitably aristocratic pieces.

Preparation

The ground should be smoothly painted with a strong, opaque orange-red. American readers can buy japan colour in just the right shade; otherwise, it can be achieved by tinting flat or mid-sheen oil-based paint with universal stainers [tinting colours] or artists' oil colours in raw sienna and scarlet.

Materials

Dark oak gloss varnish stain: this is an essential ingredient – nothing else has the right consistency to stop the streaks running all over the place; black artists' oil colour; pointed artists' brush; 50 mm [2 in] decorators' paintbrush; a wider, clean, dry decorators' brush; white spirit [mineral spirit]; paper tissues.

Method

Dilute the varnish stain, about 1 part white spirit to 2 parts varnish. Paint this over the surface. It will bubble excitedly. Fidget the brush diagonally over the wet surface, or dab with crumpled paper tissue, to distress it and remove surplus varnish. Mix a little varnish stain into the black oil colour, and streak it into the wet surface with a pointed artists' brush, using a sideways rolling motion and jerking it a little as you go, to produce highly irregular black streaks roughly 5 cm [2 in] apart, which follow a parallel course in the same direction as the diagonals. Leave to harden for just a minute or two. Then with the tips of a clean, dry brush, stroke the black streaks gently in the direction in which they were painted, teasing them out to give wispy ends. Some of the wet black will flow out over the red. Now stroke the streaks in the opposite diagonal direction. This opens them out and merges some together. Do not go on until all the original red has been darkened over. The colour ratio in this technique should be about three-fifths of the surface black and two-fifths thinned black fading into shaded red. Leave the finish to dry hard before applying further decoration.

Varnishing

Further varnishing is not mandatory, but for a more alluring surface, varnish, rub down and polish in the usual way (see pages 168–9). Do not rub down the tortoiseshell surface itself, or you may leave scars.

Tortoise-shelling with oil glazes

This effect imitates the furniture created by the French cabinetmaker, Boulle, in which a transparent veneer of tortoiseshell was laid over a green or red ground, usually in conjunction with polished wood and a good deal of ormolu for contrast. The same method is used for both green and red tortoiseshell, although the base and glaze colours are different.

The approach used here differs from the standard tortoiseshell as the colours are laid into a thin coat of transparent oil glaze, which dries more slowly than the varnish stain, allowing more time for adjusting, improving or correcting.

Red Tortoiseshell

Paint the surface with two coats of a scarlet red eggshell or vinyl silk emulsion [latex]. The method is as given for green tortoiseshell below. The colours to be used are given in brackets.

Materials

As for green tortoiseshell but artists' oil colours should be in burnt umber, burnt sienna and black.

Green Tortoiseshell

The surface should be given two coats of a mid-green eggshell or vinyl silk emulsion [latex] paint. The green should not be too bright; a cool pea green, obtained by adding a little white or cerulean blue to pea green, is about right. The golden shellac will warm the overall hue at the end.

Materials

Transparent oil glaze; white spirit [mineral spirit]; artists' oil colours in burnt umber, raw sienna, burnt sienna, and black; a standard paintbrush and soft fitch to apply initial glazes; fine No 5 or No 6 watercolour brush for smaller details; softening brush; white plate for mixing colours.

Method

Thin some transparent oil glaze with a little white spirit [mineral spirit], tint with a little burnt umber, and brush out evenly over the whole surface to be tortoiseshelled, taking one facet at a time. Tip some of this basic glaze into the middle of a plate, put dabs of the other colours round the rim, and mix these into the glaze as you go along.

Start with the lightest 'islands' using some of the basic glaze warmed with a little raw sienna and less burnt sienna (burnt umber for red finish). Dab this colour at random on the diagonal over the surface, one facet at a time. Soften with the softener. Mix up a darker glaze with more burnt umber (mix burnt sienna into existing glaze for red) and dab this on top of or in between the first patches, still at random. Soften, to blend some areas into each other. Mix up a dark brown-black glaze with burnt umber and a dot of black and use the watercolour brush to make a few little dark streaks, squiggles and blotches here and there within the previous 'islands'. Soften.

Allow to dry, then coat with orange shellac thinned with methylated spirit [denatured alcohol] or with a mid-sheen alkyd varnish lightly tinted with raw sienna (burnt umber) artists' oil colour. The shellac needs further varnishing with mid-sheen alkyd.

Tortoiseshell over metal leaf

On small objects – boxes, frames, trays – where a rich effect is not going to be overwhelming, tortoiseshell mottling over shiny metal leaf looks beautiful. Aluminium leaf makes a cheap and satisfactory substitute for the traditional silver leaf, while Dutch metal can pass for gold. The object to be leafed should have as smooth a surface as possible.

Materials   Aluminium or Dutch metal transfer leaf – as many sheets as needed to cover the object, with a little over; goldsize, on which to apply the leaf; dark oak gloss varnish stain; burnt umber and black oil colours; 50 mm [2 in] decorators' paint brush; a wider, clean, dry decorators' brush; pointed artists' brush; cotton wool [absorbent cotton].

Method   See pages 207–9 for how to apply metal leaf. When it is dry, smooth and burnished, give it a coat of quick-drying bleached shellac. When quite dry, it is ready for tortoiseshelling, which is done just as described on page 112. Do not fret if the overlapped squares of leaf are discerned through the final finish – this is hard to avoid and has its own appeal. But do smooth off any irregularities in the leaf. For a darkly glowing effect, try doubling up the technique – just enough of the silver shows through to give cool depth, like moonlight filtered through cloud.

Blonde tortoiseshell over metal leaf A blonde version of this technique gives a softer, quite different look. Use a light oak gloss varnish stain, instead of a dark one. Use your burnt umber and black oil colours a little more thinly and sparingly, and brush out the markings less.

Varnishing   Though not essential, further coats of clear varnish, rubbed and polished, will strengthen the finish.

Lacquering

A cheap wooden box has been given the works with modelling paste, gold paints, bronze powders, Dutch metal transfer leaf and chinoiserie designs.

True Oriental lacquer ware, made from the milky sap of the lac tree, must qualify as the most painstaking finish ever devised. Built up through as many as 40 separate layers, each rubbed and polished smooth with a paste of oil and bone ash applied with the fingers, it is the hardest, most lustrous surface imaginable, so rich to the eye that it looks at its most handsome unadorned.

Not surprisingly, when examples of this superb craftsmanship reached the West, European craftsmen were soon earnestly trying to imitate the prized imported wares. More confusion arose when an identically named but intrinsically different resin, 'lac' made from secretions of an insect, *Coccus lacca*, reached the West. After processing, this became 'seedlac', which we now call shellac, an ultra-fast-drying resinous varnish differing from other varnishes in being soluble only in alcohol. By combining paint with shellac, Western craftsmen came up with a variety of technically incorrect, but aesthetically pleasing, pseudo-lacquers, which they called japan. Wooden pieces were smoothly primed, painted and decorated, often lavishly gilded, and finished with many coats of shellac, to simulate the depth and richness of the Oriental wares. Japanned wares bore a superficial resemblance to their eastern models, but as time passed and innovators added further refinements, the pieces developed a style and charm of their own.

The lesson to be learned from studying examples of old lacquer and japanning is that it is quite possible to emulate their warmth of colour and patina by painting a piece in suitable colours, decorating it with Oriental-inspired motifs, and finishing it with as many coats of varnish or bleached shellac as you have the patience to apply. The result may be only a pastiche of a pastiche, but it is still extravagantly pretty. The more effort you put into it – gilt or bronze powder decoration, streaky tortoiseshell ground, stencilled or hand-painted scenes, tinted varnishes – the more sumptuous the final result. At the opposite extreme, you could explore a modern, starkly simple lacquer effect, relying on brilliant glazed colours and many coats of rubbed-down clear gloss varnish.

Furniture of a plain, strong shape is the best choice for these gorgeous lacquer treatments. Modern-style lacquer looks especially good on dining chairs and coffee tables. The wood beneath does not have to be anything special: the tattiest veneered blockboard by the time it has been gessoed, decorated and varnished to the nines is adequate.

The top of this 18th-century lacquered table has been given a witty contemporary trompe l'oeil treatment, then topped with coats of shellac for further shine.

Preparation

Acrylic gesso greatly improves the surface of open-grained or inferior wood and adds to the final appearance of your handiwork. Unless the wood you are working on is fine-grained and smooth, in which case it need only be undercoated, give the piece 4 or 5 coats of acrylic gesso, or all-purpose filler [spackle] watered-down to paint consistency (see pages 154–6). When it is dry, rub each coat down with medium steel wool or medium sandpaper. Aim for bone-hard smoothness. When the last coat of gesso is dry, brush shellac, diluted with 1 part methylated spirit [denatured alcohol] to 2 parts shellac, over the whole piece.

Materials for black 'lacquer'

Flat black oil-based paint, bought at any ironmongers or hardware store; burnt umber artists' oil colour; gloss polyurethane varnish; brush; wet-or-dry paper.

Method

The first 2 or 3 coats should be of flat black paint, the last one rubbed down with wet-or-dry paper and soapy water. For the subsequent 2 coats, mix 5 parts flat black paint with 1 part burnt umber and half a part gloss varnish. Rub these 2 coats down in the same way.

At this stage the lacquer may be gilded or otherwise decorated.

Varnishing If you want a warm black, add a little burnt umber artists' oil colour, or dark oak varnish stain, to the last of your 2 or 3 coats of protective polyurethane gloss varnish. Each coat of varnish should be rubbed down and the final one polished with rottenstone (see page 162) – for a higher lustre, wax it and polish with a soft cloth.

Materials for red 'lacquer'   Flat white oil-based paint; vermilion artists' oil colour or universal stainer [tinting colour] or, for American readers, orange-red japan colour, to colour the ground coat; white spirit [mineral spirit]; gloss polyurethane varnish; crimson and burnt sienna artists' oil colours for top coats; wet-or-dry paper.

Method   Mix the red oil colour, stainer or japan colour with just enough white spirit and flat white paint to give a little body and flow without making the colour too chalky. Paint the piece with 2 or 3 coats of this, rubbing down with wet-or-dry paper after the first 2. For the next 2 coats, make a rich transparent paint by substituting gloss varnish for the flat white paint, and adding a squeeze of crimson and burnt sienna oil colours. This changes the effect of the opaque vermilion beneath quite astonishingly.

Varnishing If the red is too bright, it can be softened before final varnishing by applying a thin burnt umber wash or glaze, or by spattering it with sepia or black ink. Alternatively, your 2 or 3 coats of protective gloss varnish – thinned 3 parts varnish to 2 of white spirit – could be tinted, as above, with a little burnt umber artists' oil colour or dark oak varnish stain, and rubbed down and finished in the same way.

Other 'lacquer' colours   As well as the classic black and vermilion, japanned furniture exhibited a wide range of colours – white, sharp yellow, olive, chestnut, blue and purple. The glow and brilliance of the final effect is greatly enhanced by brushing on a tinted varnish or, even more subtle, a glaze, in a slightly different tone of the ground colour. This can be brushed solidly over the ground, or dragged on with a brush in fine stripes, so that the two colours interact more vibrantly. Thus a ground of flat yellow – made by mixing Indian yellow into flat white – is sharpened by a glaze of chrome yellow or yellow lake; a blue ground of cobalt in flat white is made brilliant by glazing with Prussian blue or ultramarine.

Lining

Lining or striping in a contrasting colour is often used to trim painted furniture, to underline and strengthen its contours and to draw attention to decorative details. Traditionally the lining decoration used varied with the type of furniture. On curvy French and Italian provincial pieces, wide bands of watery thin colour often edged table tops and chair frames. On the whippet-slim pieces by such eighteenth-century designers as Robert Adam, the lining had a calligraphic tautness. But it was on coachwork, the supreme test of a painter's skill, that lining displayed the utmost in slender precision – all of it executed freehand with a control born of years of practice.

Anyone can manage wide decorative edge lining, which looks tremendous even when painted quite crudely, but to paint immaculately fine lining freehand, you require confidence, practice and a steady wrist. However, there are ways of cheating to get a similar effect which are worth experimenting with. Applying an intervening coat of clear varnish or thinned white shellac allows botched lines to be wiped off and redrawn. A straight-edge used with a lining fitch or a fine sable brush enables one to produce satisfactory straight lines on flat surfaces; I have even known professional decorators who simply use a felt-tip pen.

Lining is usually applied toward the end of decorating a piece, after the glazing has been done, but before antiquing (see pages 165–70). This makes for crisper definition. As always, the smoother the paint surface, the more fluently the painted lines will flow. If you are unsure of your brushwork, apply a barrier coat first (see pages 159, 160), before lining.

Paint and brushes For transparent, watery edge lining, use artists' gouache or acrylic colour diluted in a little water. To help paint to stay put, add a drop of detergent. This effect is best suited to matt-finished pieces.

For fine lining, professional decorators generally use artists' oil colour dissolved in a little white spirit [mineral spirit] and then mixed with clear varnish for body. Quick-drying goldsize is a useful substitute for varnish, since it dries fast, which means that there is less risk of smudging. Indian ink gives fine, distinct black lines but should be applied over a varnish barrier coat since it can be very difficult to remove. If you do have to remove it, wipe it off with a rag moistened with methylated spirit [denatured alcohol].

For broad edging lines, use a No 6 sable artists' brush, for fine lines, a No 3 sable brush. Professional decorators often use a swordliner (see page 232), because the curved, tapering bristles give greater control.

Other equipment You will also need the appropriate solvent for your paint; rags or cotton wool [absorbent cotton] swabs; a saucer for mixing colour. Optional: a notched card, to keep a measured line even (see drawing); a lining fitch; felt-tip pens; a straight-edge.

Make sure that the piece is placed at a convenient height. A low table, with solid legs, makes an ideal platform for most items. Test the paint mixture on a board, to get the feel of your lining brush, and to check that the paint flows nicely and that the colour is sufficiently intense. Do not overload the brush, or your neat line may blob if you press harder. The thickness of the line depends on your hand pressure as well as on the width of the brush itself. Stand a little way back, hold the brush quite far up the handle, and *draw* with a steady, relaxed sweeping movement, your eye travelling ahead of your brush. Hesitation leads to wobbles and breaks in continuity.

Correct any mistakes after you have reached an obvious break but before the paint hardens. If the paint has set, leave it to dry thoroughly, then gently rub it away with fine steel wool and retouch lines with a light hand. Rubbing down will soften less than perfect lining. Finish with a matt or semigloss clear alkyd varnish.

Preparation

Materials for lining

Method

197

Bold painted lines in dark green emphasize the interesting cut-out shape of this old pine bedhead and pick out the turned decoration to match. Lining should be scaled to the pieces it decorates, bold on rustic furniture, fine as thread on more sophisticated pieces.

Edge lining Chunky folk pieces often look good with really emphatic edge lining, anything from 12 to 25 mm [$\frac{1}{2}$ to 1 in] wide. It is the easiest kind to do, because you can use your little finger to guide the brush. Use a notched card to make little paint marks all the way along before painting, to keep the width of the band even. Slight variations do not matter.

Water-thinned paints produce delicate faded-looking lines, appropriate to antique pieces, but take care when retouching them, because thin colour builds up fast if you go over the same spot too often.

Along straight edges a helpful cheat is to set a boundary of masking tape at the requisite distance in from the edge. Peel it off immediately after painting each section, for a clean edge. To keep the old and faded look, the paint should be matt, but not so thick it builds a raised line, and the piece can be finished with matt varnish.

Fine lining This is usually painted a little way inside the edge of a piece, following the curves of a chair back or the taper of a flat chair leg. A chair back is best tackled with the chair laid on its back at normal table height, where it can be approached from three sides. Paint the inner surfaces first so that you won't smudge one line as you lean across to tackle another.

It is no good pretending that it is easy to paint a fine, even line freehand. However, confidence quickly grows with practice. Give the surface a coat of thinned shellac or clear varnish first, and strike out boldly in the knowledge that mistakes can be wiped off with a cotton wool swab moistened in solvent once you have completed the section; touch them up when they are dry.

Bambooing

During the eighteenth-century craze for chinoiserie, one of the materials in vogue was bamboo. Cheap and commonplace in the Orient, bamboo was both scarce and expensive in the West. It was not long before craftsmen were producing imitation bamboo from turned and carved wood. Made, as a rule, of inferior wood, this was painted after the style of the natural wood, and later in increasingly fantastic colours.

Most imitation bamboo kept to certain conventions. The prominent knots at the intersections were emphasized with painted lines in one, two or even three colours, and the same colours were used to add the little eyes and tapering spines characteristic of natural female bamboo. The hand-painted detail would sometimes be done in discreetly complementary colours – grey-green on yellow buff, for instance – sometimes in flamboyant contrasts like pink on white, or black and gold on vermilion.

Bambooing adds colour and fantasy to a simple painted piece, breaking up uniformly coloured surfaces in a decorative and witty fashion. First candidates are any pieces in turned imitation bamboo. Choose emphatic colour schemes for the elegant shapes that can take it – black, red, cockatoo pinks and greens – with bambooing in lighter, contrasting colours. For pieces with only a little turned bamboo decoration – on chair backs and legs, round table tops and drawers – stick to neutrals and discreet colours: sepia on buff, green on yellow, dark green or brown on green and any middle-tones on cream.

Any simple, rounded wooden moulding can be smartened up with a stylized bamboo treatment. Frames on mirrors, or screens, simple bedsteads, small tables with plain, round legs – once your eye is receptive, it is easy to pick out pieces that will gain from this treatment.

Bambooing can also be used to freshen up those spotted turn-of-the-century pieces, made of real bamboo varnished and scorched to produce a brown mottling. It would be a pity to paint fine examples, but there are many inferior pieces that would look all the better for cleaning, rubbing down and painting in a restrained colour combination.

There are two commonly used techniques for bambooing. The first, picking out in colour, can be used only where the distinctive bamboo knots, or knobbly joints, are present – either on turned wood or genuine bamboo. The decoration consists of picking out the knots with fine lines and, if you wish, adding painted eyes and spines.

A turn-of-the-century junk-shop find, bamboo-striped in tinted and thinned varnish. The wicker surfaces are painted freehand in the same three shades of blue.

The second technique is bamboo striping, which can be used on plain round mouldings, with graduated rings – in tones of the same colour – painted one on top of the other. Pieces painted in greyish-white, bamboo-striped in pink, blue, green look fresh and pretty. Shades of sepia on a straw-coloured ground, echoing natural bamboo colours, look especially effective on plain round mouldings. Over dark colours, paint bamboo striping in light, sludgy colours like white tinted with raw umber, raw sienna or yellow ochre.

Preparation

The piece needs a sleek ground coat, applied over a smooth surface (see pages 151–6). Use at least 3 coats of undercoat or flat oil-based paint, tinted to your chosen colour, thinly applied and gently rubbed down with fine wet-or-dry paper and soapy water. Turn-of-the-century scorched bamboo must be rubbed down first with steel wool and methylated spirit [denatured alcohol] to remove old French polish.

Materials

For picking out in colour, fast-drying paints with good opacity are a sensible choice. Acrylic colours or, for American readers, japan colours are both good. Flat oil-based paint tinted with universal stainers [tinting colours] or artists' oils can also be used, but will take many hours to dry.

For bamboo striping, decorators use fast-drying transparent paint made by tinting clear matt varnish with artists' oils or universal stainers, dissolved first in a little white spirit [mineral spirit]. The proportions of solvent to varnish are about half and half for the palest stripe colour, ranging to 1 teaspoon of solvent to 1 tablespoon varnish for the darkest tone. The palest stripe should be transparently thin; over a dark colour it must contain some white pigment to show up sufficiently.

You also need fine, pointed sable artists' brushes, Nos 3 and 6, for painting details; a square-cut oxhair artists' brush for stroking on transparent colour and, for bamboo striping, two standard decorators' paintbrushes or fat soft-bristled artists' brushes 12 mm [½ in] and 17 mm [¾ in] wide; rags; saucers for mixing.

Method for picking out in colour

Mix up a little paint in a saucer – a couple of tablespoonfuls is enough to do a chair. The mixture should be opaque enough to cover the ground colour, but thin enough to flow smoothly from the brush.

With the fatter brush (No 6), paint a neat band of colour round each knot, pressing on the bristles so that the colour extends a fraction over either side of the ridges. Fine spines and speckled eyes may be painted in with the No 3 sable brush. The spines should be painted with two curving lines joining to form a delicate spike, not more than a third of the bamboo section in length. In nature the eyes appear either side of the spine. They are slightly oval dots, surrounded by tiny freckles of colour. Paint a few sparingly on the more prominent sections, placing them asymmetrically.

When the paint has dried hard, you can add a little tinted varnish to bring out the modelling of the bamboo. Dip the square-ended brush into the mixture, brush off the excess on rough paper, and stroke it in fine

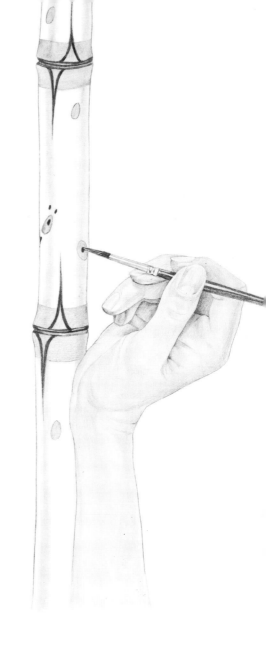

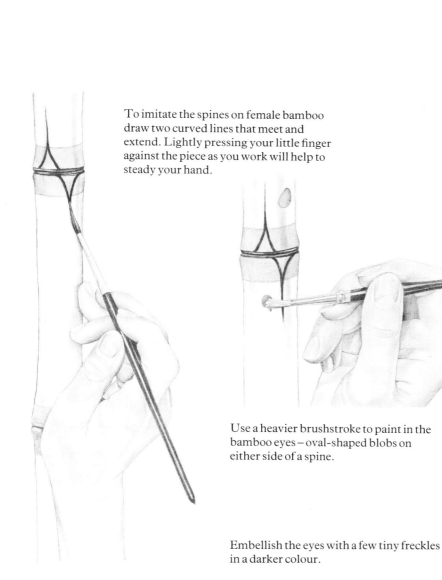

To imitate the spines on female bamboo draw two curved lines that meet and extend. Lightly pressing your little finger against the piece as you work will help to steady your hand.

Use a heavier brushstroke to paint in the bamboo eyes – oval-shaped blobs on either side of a spine.

Embellish the eyes with a few tiny freckles in a darker colour.

stripes over the plain sections between the painted knots. Keep the brush pressure light, and the colour unemphatic.

Method for bamboo striping

The widest stripe is painted in the lightest tone of your transparent paint, usually about 25 mm [1 in] wide, using the wider brush. Centre it over the bamboo knot (or where a knot would be), and paint a smooth ring of the thinnest possible colour right around it. Paint all the wide rings on the piece in one go, and wait a moment for them to dry.

Now tint the paint a few tones darker, and paint a second narrower ring in the centre of the wide ones, about 12 mm [½ in] wide. Then make the remaining paint decidedly dark and, using the No 3 brush, paint in a slender central ring, about 6 mm [¼ in] wide.

You can also use this darkest tone to paint in eyes, and for lining on chair backs and table legs (see pages 196–9). When it is dry, you can brush or drag on a darker tinted varnish (see pages 45–9).

Varnishing

When the surface is completely dry, give the whole piece 2 protective coats of clear matt varnish. To add a soft sheen, give it a light coat of soft, colourless wax. Bambooed pieces finished in dark, Oriental colours may look better covered with gloss varnish for a lacquer effect.

Decorative painting in watercolour

Watercolour decoration over a chalky gesso base creates the attractively worn and 'threadbare' effect of this small panel of birds and foliage.

One unexpected spin-off of the current interest in fast, water-based paint for furniture is a revival of the gentle art of decorating furniture with flowers and motifs in watercolour, practised by the young ladies of the eighteenth century. Experienced furniture painters often use watercolour in its simplest dried form, the little blocks or pans one associates with school art classes. Others will find it easier to work with gouache colours dissolved in gum arabic, a clear fluid with a gluey consistency which brushes out smoothly and as transparently as needed, but which can be overpainted with less risk of 'lifting'. Two points need emphasizing in connection with watercolour decoration. First, a pale base colour – a creamy or ivory shade, or a gentle pastel – is the best suited to transparent decoration, as it will not affect the colours used over it to any great extent. On mid or darker shades it is first necessary to 'white out' the motifs, with white acrylic tube colour, or acrylic gesso. Secondly, because the watercolour is so fine and fragile, it is essential to seal it immediately on completion, before proceeding to any antiquing or further varnishing. Use a clear spray varnish for this, just on the watercolour work itself.

Materials

Gouache colours, which come in a wide colour range and are available from most artists' suppliers – they are very concentrated, so small tubes go a long way; gum arabic, sold in small bottles by the same shops; white paper, or a white plate for mixing colours; brushes – soft, pointed watercolour brushes are esential, in fine, medium and fatter sizes, and one soft, flat-ended brush is useful for petals; a can of clear spray varnish, which can now be obtained in 'green' formulations, without aerosol; chalk. You will find that sable brushes are the most resilient, squirrel is satisfactory, and synthetics are cheap but apt to lose their shape. Clean brushes well, and never leave them standing in a jar of water; to preserve their shape run them over a cake of soap before twisting back into a point after cleaning. Wash out soap before reusing.

Motifs and designs

Watercolour is perfect for floral subjects, and there are innumerable sources of inspiration for these, from botanical prints to postcards and stationery, painted china, chintzes, wallpapers and borders. In some ways it is easier to transpose from existing designs than it is to copy nature, but this is up to you. Other appealing subjects might be seashells, feathers, birds and butterflies or cherubs. Simple lines look soft and pretty when painted in watercolour, perhaps just as an outline, or crisscrossing to form a lattice. Rococo curlicues and scrolls, and blue-and-white chinoiserie motifs are other possibilities. A browse round the postcard section of a good museum should give you lots of ideas, cheaply. But don't aim too high to begin with: choose a simple motif and leave the design understated.

Method

First chalk in the main outlines of the design. Then begin by painting the mid-tones: pink, for rose petals, mid-green for leaves, for example. Next

Two shades of blue gouache – cobalt and ultramarine – mixed with differing quantities of gum arabic give the range of tones shown in this spray copied from an old Export Chinese plate. The gum dries to a glassy surface, which for permanency must be sealed with a spray varnish.

add darker accents, a touch of crimson (always diluted in gum arabic on either paper or your plate palette) or for leaves, a green 'dirtied' with raw umber or burnt umber. Tip a little gum arabic into the middle of the plate, with your dabs of gouache around the rim, and play with different combinations and intensities of colour. For highlights mix a little white into the mid tones; highlights should be added sparingly at first, since the white will tend to make the colours more opaque. Next stand back, half-close your eyes and decide whether you have the balance right – perhaps the pink roses need a little warmth of tone, a nuance of burnt sienna. Or the leaves might enjoy a faded yellowish tone. Add details such as leaf veins, thorns and stamens with a fine brush. A delicate shadowing around a motif, in one of the umbers much diluted in gum arabic, will help throw it into relief. Bear in mind that painted decoration of this kind is properly playing a supportive role, not clamouring for any attention. It should enrich a piece visually, adding a graceful shape and soft colour, but not compete for primacy. Very effective watercolour decoration can be done in one basic colour.

When the decoration is thoroughly dry to the touch, spray varnish to seal it. Then wash over with an antiquing colour or finish it with craquelure (pages 172–3); both effects help to 'tie in' the decoration to the background and enhance a piece of furniture, suggesting a look of casual elegance. On the whole this sort of work looks best given an unobtrusive varnish finish, in matt or eggshell alkyd.

Gilding

Something of a mystique surrounds the art of gilding – understandably, in view of the expense and fragility of the true gold leaf, and the elaborate technique involved in traditional water gilding. The current price of gold leaf certainly puts it outside the reach of amateur furniture decorators – there is no fun in experimenting with a material so expensive that every mistake you make hurts.

There are other ways of adding a rich metallic gleam to a painted surface, using lesser metals in the form of transfer leaf or metallic powders. These are far cheaper, as well as being easier to apply, and can be boosted with various professional tricks to give a pleasing suggestion of the real thing.

Fake gold materials look best treated in a throwaway fashion, distressed to let red ground colour show through and then antiqued with a raw or burnt umber wash or dark tan shoe polish. A touch of gold or silver, outlining drawer fronts and table tops or highlighting relief carving, turned chair legs and backs, adds considerable class. Delicious effects can be obtained by using aluminium leaf or Dutch metal transfer leaf as a luminous ground for tortoiseshell finishes – a treatment that makes smaller objects like picture frames and boxes look precious and important. The simple gilding techniques described here are not so costly as to be inhibiting and can be confidently undertaken by any reasonably neat-fingered person.

Metallic powder decoration

Bronze, silver and aluminium powders come in a wide range of colours – from silvery white to rich bronze gold – and look most attractive when several colours are used together. Use them for stencilling, freehand decoration or spattering. They can be applied straight over a tacky surface, usually painted in a dark colour such as black or red to set off the metal, or over motifs filled in with a sympathetic colour, say yellow ochre or Venetian red, which enriches the metallic finish.

Metal powders tarnish, so should be varnished for protection. They look effective shaded with tinted varnish or antiquing glazes, to suggest patina and modelling. Knocking back the metallic gleam in this way makes the untreated areas, paradoxically, shine more brightly.

Neatness and patience are the chief requirements for handling metal powders. They are so light and clinging that some care is needed to stop them from going where they are not wanted. (*Warning*: wear a mask when working with fine, powdery materials – especially metallic ones.)

Preparation

Surfaces for powder decoration should be covered with opaque flat or mid-sheen oil-based paint. Rich, dark colours set it off best – brownish red, black, dull green, chestnut or fake tortoiseshell. The ground colour must be left to dry completely hard, without a hint of tackiness.

Nervous practitioners might like to give the surface a coat of clear semigloss varnish or thinned shellac; this not only allows more scope for correcting mistakes but will encourage even drying in the varnish subsequently used as a size. This barrier coat should be rubbed down lightly with very fine steel wool, and wiped clean with a rag moistened with white spirit [mineral spirit].

Stencilling with metal powder

This way of using metallic powders produces great subtlety of shading and highlight. Stencils and metal powders were traditionally used for lacy borders, but also make effective allover patterns and large single motifs. The stencils should be neatly cut, since any raggedness shows more with powder than it does with paint, and should be small enough to be easily controlled. Press them flat before use – ironing with a warm iron over paper flattens them quickly.

Materials for metal powder stencilling

Stencils (see pages 69–73); metal powders; clear semigloss or gloss polyurethane varnish; small pieces of silk, velvet or chamois leather; varnish brush; small brush for shading; square-tipped artists' hogshair brush, for floating on colours; artists' oils, or japan colours (for American readers) for tinting varnish; saucers or plastic jam jar lids; paper to hold excess powder; rags; masking tape.

Method for powder stencilling

First varnish the entire surface with semigloss or gloss varnish. Leave this to dry until there is a just perceptible 'tack' left – if you press the stencil on a corner it should come off with a faint pull but leave no mark. The tacky varnish will act as a size or adhesive for the metal powders.

205

Tip a little powder into a saucer or jam jar lid – if you are using more than one powder, use a separate container for each one. Place your stencil on the varnished surface, masking off the surrounding area, if possible, with paper fixed with strips of masking tape. The stencils should cleave tightly to the surface or powder may seep underneath.

Wrap a piece of velvet or chamois leather round your index finger, adjusting it so no creases appear. Dip the covered finger into the powder, then rub it on a piece of spare paper to remove the excess - very little powder is needed at any time. Place your finger on what is to be the highlight of your stencil design and, starting from there, rotate it gently, to polish in the highlight. From there work outwards, lessening the finger pressure so that the solid highlights blend to a softer bloom at the edges. When you need to pick up more powder, use the surplus on your spare paper first.

Use a different piece of fabric for each powder colour. Pale colours can be shaded with a darker one – use the lighter shade as highlight, and blend the two colours gently into each other for a modelled effect.

When your motif is completed, lift up the stencil and move it along to the next spot; repeat in the same way until the design is complete. Leave the varnish to dry hard – this usually takes about 24 hours. Then wash it gently with soapy water and a rag to remove any loose powder. Any powder that has landed on the wrong areas can be rubbed off patiently with a cotton bud dipped in a little household scouring powder.

Floating on colour When the powder stencilling is dry and clean, brush on a barrier coat of bleached shellac, to give yourself leeway for experiment.

Floated colours are made by mixing a little artists' oil colour with clear alkyd or polyurethane varnish. Apply this tinted varnish smoothly over the metallic motif with a soft, square-tipped artists' brush. Keep the colour intense in, say, the deeper folds of petals or the crease of a leaf, and thin it out over the rest. The effect should be very smooth and a little melodramatic. It does not matter if the floated colour goes over the edges, since being transparent it will scarcely show over a dark ground colour.

Use this technique with raw or burnt umbers or siennas, if you want to add richness to metallic decoration without too strong a contrast.

Above Though it has the sultry glow of antique gilding about it, this obelisk is new plaster covered with Dutch metal transfer leaf, a cheaper imitation of gold leaf. The secret of its allure is distressing, which reveals some of the red base beneath, and it has been antiqued with a murky rub of burnt umber oil colour.

Opposite Nothing becomes a handsome old painted piece so well as details picked out in burnished gold leaf. Gold on white is a favourite neo-classical combination, especially contrasted, as here, with dark green.

Transfer metal leaf

This consists of squares of leaf mounted on sheets of waxed tissue, which come in booklets. It is much easier to handle and lay than loose leaf, which is so light and fragile that it readily disintegrates. The most suitable types for use on furniture are Dutch metal – an alloy that closely resembles gold in colour and gleam – and aluminium. The latter is considerably cheaper, and can be coated with button polish (orange shellac) to imitate gold, or shaded with a little umber to suggest aged and tarnished silver.

Transfer leaf can be applied over small or large areas, as fine line trimming, and on raised or carved surfaces as well as flat ones. Once laid, it can be etched through with a sharp stylus or pointed instrument to reveal the paint colour beneath. It is not particularly difficult to lay – provided the degree of tackiness is right (see below), and the size accurately applied, it goes on as easily as any other type of transfer. To avoid waste, transfer leaf can be cut into smaller pieces with scissors or a sharp knife, cutting from the waxed paper side.

Preparation   As for metal powder decoration.

Materials   Dutch metal or aluminium transfer leaf; quick-drying goldsize or 'Wundasize', and soft artists' brush in suitable size for applying it; soft cotton wool [absorbent cotton]; orange shellac or diluted Indian ink.

Method   Use chalk to sketch out your design. Colour in the areas you intend for gilding or leafing, using ready-made red gesso or red casein paint for Dutch metal, and cobalt blue casein for silver/aluminium leaf. When dry, cover these areas thinly with goldsize or 'Wundasize'. The great advantage of the latter is its flexibility – it is ready for leafing after 20 minutes, but it is still tacky enough to work with up to 24 hours later. For standard goldsize, follow the maker's instructions.

The leaf is more lustrous when laid at the right time - if the size is too wet, it will tend to look dull. The time this takes depends on the conditions in which you apply it and the type of size used; the way to be sure is to test it. Extract a sheet of waxed paper with leaf attached from the booklet, and turn it leaf side down on the sized area. Rub over the back quite firmly with a pad of cotton wool or your fingertips. Then lift the paper off gently – if the tack is right, and your pressure even, the leaf will be stuck to the sized portions. Lay the next sheet to slightly overlap the first, and repeat the procedure, continuing until you come to the end of the design. Carefully brush off any loose metal with a soft paintbrush. Repair any 'skips' in the leafed surface by pressing on scraps of metal while the size is still sticky. When the size has dried, rub the surface over with soft cotton wool to smooth it and remove any loose bits, taking particular care with the overlaps.

To turn applied aluminium leaf a convincing bright gold, give it 1 or 2 coats of orange shellac, which dries in less than an hour. Brush diluted Indian ink over it for a soft, silvery finish. Shading and antiquing can be added by applying raw or burnt umber oil colour mixed into a little thinned varnish.

Applying metal leaf over carving Over raised or carved areas, such as picture frames, paint the surface first with red, blue or ochre casein paint. When that is dry, apply the goldsize and wait for it to become tacky. Then apply the leaf to the prominent areas of the carving, not attempting to cover every crevice, but just to suggest gilding worn and weathered over the years. This selective use of leaf used to be known as 'parcel gilding' and has always been a sensible economy – no sense in wasting gold where it will not show. When the size has dried, any surface patchiness can be

208

softened by rubbing down very gently with fine steel wool to reveal a little red, blue or yellow underlay here and there.

Finish off by varnishing the whole surface with clear semigloss alkyd varnish (see pages 160–2). **Varnishing**

Using metallic paints, creams and pens

These are among the easiest metallic finishes to apply, come in a good and convincing range of colours, and are useful combined with transfer leaf and metal powders, where their particular texture acts as a foil to the bright gleam of leaf and the soft but rich bloom of the powders. I find metallic paints handy for fine, brushed-on detail, twigs, stems, and leaves, such as might form part of a japanned scene. The creams are excellent for patching gilt frames quickly or for adding a smooth band of gold, silver or whatever to a painted piece. I would avoid using either over a large area, where their effect begins to look artificial.

Metal paints

These are available in both solvent- and water-based forms and should be applied with fine watercolour brushes, or lining brushes for line decoration. Metallic gouache colours are especially effective used over a dark base, so that the base 'ghosts' through to give a shaded effect. Practise this on a spare card or board first, painted in the same colour as the object to be finished. Being water based, metallic gouache is fast drying, and makes cleaning up quick and easy, but it must be sealed with shellac on completion, and before brushing over an antiquing wash of say, diluted acrylic, which would simply wipe it off again. Solvent-based metallic paints are a shade cruder in effect, but their consistency makes them especially useful for fine lining or details. They do not require special sealing (see maker's instructions).

Gilt creams

Unbeatable for an instant touch of metallic lustre, these can be applied over virtually any finish with fingertips or with a flat, soft artists' brush. The brand I use has the disadvantage that it needs its own special sealant but this is a small hiccup set against its splendid ease of application and pleasing texture. A small jar lasts an impressively long time.

Metallic felt pens

Metallic felt pens have their place in the panoply of new tools and materials designed to make specific tasks easier. They can be used, sparingly, to add a touch of helpful richness where their neatness and direct results are effective and suitable. Picture framers use them with rulers for gold lines round mounts. They are also suitable for 'lining', on painted furniture, but rub them over lightly with fine wire wool for an aged effect, and spray with varnish to fix before proceeding to other treatments. Metallic felt penwork looks richest applied over strong colours. A Greek key pattern, for instance, bordering a mount, has real impact if you paint in a band of terracotta, dark green, royal blue or black first, and then ink in the pattern on top.

Fundamentals

Paints, stains and varnishes

A little background knowledge about the way paints, stains, varnishes and so on are made, and why some do some jobs better than others, is helpful to anyone contemplating the bewildering array of cans displayed in most paint shops and do-it-yourself centres. I have not attempted to give an all-inclusive list of every variety of paint available, since many of these fall outside the scope of a book concerned with paint used decoratively rather than functionally, that is, as a protection from weather, rust or damp. Practicality does come into the picture, of course, since no one wants to be left with peeling, flaking walls, but decorative painting is concerned first with the look of a finish.

I have therefore classified the paints, varnishes and so on in this book

Flat finishes

Type	Composition	Appearance	Solvent
Undercoat (UK)	Pigments, drying oil or oil-modified alkyd	Perfectly flat, slightly chalky texture. Gives a thick, opaque film that fills small depressions in the surface	White spirit [mineral spirit]
Flat finish/flat oil paint [alkyd flat paint]	Pigments, drying oil, alkyd resin	Perfectly flat, a thinner and more uniform film than undercoat. Good coverage	White spirit [mineral spirit]
Vinyl matt emulsion/matt emulsion [latex flat paint and latex flat enamel]	Pigments, synthetic resins – usually polyvinyl acetate (PVA) or copolymer or acrylic polymers or a combination of the two – dispersed in water to form an emulsion binder	Less matt than flat paint. Some makes tend to have faint sheen. Gives a thick, slightly plastic coat that looks better in pale colours – dark or bright ones lack resonance	Water
Whitewash (generic name for soft distemper, oil-bound distemper and limewash)	Pigments, whiting, glue size, water. Limewash contains slaked lime instead of whiting. Oil-bound distemper has a binder of an emulsion of oil in water. Casein-bound distemper is a similar product more widely available in the US than in the UK	Absolutely matt. Soft, powdery texture. Good cover and clear colour	Water
Buttermilk (casein) paint	Soaked dry pigments, buttermilk	Perfectly flat, but not as powdery as distemper. Exceptionally clear colour since no white pigment is present	Water
Quick-drying floor paint	Pigments, acrylic resin	Non-shiny. Dull in colour	Water

simply by their finish – flat, mid-sheen, glossy or transparent. Primers have not been included in these paint charts, since they are not used as final finishes: follow the maker's instructions when using them.

The secret of using paint finishes successfully today, when there are so many formulations available, seems to me to lie in intelligent experiment plus common sense. There may be several ways of achieving a similar effect – you must decide which one best suits your taste, the sort of wear it can expect to get, and the amount of time and money you can invest in it.

Flat finishes

Look here for information about paints with matt, or flat, finishes. The most versatile and stylish one is the oil- or alkyd-based 'flat paint', which can be used on walls, woodwork, floors and furniture. Widely available in the United States, it is difficult to find in the United Kingdom, but British readers can use standard undercoat as a satisfactory substitute, although it will require protective varnishing. Incidentally, American enamel undercoater should not be used as an alternative to flat paint, as it dries to a hard, slightly shiny film, instead of a matt, chalky softness.

Uses and advantages	Disadvantages
Not intended to be a finish but has come to be used as a readily available substitute for flat paint. Cheap, easy to apply, dries in 8 to 12 hours. Highly pigmented. Pleasant, matt, dry texture. Can be bought anywhere, and although it comes in a limited range of colours it can be tinted and takes colour well	Needs matt varnish protection on surfaces that get scuffed. Poorer quality undercoat is more absorbent than flat paint, and so takes decoration less cleanly and smoothly
Can be used for most interior purposes. The best flat finish available – opaque and elegant. Takes colour well, dries in 6 to 12 hours. A favourite with decorators, either as a paint finish or as a glaze (thinned with solvent and with added drier). Alkyd flat paint is widely available in the United States	In Britain, obtainable only through specialist paint suppliers. Shows scuff marks. Must be used over undercoat
Quickest, cheapest, easiest and fastest drying finish for walls and ceilings. Can be bought anywhere. May be tinted with stainers [tinting colours]. Can be used as a base for some decorative finishes, or thinned with water to make a wash. Recoatable in about 4 hours, washable. Can be used on new dry plaster or rough, porous surfaces such as interior brickwork. Has almost no smell. Some types have been formulated for one-coat coverage for speed, and in gel form for no drips	Too absorbent to take most decorative finishes really well but can be used as a ground for stencilling. Not as soft or matt as distemper. May soil unless protected with matt varnish. Not recommended for steamy rooms such as kitchens and bathrooms; cannot be used on bare metal, since it can cause rust. A wash of thinned emulsion paint dries almost too quickly
Very cheap – you can even make it yourself, see page 37. Easy to apply, delicious texture and particularly pretty colours. Can be tinted with gouache, dry pigments or stainers. No smell, easy to clean up, soft distemper can be scrubbed off. Ideal for colourwashing or for any simple rustic effects. Limewash can be used on exteriors	Difficult to buy, since the do-it-yourself market rejects it as being short-lived, non-washable and susceptible to damp. Limewash and soft distemper require alkali-resistant pigments. Soft distemper is liable to rub off, and must be removed before applying oil-based or emulsion paints on top. Limewash should be given a coat of alkali-resisting primer before overcoating with oil-based paints
A 'cousin' of casein-bound distemper. The easiest paint to make – just mix soaked dry pigment into buttermilk, bought or homemade, with a little fungicide to prevent mould growth. Good, clear colour. Easy to apply; smells nice (not cheesy). Used in many early American stencilled rooms and still good for the purpose	Better in paler shades – bright or dark colours look streaky. Non-washable and susceptible to damp. Must be removed before overpainting with oil-based or emulsion paint
Quick-drying, tough, hardwearing paint, especially formulated for floors – wood or cement. Washable and requires no varnishing. Fairly good colour range	Available only in large quantities (5 litre cans) in UK

Mid-sheen finishes
These are the finishes that come midway between flat and gloss. If you can get trade eggshell, do, because it is a splendid all-purpose paint – strong and non-absorbent with an elegant soft sheen when dry. It makes the ideal base for many of the decorative finishes described in this book, particularly for glazes. If it cannot be found, one of the oil- or alkyd-based mid-sheen paints formulated for the do-it-yourself market will serve almost as well.

Mid-sheen finishes

Type	Composition	Appearance	Solvent
Trade eggshell/Eggshell	Pigments, synthetic alkyd resin, drying oil	Like thin cream, with a smooth, hard opaque surface and a dull sheen. An elegant finish for woodwork	White spirit [mineral spirit]
Quick-drying eggshell/ Acrylic eggshell	Pigments, waterborne copolymer emulsion	As above	Water
Oil- or alkyd-based mid-sheen, semi-sheen, or satin finish paints [velvet, eggshell, low-lustre and satin finish paints]	As previous two entries, but some are modified for faster application and opacity in one coat. Some may be thixotropic (gel-based), for non-drip, non-stir properties	Much as previous two entries, but thicker, slightly less attractive appearance. The list is in ascending degrees of sheen, i.e. satin is the shiniest	White spirit [mineral spirit]
Water-based silk or satin emulsion, vinyl silk or silk vinyl [latex velvet, eggshell, low-lustre and satin finish paints]	As for matt emulsion but with more PVA added to give extra sheen and washability	A soft but definite sheen (listed in ascending degrees of sheen)	Water
Floor paint, liquid lino [UK]	Pigments, epoxy resin	Very thick, rubbery coat. Dull colour	White spirit [mineral spirit]

Gloss finishes

Type	Composition	Appearance	Solvent
Semigloss, gloss, high gloss and hard gloss paint and enamel	Usually based on oil-modified alkyd resin, lightly pigmented with finely ground, highly opaque pigment	Brilliant gloss, hard, tough surface film. Semigloss is less shiny	White spirit [mineral spirit]
Acrylic, quick drying gloss [latex enamel]	Based on polycrylic resin plus pigments. May be thixotropic (gel-based) for convenience	Shiny, but not brilliant, gloss	Water
Aerosol spray-on paint and enamel	Pigmented nitro-cellulose medium or acrylic lacquers	Very hard, shiny, thin surface film – as on car bodywork	Benzol, acetone
Floor enamel [US]	Available in both alkyd- and latex-based types	Alkyd type has a high gloss finish, latex type a mid-sheen	Alkyd – white spirit [mineral spirit]; latex – water

Gloss finishes

Glossy paint finishes are seldom used in high-class decorating circles, except perhaps for children's playrooms, kitchens, bathrooms and other places where hard-wearing properties are the first requirement, since they are the toughest of the finishes and can be washed down frequently.

In decorative painting, a shiny finish – such as that on 'lacquered' walls or furniture – is usually achieved by applying coats of gloss varnish over flat or mid-sheen paint, rather than a simple one-step shiny paint. The result is a more subtle texture, with greater colour depth.

Uses and advantages	Disadvantages
As a finish for interior walls, woodwork and furniture, as a base for decorative treatment of any kind on a smooth, sound surface. Takes tinting well. Gives a fine, non-porous, porcelain texture that looks and feels nice, wears well and is lovely to paint on	More expensive than other mid-sheen paints. Takes 12 to 16 hours to dry, and needs careful brushing on and laying off
As above. Quick-drying	As above, but water-based takes only 2–4 hours to dry.
As previous two entries, though with a less satisfactory texture. Needs less brushing out. Easily available	Gives less coverage. Professional decorators prefer trade eggshell
Very fast-drying, recoatable in 2 to 4 hours. More suited to walls than woodwork. Can be used as a base for decorative finishes. Tougher than matt emulsion	Not as hard-wearing as oil- or alkyd-based paints
Exceptionally tough, hardwearing paint especially formulated for floors – wood or cement. Needs 2 coats minimum. Washable, does not require varnishing. Ideal where a strong, cheap coat of colour is called for – bathroom, landing. Fairly widely available	Poor colours, although they can be intermixed for greater subtlety. Not to be used with stainers or other pigmented media

Uses and advantages	Disadvantages
Gloss is for any surface requiring a strong, shiny, dirt-resistant finish. Hard gloss is for places that get extra wear – exterior woodwork, kitchen fitments. These paints are all long-lasting, moisture-resistant, easy to wipe down and reasonably proof against scratching and chipping	Must be used over proprietary undercoat for proper colour solidity. Takes between 12 and 16 hours to dry. Shiny finish exaggerates surface flaws, so thorough preparation is essential. Hard gloss finishes contain less oil; this makes for harder surface film, which chips more since it is less elastic
Dries in 2 to 4 hours. Easy to apply	Not as durable as oil-based gloss finish, nor as hard and shiny. Brushmarks show. Plastic-looking
Sold at do-it-yourself centres for touching up car bodywork. Can be used for spraying large, simple stencil patterns, where it can give a softly graduated colour effect	Expensive, tricky to use evenly, apt to spatter everywhere. Unpleasant smell; requires special solvent for cleaning up. Can be applied over emulsion [latex] or acrylics, but not over oil-based paints
Fairly quick-drying. Hard-wearing. Latex floor enamel can be applied to damp (though not wet) surfaces	Fairly expensive

Transparent finishes
Polyurethane varnishes, still the most widely available, are increasingly being challenged by newer formulations, like alkyd and acrylic varnishes. Shellac is not used as a finish as it is not alcohol- or water-proof but it is immensely useful as a fast-drying (20–30 minutes) isolating coat between paint layers and under applied decoration.

Transparent finishes

Type	Composition	Appearance	Solvent
Polyurethane varnish	Clear or pigmented polyurethane/alkyd	Clear, only a faint yellow compared with older type varnishes. Matt, semigloss or gloss according to need	White spirit [mineral spirit]
Alkyd varnish	Clear or pigmented alkyd or modified polyurethane/alkyd (uralkyd)	Clear. The uralkyds (including yacht varnishes, which have built-in UV filter) tend to be tougher than the more old-fashioned alkyds	White spirit [mineral spirit]
Acrylic/solvent-free quick-drying varnish	Water-based acrylic resins	Clear	Water
Emulsion glaze	Polyvinyl acetate copolymer or acrylic polymer	Milky white fluid which dries to a clear finish. Available in matt, eggshell, satin or gloss	Water
Shellac; button polish or orange shellac; white polish; knotting [knot sealer]	Natural shellac in alcohol	Transparent. Shellac itself is yellowish-brown; button polish or orange shellac is orange, as is knotting; white shellac or white polish, made from bleached shellac, is almost clear	Methylated spirit [denatured alcohol]
Proprietary floor seal	Alkyd resin or polyurethane base	Clear, slightly yellowy, hard and shiny surface film	White spirit [mineral spirit]
Goldsize, japan goldsize	Rapid-drying, short oil varnish with high drier content	Clear, slightly yellowy	White spirit [mineral spirit]

Stains

Type	Composition	Appearance	Solvent
Water stains	Water-soluble dyes or pigment usually bought in powder form to be dissolved in boiling water and diluted to strengh required	Clear, vivid colour, as with all colour using water as a medium. Can be bought in wood colours or made up from dry pigments (household dyes will do) and water	Water
Spirit or alcohol stains	Spirit-soluble dyes in shellac solutions thinned with methylated spirits	Come in woody and other colours. Less brilliant than water stains	Methylated spirit [denatured alcohol]
Oil stains	Pigments in oil or synthetic resin	More transparent than water stains	White spirit [mineral spirit]
Varnish stains	Mixture of oil stain and hard-drying oil varnish	Thicker, more opaque colour, which is less flattering to woodgrain	White spirit [mineral spirit]
Wax stains	Can be made by mixing artists' oil colours into beeswax or paraffin wax melted in a double boiler; allow it to cool to a soft paste. Shoe polish is a handy readymade alternative	Transparent and shiny, with a rich, waxy gloss after polishing	White spirit [mineral spirit]

Stains

There are a number of stains available for use on wood. You can also try applying fabric, carpet or leather dyes, made up according to the instructions on the packet but with only half the recommended amount of water. Another idea is to make your own wax stains – they give a rich glow to any wood, but require a lot of elbow-grease to maintain.

Uses and advantages	Disadvantages
The most versatile, easily used and widely obtainable varnishes for most decorative purposes – walls, woodwork, floors and furniture. Hard, clear, almost non-yellowing, strong. Touch-dry in 6 to 8 hours, should be left overnight before recoating	Not as elastic as traditional varnishes, less suited to rubbing down. Has a tendency to yellow
Some specialist types are less yellow than polyurethane varnishes. Very useful over glazed finishes. Uralkyd varnishes are generally very durable and clear	Alkyds tend to be weaker than uralkyds
Quick-drying. Some durable enough to use on floors and exteriors. Generally colourless, although some can yellow in contact with 'refined' linseed oil mediums	Not all are as tough as oil varnishes
Protective coating on wallpaper can be tinted with universal stainers for use as a glaze. (Thinned PVA can be used in the same way)	Not very strong. Some cannot be used in kitchens and bathrooms because of steam
Almost instant-drying sealing varnish for use in French polishing and as a barrier coat in furniture painting. Button polish or orange shellac can be used over metal leaf to simulate gold. Knotting is used to seal knots in new wood. Waxing can give greater protection	Must not be bought in large quantities, as it does not keep well. Does not make a strong final finish, since it is not alcohol- or water-proof
Easily applied, with rags or brushes, water-thin protective coat for decorated floors. Hard and durable if 4 or 5 coats are superimposed	Needs dry conditions. Not as tough, and slower-drying than polyurethane/alkyd varnish
Used as adhesive for metal leaf, and as medium for some quick-drying paints. Very fast-drying – 'quick goldsize' especially so – almost clear, easily applied	Brittle, becomes tacky at temperatures above 43°C [110°F]

Uses and advantages	Disadvantages
Cheap, easily applied, allow great range of colour effects, especially on light-coloured, close-grained woods	Lift woodgrain, so need rubbing down. Surface must be free from grease. Penetrate unevenly on porous softwoods, need sealing with shellac or goldsize before waxing
Best stains for use under French polish, penetrate deeply. Ideal for oily or hard, fine-grained woods. 2 or 3 pale coats give better results than 1 bright or dark one	These dry so fast that they are difficult to apply evenly. They may lift the grain a little
Easier to apply than spirit stains, give a more even, less penetrating colour. Ideal for softwoods, will take any superimposed clear finish when dry	Slow-drying, must be left overnight
Cheap, easily available and quick to apply	May be brittle. Very hard to remove
Easy to apply – simply rub in and burnish. Give a mellow, antiqued look – restorers use shoe polish on pieces of non-matching woods	Hard work to polish, harder still to remove. Will not take any other finish on top

Making colours

Although these days a paint stockist can mix most of the colours that you are likely to require, learning how to mix your own precise colours and tones is an excellent way to develop a colour sense – probably the definitive step toward becoming a decorative painter. With a small stock of concentrated pigments and a tin of basic white, or coloured, paint you can mix up most colours you are likely to need as you require them.

Pigment, or raw colour, is available in many forms – as loose powder, compressed blocks or cakes, or bound with oil, varnish, and other media

Type	Composition	Appearance	Solvent
Powder paint, artists' quality	Finely ground pigments	Matt colours, vivid, clear (unless mixed with white) and intense	Water (for water-based paints – can be mixed with oil to tint oil-based paints)
Poster colours	Powdered pigments, not so finely ground as artists' quality	Matt, rather thick colours, not so vivid or rich as above	Water
Universal stainers [universal tinting colours or colorizers]	Concentrated colours bound in high boiling point solvent which is compatible with oil-, water- and spirit-based paints	Very strong, matt colours, clear unless mixed with white	White spirit [mineral spirit]
Artists' oil colours	Highly refined pigments bound with linseed oil	Rich, varied and finely differentiated colours, matt if thinned with white spirit, otherwise the oil gives some sheen	White spirit [mineral spirit]
Students' oil colours	As above, but generally cheaper mixes	As above	White spirit [mineral spirit]
Watercolours	Pigments in a gum base, available in tubes and in semi-solid form in pans	Sharp, clear, translucent colours	Water
Alkyd colours	Pigments suspended in alkyd resin and solvent	Similar to artists' and students' oil colours	White spirit [mineral spirit]
Gouache colours	Concentrated colours in a water base	Particularly sharp, clear and fresh matt colours of great staining power. The white-pigmented base gives more opacity than ordinary watercolours	Water
Artists' acrylics	Pigments in a water-soluble polyacrylic base	Watercolour-clear when thinned; juicy *impasto* used neat. Matt colours, a little less vivid than gouache	Water
Signwriters' colours [bulletin colours]	Pigments in quick-drying varnish medium	Matt, intense, opaque colours	White spirit [mineral spirit]
Japan colours [US only]	Pigments in quick-drying varnish medium	Similar in texture and appearance to signwriters' colours	White spirit [mineral spirit]
Casein colours	Pigments in casein medium	Matt, powdery, opaque, very intense but hard colours unless mixed with white casein paste	Water

in tubes, jars and tins. One rule to bear in mind is that like should be mixed with like – thus you mix solvent-thinned pigment with solvent-thinned paint, water-thinned pigment with water-thinned paint. But this is only a rough guide, since there are exceptions – universal stainers [tinting colours], for instance, can be used to colour both water and oil-based paints. However, do not add more than 10% of stainer to the total volume of paint, or the mixture may start to gel and drying may be retarded.

Most of the colours listed below can be obtained from artists' suppliers; many paint suppliers stock universal stainers.

Uses and advantages	Disadvantages
Can be used to tint oil- or water-based paints, or varnishes. Dark colours stain wood. Pale colours make lovely washes	Cannot be used satisfactorily by themselves. In most cases they need a protective finish to prevent the colour washing off. Can be difficult to dissolve completely – need to be soaked first, in water or oil, depending on the paint to be used
Cheap, easily soluble colours, used mainly by children. Can be mixed with water-based paints	Limited range of colours in rather crude shades, thick pasty texture. Not easily mixed
Cheap, highly concentrated colours that mix easily and quickly with almost every type of paint or glaze. Limited colour range, but intermixing gives much greater colour possibilities	Rather hard colours that tend to need a touch of their complementaries to soften them. No raw umber in some ranges
Decorators use these for a lot of smaller scale decorative painting, because the colours are excellent, comprehensive and the texture is fine. Can be used thinned with solvent or oil, or mixed into clear varnish	Not cheap. Relatively slow-drying as compared with acrylics
As above	As above
Can be used for small-scale tinting of water-based media	Expensive and not easy to mix
Fast and even drying. Clarity of resin allows brightness of pigment to show through	Limited range of colours. Not widely available
Really beautiful colours, especially in strong pastel range. Ideal for colouring water-based paints and washes. Mix easily. Concentrated, so a little goes a long way. Used often in past to decorate furniture, on a gesso ground	Expensive
Amazingly quick-drying, so stencils or painted decoration can be finished in one session. Can be used diluted with water for a transparent effect, or in a special acrylic medium for transparency with body, or straight from the tube for thick, opaque cover	Expensive. Less rich textured than oil paints. Less mellow colours too. Dry so fast they need constant wetting in use (a retarding medium is also available). There tends to be wastage because of this very rapid drying
Very opaque, thick colours, so give good coverage with one coat – ideal for floor stencils. Large colour range	Not so rich or mellow as artists' oil colours. Need varnishing to bring out the colour. Available only from specialist suppliers
Rapid-drying, good flat texture and excellent colour range. Ideal for furniture decoration and any stencilling; use thinned with solvent, and with clear varnish – to bind colours and improve adhesion	Give reasonable opacity when thinned, but not full coverage. Though touch-dry in less than half an hour, must be left considerably longer before applying second coat or this dissolves the first
Use thinned with water only (about 1 part colour to 2 parts water) for a wash, or added to white casein paste or other water-thinned paints for creamier and pastel shades. Dry very quickly, excellent opacity and therefore economical to use. Hard finish	Must be left for some time and sealer applied before painting on second coat. Tend to solidify if not used up quickly. Unpleasant smell. Limited availability in UK

Reds

Burnt Sienna + Alizarin Crimson +

Cadmium Scarlet =

Raw Sienna + Cadmium Scarlet +

Venetian Red + Cadmium Scarlet =

Pinks

Burnt Sienna   + White =

Mixed Pink No 1

Mixed Pink No 1 +

Yellow Ochre = Mixed Pink No 2

Mixed Pink No 1 +

Black +

Cobalt =   Mixed Pink No 3

Crimson + White =

Yellows

Yellow Ochre + White =

Lemon Chrome + Chrome + Burnt Umber =

Greens

Chrome Yellow + Black =

Mixed Green No 1 + White = Mixed Green No 2

Chrome Green⋆   Sap Green⋆

Raw Umber + Chrome Yellow + Indigo +

White =

Blues

Cobalt +

Raw Umber =   Chrome Yellow =   Scarlet =

Cerulean +   Chrome + Raw Umber +

(varying amounts of) White =

⋆These bright colours cannot easily be mixed, but may be bought from artists' suppliers

Colour mixes

If the ability to combine colours inventively is a largely instinctive process, knowing what to mix with what to get a specific colour is something you pick up as you go along, making notes of happy combinations you come across. Here are some rough indications of how to get what decorators call 'good' (that is, gutsy, lively, distinguished) colours. It would take a book to go into the subject in depth, but half a loaf is better than no bread and you may find these notes helpful.

Don't be frightened of experimenting with colours. But don't mix large quantities while you are experimenting; a few spots of likely shades on a plate or sheet of paper can be worked together with a fingertip to give a good idea of what they look like when mixed. Once you know you are on the right lines, it's safe to proceed with larger quantities.

Don't run away with the idea that there is only one way to get a particular colour. If your requirements are not too precise, if you are after a warm earthy red rather than the exact shade to match a piece of fabric or an old tile, there are probably half a dozen or more ways of arriving at a colour in that general area. Most interesting colours in decorating are, literally, mixed-up ones, but there are exceptions, generally in the pure and paler shades: for example, a mix of cobalt blue, white and a tinge of yellow does not give quite the same cerulean tint as the paint of that name, nor do cobalt, chrome yellow and white give quite the lettuce green of chrome green. But it is nevertheless sound practice and training to begin with a fairly limited standard range – such as the universal stainer [tinting colour] range plus raw umber and crimson – and see how far you can get by combining these in various proportions. Some decorators swear that they can get all the colours they want this way. Others insist that some shades can be prepared only from bought pigment. But you can always add these special colours to your collection as you need them.

Dirty, or off-whites Raw umber plus white gives a cool greenish grey, a very safe colour. A spot of yellow ochre warms it, a dot of black intensifies it – easy on the black, though, as a little goes a long way. Yellow ochre plus white gives a warm cream, which is lightened to ivory by adding more white. A dot of umber shades it to parchment. White plus ivory black gives a cool grey, known as French grey.

Pinks You can make good pinks by mixing burnt sienna with white. This gives delectably warm, but not sissy pinks, like faded cottage walls. Adding more white lightens them, a little yellow ochre (earth colours are mutually compatible) gives an apricot cast, a touch of cobalt and black takes them toward terracotta. Venetian red and white also make a good strong pink. Use the crimson reds to get sky blue pinks, because they contain a little blue.

Reds It is rare to find a really good commercial red, they tend to be too brash and hurtfully bright. But it is easy to mix your own. Composite reds always work better on walls, floors, woodwork and furniture than pure ones, in my experience. Burnt sienna, alizarin crimson and a little cadmium scarlet, vermilion or bright red stainer give a magnificently vital, rich but not hard red with a brownish cast. More crimson makes it deeper, cooler, more sienna makes it earthier and browner, more vermilion brings it nearer to old lacquer. Raw sienna mixed with scarlet gives a soft, warm orangey red. Venetian red, red oxide and Indian red are all good strong sympathetic slightly brownish reds. Add a dash of cadmium or one of the other red reds above to make them brighter and less earthy. A spot of green softens red red; umber will age it.

Yellows Yellow ochre and Indian yellow are both warm friendly earthy yellows, with a creamy tone when mixed with white – nice wall colours. Chrome yellow is a hearty, sunflower colour with more orange to it. It is also the best, most opaque, one for mixing other colours, but you can also use cadmium yellow. For the sophisticated yellow often used for lacquer wall effects, try a glaze of mixed yellows: lemon chrome (or cadmium lemon), chrome and a touch of burnt umber, over primrose: white tinted with chrome yellow.

Greens Yellow ochre mixed with lamp black gives a strong, drab olive green much used in the eighteenth century, on woodwork and furniture. Adding white to this produces a Dijon mustard colour. Cobalt and chrome yellow again give a green of olive tone. Indigo, chrome yellow, raw umber and white give strong greens paling to duck egg green as one adds more white. Some greens cannot be successfully mixed, and must be bought as tube colours. The sharp, light yellow-greens are a case in point. Chrome green is the juiciest but sap green is another good one.

Blues Cobalt is the blue most used by decorators, a nice clean but soft blue, less strident than ultramarine and Prussian. A little umber dulls it, chrome yellow warms it, a spot of red knocks it back. I like indigo, a very distinguished blue, darker than cobalt, with purply sloe-berry overtones. Mixed with the above colours it gives similar, but moodier effects. To make the ethereal cerulean/thrush egg blues, best start with a bought cerulean, adding a spot of chrome and raw umber, or yellow ochre, to give the greeny cast, and then lots of white. For a terrific, vibrant stained-glass sort of blue, with green tones, use ultramarine or Hortensia, but don't try to get it in one, use a tinted glaze in one tone over a ground coat of another. To make a very pure violet, mix ultramarine and crimson, rather than Prussian blue and scarlet, which both contain yellow.

Glaze is a word that crops up repeatedly in this book, as it is a key ingredient of many decorative finishes, for walls, woodwork and furniture. Broadly speaking, a glaze is a semi-transparent film of oil-based colour, while a wash is a semi-transparent film of colour diluted with

Glazes and washes

water. There are subtle visual differences between the two; oil-based colour tends to be richer, sleeker and more transparent, while colour in water is fresher, purer, still diaphanous, but 'brushier' looking. Both can be used over painted surfaces to soften, enrich, and otherwise modify the colours beneath.

Glazes, being slower drying, are more easily manipulated than washes. Classical painting used glazes routinely, to float delicate tints on hair and skin, deepen shadows, suggest the fragility of flower petals, the lustre of pearls. In the decorative field, the concept of colour seen through transparent colour has countless applications. Woodgrainers and marblers use glazes, and washes, to suggest patina, depth and the complex layering of colour and markings in natural materials. Furniture restorers often use murky tinted glazes to give an instantly 'aged' look, suggestive of centuries of use and wear, to newly painted furniture. Decorators use glazes, and washes, to get subtle colour effects or for distressed finishes that give a soft, rich, spaced out look to interiors. A wash has a particularly vivid spontaneous effect. Whether as a glaze or a wash, transparent colour over white gives glowing pastels; over toning colour it gives a richer version of the same; over contrasting colour it creates effects of astonishing sophistication considering the simplicity of the means. Glazes are a help, too, in keeping one's colour options open – wall colours that have come out wrong can be corrected by applying a suitably coloured glaze on top, distressed or plain. Since thin glazes can be applied over walls in less than half the time it would take to repaint them, this is worth knowing.

Terracotta has been one of the favourite colours in recent decoration, providing a strong but friendly background to the eclectic mix of furnishings so characteristic of today's interiors. The colour here has been applied using several coats of tinted oil glaze for a rich but matt finish.

Glazes

Depending what goes into a glaze, it can be shiny or matt and more or less transparent, according to the amount of white pigment it contains in proportion to the other ingredients. It should not be confused with that other transparent medium, varnish. Varnish is designed to give a hard, clear, protective coating and though it is sometimes tinted (as with lacquered walls or in furniture decoration) to give a glazed effect, it is not suited to distressing.

Glazes can be bought ready made, requiring tinting, or they can be made up from ingredients available from most artists' suppliers.

Transparent oil glaze

Transparent oil glaze, sometimes sold under the name 'scumble glaze' in Britain [glazing liquid or glaze coat in the United States], is a ready-mixed glaze base to which colour is then added. This can come in the form of universal stainers [tinting colours], which are powerful and cheap, but are available in a limited colour range, or artists' oil colours, which offer much subtler and purer colours, but are more expensive. To tint oil glaze, squeeze a blob of colour into a cooking tin or pan and add a little white spirit [mineral spirit] to dissolve it, stirring hard to blend. Next spoon in a cupful or so of the unthinned glaze and stir well, then add the rest of the glaze, still stirring continuously.

Proprietary transparent oil glazes are convenient and easy for beginners to work with because they stay 'open' and malleable long enough to be distressed with rags, brushes and other equipment. However, it must be said that their very ease and convenience has led to some confusion among amateur painters, who are thereby misled into thinking that proprietary glaze needs only the addition of colour to create a sophisticated wall finish. Used almost neat like this, oil glaze looks like thick jam; wood graining is the sole technique where these products are used full strength. For special effects on walls, woodwork or furniture, professionals make up a glaze using a relatively small amount of proprietary glaze, much thinned with white spirit [mineral spirit], tinted with oil colour and, more often than not, modified by the addition of a spoonful or so of standard white undercoat. The undercoat softens the glaze colour, giving a slightly blurred rather than hard-edged imprint when it is ragged, dragged or whatever. The linsed oil content of a proprietary glaze does contribute to the eventual yellowing and darkening of the tinted colour, which is another good reason for minimizing its use in the modified glaze recipe. Here is a standard glaze recipe, which you should find adequate for many purposes:

> 1 part proprietary oil glaze
> 3 parts white spirit [mineral spirit]
> universal stainers [tinting colours] or artists' oil colours
> 1 tablespoon undercoat, flat white or eggshell white paint per ½ litre [1 US pint]

It is quite possible to make up your own glaze – artists have done so for centuries. Here is a basic recipe to try:

> 1 part raw linseed oil
> 1 part white spirit [mineral spirit]
> 1 part clear matt varnish (for a softer effect, add one tablespoon or more of white undercoat per ½ litre [1 US pint]

Linseed oil may be purchased 'raw' or 'boiled' and it eventually dries to a hard finish. Boiled linseed oil is a refined and faster-drying version of the raw form. *Do not boil it!* Yet in either form linseed oil can take an impractically long time to become hard dry, and it may be advisable to add a proprietary product known as 'drier', obtainable from trade suppliers, which helps the glaze to dry hard more quickly.

The above recipes are guidelines, and I use this term deliberately. Beginners find cut-and-dried recipes encouraging, but anyone who works with oil glazes constantly knows that many variables may need to be taken into account. These include the climate, room temperature, type of wall (whether it is an exterior or party wall), depth of the previous finishes, type of base coat and number of layers of base coat. So keep an open mind and critical eye on your glaze and be prepared to play around with it, adding and modifying, till it behaves as it should, taking impressions clearly but not 'jammily'. If dragged markings run together, it is too thin; add a little more transparent oil glaze. Often leaving a wet glaze to 'set up' a moment or two longer before distressing will correct a tendency to blur.

Be prepared to experiment on boards or on a patch inside a cupboard – you can always wipe off the wet glaze with a cloth dipped in solvent if you are not happy with the effect.

Ground Transparent oil glaze should be applied over a ground of non-porous paint. Two coats of eggshell (mid-sheen) oil-based paint is the standard professional specification. Today many people cut corners with 1 coat of eggshell over undercoat, or at a pinch 2 coats of vinyl silk emulsion [latex] which is cheaper, easier to apply and has a similar non-porous effect.

Applying a glaze

Keep the glaze coat to a thin film for maximum transparency. Take up a small amount of glaze on the bristles of a decorators' paintbrush, brush it on quickly and then smooth out lightly with the bristle tips. On a very smooth, eggshelled surface, glaze can be applied with a bunched-up rag – *smeared* on thinly. If a glaze seems too fluid, leave it a few moments to harden off slightly before distressing.

Where a glaze threatens to dry off too quickly, as it might on a hot day, one solution is to add a little clarified raw linseed oil – a teaspoon to ½ litre [1 US pint]. Remember to allow longer for overall drying, up to 48 hours.

Washes

Washes of colour diluted in water are trickier to apply and handle than oil-based glazes, just as watercolour is a more difficult medium to excel in than oil painting, but they give such luminous colour and airy transparency that some decorators find them irresistible. Walls washed over with clear colours have something of the ethereal freshness of old fresco painting.

A wash can vary in consistency, all the way from emulsion [latex] paint thinned to milkiness, to a mixture that is little more than tinted water, with a dollop of emulsion for 'body'. Thinned and tinted emulsion paint can be dragged, rag-rolled, sponged or slapped on every whichway for a dappled look. The effect is never going to be as delicately modulated and controlled as if you were working with an oil glaze, but it gives a streaky homespun effect and powdery texture that you might prefer. Use the ultra-thin colour washes for loose brushing on only, not distressing, as they dry too quickly to manipulate. Besides, colour applied like this has its own built-in distressing, a brushy quality, especially when the colours are at all strong. If you dislike this effect stick to pale colours – yellows, pinks, pale blues and greens.

Decorators invariably use the purest colours for making washes, favouring gouache colour especially for its vividness. I find powder colours, either artists' quality or the poster colours sold for children's use, make effective washes too, a bit cruder looking perhaps, but nicely reminiscent of those casually coloured old interiors one sees in France and Italy. Acrylics, also soluble in water, are another possibility, but more expensive.

Ground A wash is most satisfactorily applied over a flat emulsion [latex] base paint; it tends to trickle off an oil-based ground. The flatter the emulsion base is, in my experience, the more absorbent, and therefore the easier it is to apply an emulsion wash over it. If you have to apply an emulsion wash over a mid-sheen surface, adding a drop of liquid detergent will help the wash to 'stick'. Preferably, over any mid-sheen or gloss surface, use a more compatible oil-based glaze thinned to transparency, which will also dry matt.

Thinning An emulsion [latex] wash suitable for such techniques as dragging, rag-rolling and sponging should be thinned about 1 part paint to 3 or 4 parts water. Use a much thinner version for colourwashing: 1 part paint to 8 or 9 parts water. For the 'tinted water' washes, the proportions of colour to water will obviously depend on how vibrant you want the effect to be. A rough guide for a wash of this kind is to use 1 small tube of gouache to ½ litre [1 US pint] water, plus a tablespoon of emulsion paint.

Tinting washes Tint thinned emulsion [latex] washes with gouache colours, acrylic colours, powder colours, or with universal stainers [tinting colours]. Dissolve the colours in water, then mix with full-strength emulsion paint before thinning as required. The critical part of mixing your own colours is to mix *thoroughly* – undissolved specks of pure colour can emerge as huge streaks on a wall.

Applying a wash The most important thing when applying a decorative finish over or with emulsion [latex] paints is to make sure the surface beneath is well cleaned of grease and grime. Water-thinned colours simply won't stick over greasy patches. Use a weak solution of a proprietary paint cleaner, or, if you feel the finish might rub off, wipe over with warm water plus something to cut the grease – ammonia, washing soda, vinegar. Rinse afterwards, and leave to dry out completely before putting on a wash.

The most likely problem in applying a wash, especially in hot weather, is that the wet edge will dry, leaving hard lines of colour that are difficult to disguise. If this happens, adding a spoonful of glycerine – bought from a chemist or druggist – to the wash can help keep the paint 'open' and workable longer. Start with a teaspoon per ½ litre [1 US pint], adding a little more if needed.

When you apply two washes on top of each other for richer colour, leave the first wash to dry for at least 24 hours before painting on the second, or the top colour may lift off the one beneath leaving bald patches of base coat showing through, which are not easy to touch up afterwards. If you do have this problem, try sponging on the second wash, using quick pecky movements so as not to disturb the wash below. If the second wash runs and drips too much, add a little more emulsion to make it thicker. You can drag one wash on top of another, but again brush it on quickly and lightly and try not to go over the same place too much or the wash beneath will soften and begin to lift.

Decorating equipment
For descriptions of the equipment
illustrated here see overleaf.

1

2

3

4

5

6

7

8

9

10

11

12

13

Don't panic   When a glaze or wash doesn't behave quite as you expected, don't panic. Check through various possible explanations – is it too thin, too thick, is the base coat too slippery or greasy, is the weather exceptionally hot or are the walls damp? If it doesn't brush out evenly and looks messy, try sponging or ragging the wet glaze to even it up – use a sponge dampened with solvent if a glaze has hardened. Really patchy effects can be rescued by sponging a darker or lighter colour on over the top, glazing overall with a creamy colour, dragging with a darker colour, or adding a stencilled border. But before resorting to any of these measures, try hanging a few pictures and putting back some furiture – it is amazing how re-populating the space relegates the wall finish to second place. All decorators agree that some of their happiest effects have been part accidental – some unforeseen reaction that they had the wit to take advantage of.

Equipment

Apart from basic paints and brushes, you will find it pays to keep a supply of general decorating equipment. The following (illustrated on page 227) are used for preparation and for many of the techniques described in the book.

1 Chamois Leather   An alternative to rags for ragging wet glaze. It makes crisper 'prints' than rags but is more of a nuisance to clean. Use white spirit [mineral spirit] for this. Rags can be junked.

2 Mutton Cloth (also called stockinette)   For cleaning up; can also be used for ragging and breaking up wet glaze. It will leave some loose fibre but this can be brushed off when the glaze dries.

3 Cotton Rags   Used to lift off glaze when ragging and rag rolling, to create distinctive 'prints'.

4 Sandpaper and Wire Wool Available in different grades for rubbing down and finishing. As well as standard abrasive papers, keep some wet-or-dry paper in various grades.

5 Sponges   Natural, marine sponges are best for sponging on and off and for dabbing and distressing wet glaze. Synthetic sponges can be used in stencilling and to apply washes.

6 Jam Jar   Endlessly useful for storage, keep a box full of spares.

7 Acetate   Transparent plastic film can be used instead of card. Its transparency is somewhat illusory since paint soon masks this. But it is immensely tough and usefully bendy for corners, etc. Apt to split while hand-cutting. Commercial stencils are stamped out with dies.

8 Stencil Card   Oiled manila card is good for making your own stencils as it is easier to cut smoothly without splitting. Not indestructible because water eventually softens it, so make 2 or more of each pattern on large scale jobs.

9 Rollers   Heads available in a variety of materials including mohair; foam-headed and lambswool heads are shown here. Use to cover a background faster, where absolute smoothness is not critical – such as applying primers, undercoats, emulsion [latex] paints. Some painters use a roller to put glaze on, together with a stippling brush.

10 Cutting Mat   Helpful if you are intending to cut a lot of stencils, though I often use layers of newspaper instead.

11 Stanley Knife and Craft Knives   For cutting stencils in acetate or card; it has many other uses. Make sure you never run out of sharp new blades.

12 Trowel   Used for plastering and applying skim coat materials like proprietary filler.

13 Scraper   Scrapers are multi-purpose tools; depending on size, they may be used for mixing filler [spackle], applying skim coats, stripping wallpaper and loose paint. Choose one with a rigid steel blade. In addition a flexible spatula or artists' palette knife is neat for small filling jobs.

Brushes

A brush consists of a handle, bound at the stock [block] to a filling previously 'set' in resin or vulcanized rubber. The filling is usually referred to as the 'bristles', although in fact bristle is only one of the available fillings, which also include hogshair, badgerhair, oxhair and synthetic filaments. Indications of quality in a brush are a thick, silky, flexible filling, well bonded to a handle that is balanced and pleasant to hold. You can tell an expensive brush from a cheap one, as the latter has a wide stock [block] running between the bristles. A selection of brushes is illustrated on pages 230–1, and discussed on page 232.

Working with well-made equipment, scaled to the job in hand, is pleasurable and fast. Go to a trade supplier, rather than a do-it-yourself centre, and ask the experts which brushes they recommend. It pays to buy the best and look after them well – a good brush will last twice as long as a cheap one and does the job more efficiently.

It is worth investing in a proprietary cleaner, too, to keep brushes in shape. These cleaners contain stronger solvents than white spirit [mineral spirit] and they clean the bristles faster. Amateurs invariably skimp the tedious soaking and rinsing ritual, so the use of a brand cleaner will counteract any laziness here. Keep plenty of well-washed glass jars for the purpose – with the lid screwed on tightly to prevent evaporation, the same jar of cleaner can be used over and over again. Brushes used in emulsion [latex] paint must be cleaned immediately after use – either in soap and warm water or in proprietary cleaner. An old-fashioned scrubbing brush, with stiff bristles, is useful for dislodging paint that has worked up the bristles. Lay brushes flat in the sink and scrub away from the handle end under a tap. Never leave a brush standing in solution for days on end – this bends and weakens them. One professional dodge is to drill a hole through the handle, and slot a wire or pencil through, laying it across the top of the jar so that the bristles are suspended in the cleaner without touching the sides of the container, which will bend them. It is worthwhile drilling holes anyway, since hanging brushes from nails is a good way to store them when not in use.

To extract loose hairs from a new brush, bang it hard a few times on the edge of a horizontal surface, or spin it between the palms of your hands. The hairs soon work their way into sight, so you can easily pick them out. Traditionally, new brushes were 'worked in' on primers, then undercoats for several days – a loose hair stuck in a priming coat is less of a problem than one stuck in a last coat of gloss.

Brushes
A selection of useful brushes which are described overleaf.

1

2

3

4

5

6

7

8

12

13

14

15

16

17

18

9

10

11

25

27

23

24

26

28

19

29

20

21

22

30

31

1–3 Standard Decorators' Brushes
Part of any painter's kit. Buy more as
special needs arise. A wide, thickly
bristled brush (1) is essential for walls –
100 or even 125 mm [4 or 5 in] wide,
depending on how large your hands are.
For painting woodwork, use a medium-
sized brush (2), between 50 and 75 mm [2
and 3 in] wide.

For fiddly 'cutting in' on such surfaces
as window frames and door panels, a small
brush 25 mm [1 in] or narrower is easier to
control. You can use it for painting
furniture and other precision work, too.
Brushes cut on the diagonal (3) are
available for cutting in.

4–7 Artists' Brushes A selection of
artists' brushes is necessary for decorative
work. Soft pointed watercolour brushes
are used for fine work in all media. Get the
best you can afford in 2 or 3 sizes,
including one very fine one. Hogshair
brushes for oil painting are versatile too. A
rounded fitch makes a handy stencil brush
for small-scale work, while flat-ended
bristle brushes are good for broad lining.
Store all these like wooden spoons, handle
down in a jar.

8 Dusting Brush Useful, versatile and
inexpensive. It has soft, medium-length
bristles set in a wooden handle.
Decorators use it for stippling work on a
small scale – furniture, woodwork. You
can also use it for softening glazes and
washes, although it won't give as fine
control as will the badger softener. It
should be cleaned carefully – never
immerse the stock [block] in cleaner: the
solvent will dissolve the resin, causing the
bristles to drop out.

**9, 10 Badger Softener or
Blender** This is the finest brush for all
softening purposes. Expensive, because it
is made of badger hair, but smaller sizes
are affordable. It can be used with oil and
water media, for softening brushmarks,

graining, etc. but should be carefully
cleaned after use. Rub bristles as clean as
possible on paper or rags, dip into solvent
as briefly as possible, then wash in warm
water with soap rather than detergent,
which dries out the bristles. Rinse, shake
and dry flat.

11 Stippling Brush This hogshair
brush comes in various sizes, all with a
fixed bridge handle, and is purpose-made
for stippling wet glazes, paints and
varnish. Because of its size the stippling
goes faster and the handle makes it less
tiring to use. It is also expensive as brushes
go because of the quantity of bristles and
should be carefully cleaned and stored so
the bristles don't get bent out of shape.

12, 13, 14 Brushes for Varnishing
Varnishing requires clean brushes, so buy
and keep particular ones for that purpose
only. You can use a standard decorators'
brush, or a glider, a light brush with thin
silky bristles which is good for applying
thinned varnish and shellac, or an oval
varnish brush, which painters use for
larger jobs because the generous head of
bristle holds more varnish and brushes it
out smoothly. Check instructions on
varnish tins to determine the correct
solvent – white spirit [mineral spirit] for
oil-based varnishes, water for acrylics and
methylated spirit [denatured alcohol] for
shellac. Try to keep a separate brush for
each type.

15 Camel Hair Mop An ultra-soft
brush, like a cosmetic brush, which can be
helpful in work using metal powders. I
would substitute a cosmetic brush.

16, 17, 18 Fitch A rounded brush with
flexible but firm bristles, the fitch comes in
sizes ranging from 4.5 mm [⅛ in] to about
30 mm [1¾ in] wide. Traditionally used
with oil paints, it is suitable for spattering,
stippling and painting small-scale
stencils. Not expensive and useful.

19–22 Stencilling Brush The
traditional stencilling brush (20–22) looks
like a man's shaving brush – short and fat,
with hogshair bristles, blunt cut at the
end. It comes in various sizes, between 6
and 50 mm [¼ and 2 in] across. With this
kind of brush the paint is 'pounced' on, a
tiring procedure, and stencillers now often
prefer to use a softer, mop-headed brush
(19) which allows the paint to be applied
in a looser, more swirling fashion that is
faster and creates a fine dry image. An
artist's fitch is another alternative.

23, 24 Lining Brush Special lining
brushes can be bought with long, soft
bristles which hold more paint so your line
goes further. The swordliner (24) is also a
good brush for making fine straight lines
freehand. For fine line work I often use a
sable artists' watercolour brush. A
signwriter's lining fitch has the advantage
that you can use it with a straight edge.
Lining brushes should be coaxed back
into shape after cleaning – fuzzy lines are
useless. A trace of soap makes a good
setting agent. Store flat.

25–31 Graining Equipment Metal
(25) and rubber (26) combs are used for
creating the distinctive graining effects,
and can also be used for other types of
decorative painting. The 'rocker' or heart
grainer (27) is used specifically to suggest
the whorls of heartwood. An ordinary cork
can be whittled to make a knot tool (28).
The flogger (29) is primarily a graining
brush. Its long, flexible horsehair bristles
are flicked against wet glaze to create a
woody fibrous texture and also to drag
straight grain marking, to which a slight
wobble of the handle imparts a naturalistic
ripple or bend. This brush can also be
used for decorative dragging on
woodwork or smaller items. Beginners
will find a 'glider' (12–13) can substitute
satisfactorily. Overgrainers (30 and 31)
are used to put in detail on a dry,
previously grained surface.

If you cannot find paints and painting sundries at your local dealer, the dealers and manufacturers on this list will be able to help you. Those marked with an asterisk offer a mail order service. Artists' suppliers appear in italics.

List of suppliers

EAST COAST───────────────────

Wolf Paints (S. Wolf's Sons)
Janovic Plaza
771 Ninth Avenue
New York, NY 10019

Tel: 212 245-3241

Arthur Brown & Bro. Inc.
2 West 46th Street
New York, NY 10036

Tel: 212 575-5555

Janovic Plaza
1150 Third Avenue
New York, NY 10022

Tel: 212 772-1400

SOUTHEAST───────────────────

Kurfees Coating, Inc.
201 East Market Street
Louisville, KY 40202

Tel: 502 584-0151

Janovic Plaza
30–35 Thomson Ave.
Long Island City, NY 11101

Tel: 718 392-3999

Flax Artists and Drafting Supplies
1460 North High Drive
Atlanta, GA 30318

Tel: 404 352-7200

MIDWEST───────────────────

Kurfees Coating, Inc.
1380 Mark Street
Elkgrove, IL 60007

Tel: 708 595-0893

Charrette Favor Ruhl
23 South Wabash Avenue
Chicago, IL 60603

Tel: 312 782-5737

SOUTHWEST───────────────────

Texas Art Supply
2001 Montrose
Houston, TX 77006

Tel: 713 526-5221

Dan Lee (suppliers of Woodwash
and proprietary colorwash)
The Plaza at University Park
4020 Villanova
Dallas, TX 75225

ROCKY MOUNTAIN AREA───────────────────

Diamond Vogel/Kormac Paints
1201 Osage Street
Denver, CO 80204

Tel: 303 534-5191

WEST COAST───────────────────

Standard Brands
3 Masonic Avenue
San Francisco, CA 94118

Tel: 415 922-4003

Paint Magic
2426 Fillmore Street
San Francisco, CA 94115

Tel: 415 292-7780

Flax's
1699 Market Street
San Francisco, CA 94103

Tel: 415 552-2355

*Pottery Barn (suppliers of Woodwash
and proprietary colorwash)
Williams Sonoma
100 North Point Street
San Francisco, CA 94133

Tel: 415 421 7900

This book features the work of the following designers and decorative artists.

Tania Backhouse
359 Portobello Road
London W10 5SD
Tel: 081 968 4622

Kitty Beamish
117 Sudbourne Road
London SW2 5AF
Tel: 071 274 7919

Suzanne Bellehumeure
295 Sound Beach Avenue
Old Greenwich
Connecticut 06870
USA
Tel: 0101 203 698 1121

Colleen Bery Designs
157 St. John's Hill
Battersea
London SW11 1TQ
Tel: 071 924 2197

Angeles Blasco
82 Cavendish Road
London SW12 0DF
Tel: 081 673 2779

Sarah Delafield-Cook
7A Anhalt Road
London SW11 4NZ
Tel: 071 247 9462

Nicholas Fer Specialist Paint Finishes
29 Winterwell Road
London SW2 5JB
Tel: 071 737 4574

Cicely Gattagher
44 Victoria Road
London W8 5RG
Tel: 071 937 2742

Gonzalo Gorostiaga
48 Brushfield Street
London E1 6QG
Tel: 071 375 0779

Saul Greenberg
3 Rosslyn Mansions
21 Goldhurst Terrace
London NW6 3HD
Tel: 071 328 2090

Emma Hardie
25 Leighton Grove
London NW5 2QP
Tel: 071 482 6654

IPL Interiors
308 Fulham Road
London SW10 9UG
Tel: 071 352 8360

Thomas Lane Painted Interiors
57 Wellington Row
London E2 7BB
Tel: 071 729 6195

Rachel Macfadyen
Specialist Paint Finishes
The Conservatoire
19–21 Lee Road
London SE23 9R4
Tel: 081 297 9108

Ray McNeill Furniture Design
117 Fairfax Road
London N8 0NJ
Tel: 081 340 7871

Steve Marsh
8 Windsor Court
Catsey Lane
Bushey
Herts WD2 3HY
Tel: 081 950 4318

Christopher Nevile
Design Partnership
55 Endell Street
London WC2H 9AJ
Tel: 071 240 5844

Mauro Peruchetti
RMC House
15 Townmead Road
London SW6 2QL
Tel: 071 371 5497

Richard Sleeman
c/o The Diarama
Park Square East
Regents Park
London NW1

Fiona Sutcliffe
13 Crescent Place
London SW3 2EA
Tel: 071 581 1083

Reading list

Painting techniques

A. Bishop and C. Lord *The Art of Decorative Stencilling* Thames and Hudson, London, 1976, revised edition, Viking Penguin, New York, 1985

Jocasta Innes *The Complete Book of Decorating Techniques* Macdonald Orbis, London, 1986
Paintwise: Decorative Effects on Furniture Pyramid Books, London, 1991
Paintability Weidenfeld and Nicolson, London, 1986
Scandinavian Painted Decor Cassell, London, 1990

Miranda Innes *The Country Home Decorating Book* Dorling Kindersley, London, 1989, Collins and Brown, London, 1991

Ralph Mayer *The Artist's Handbook of Materials and Techniques* 5th edition Faber and Faber, London, 1991

Kevin McCloud *Kevin McCloud's Decorating Book* Dorling Kindersley, London, 1990

I. O'Neil *The Art of the Painted Finish for Furniture and Decoration* William Morrow, New York, 1971

John P. Parry *Parry's Graining and Marbling* 3rd edition, revised by Rhodes, B. and Windsor, J. Sheridan House, New York, 1985 and Blackwell Scientific, Oxford, 1987

W.J. Pearse *Painting and Decorating* 9th edition, revised by Goodier, J.H. and Hurst, A.E. State Mutual Book, New York and Charles Griffin, London, 1980

Annie Sloan *Simple Painted Furniture* Dorling Kindersley, London, 1989

Annie Sloan and Kate Gwynn *The Complete Book of Decorative Paint Techniques* Ebury Press, London, 1992

Stuart Spencer *The Art of Woodgraining* Macdonald Orbis, London, 1989
Marbling Ward Lock, London, 1990

Bill Stewart *Signwork: A Craftsman's Manual* Sheridan House, New York, 1985 and Blackwell Scientific, Oxford, 1987

Janet Waring *Early American Stencils on Walls and Furniture* Dover Publications, New York and Constable, London, 1968

Paint techniques in an historical context

Isabelle Anscombe and Howard Grey *Omega and After: Bloomsbury and the Decorative Arts* Thames and Hudson, London, 1981

Alexandra Artley (editor) *Putting Back the Style: A Dictionary of Authentic Renovation* Evans Brothers, London, 1982

Patricia Bayer *Art Deco Interiors* Thames and Hudson, London, 1990

Jonathon Bourne *Lacquer: An International History and Collectors' Guide* Studio Editions, London, 1990

John Cornforth *The Inspiration of the Past: Country House Taste in the 20th Century* Viking in association with *Country Life*, London, 1985

Florence de Dampierre *The Best of Painted Furniture* Weidenfeld and Nicolson, London, 1987

D.A. Fales Jr. *American Painted Furniture 1660–1880* Crown Publishers, New York, 1988

Chester Jones *Colefax and Fowler: The Best in Interiors* Barrie and Jenkins, London, 1989

Hugh Lander *The House Restorers' Guide* 2nd edition, David and Charles, Newton Abbott, 1992

Jean Lipman *Techniques in American Folk Decoration: With Practical Instruction by Eve MeLendyke* Peter Smith, 1984

Hiram Manning *Manning on Découpage* Dover Publications, New York, 1981

Miriam Millman *Trompe L'Oeil Painting: Illusions of Reality* Macmillan, London, 1982

Mario Praz *An Illustrated History of Interior Decoration from Pompeii to Art Nouveau* Thames and Hudson, London, 1964

Peter Thornton *Authentic Decor, the Domestic Interior 1620–1920* Weidenfeld and Nicolson, London, 1984

General

Phillipa Lewis and Gillian Darley *The Dictionary of Ornament* Macmillan, London, 1986

Country House Floors 1660–1850 Temple Newsam Museum Country House Studies Catalogue, 1987, available from Temple Newsam House, Leeds LS15 0AE

Index

Page numbers in *italic* refer to illustrations. Where illustration and caption appear on different pages, the reference is to the caption.

Editors Margaret Crowther
and Judith Warren
Design Anne Wilson

Picture Editor Anne Fraser
Picture Research Sue Gladstone

Editorial Director Erica Hunningher
Art Director Caroline Hillier
Production Adela Cory

Author's acknowledgments

A seriously revised edition calls for updating in the acknowledgments, inevitably, because so many newcomers have joined the original cast – Graham Carr, Stewart Walton, my sister Miranda, Roger Seamark, Karl Wizard and Jeffrey Ratcliffe – to whom my gratitude remains unaltered. First, a big thank you to Patrick Baty, of Papers and Paints, whose unsparing critique and great erudition helped blast the project off its launch-pad. Mauro Perruchetti and Suzanne Bellehumeure generously shared their professional discoveries with us, the fruits of which are to be found in the faux fresco section. Fleur Kelly guided me, in her own backyard, into the mysteries and beauties of *buon fresco*. Ricardo Cenalli and Gonzalo Gorostiaga, both neighbours, added to the book painterly wit and brio. For patient problem-solving at a technical level, I am indebted to everyone at Foxell-James, and to Stuart Stevenson. Nearer home, a fond squeeze to Spitalfield Studio's three graces, Sarah Delafield-Cook, Emma Hardie and Cicely Gattagher, who expended time and talent on the new 'paint magicking'. Angeles Blasco, House Style's fiery particle, gets the maverick award for chucking my Colourwash shades together with such outrageous success. The team at Frances Lincoln defused the occasional tantrum with exemplary patience. To all of them, Anne, Judith, Margaret, must be attributed much of the vitality of the born-again version of a manual which began by hoping to be useful but seems to have achieved the status of a classic. It is something of a treat to be allowed to have new thoughts about a book, and a real indulgence to see them fleshed out in glorious (and to me it is) colour.

Publishers' acknowledgments

The publishers would like to thank all those who contributed their help and advice: Berger Decorative Paints; Graham Carr; Jeffrey Ratcliffe of J. H. Ratcliffe & Co (Paints) Ltd; Patrick Baty of Papers and Paints Ltd. Thanks to E. P. Dutton Publishers for permission to reproduce photographs from *American Painted Furniture 1660–1880* by Dean A. Fales Jr. We are grateful to everyone who allowed their houses to be photographed: Mr and Mrs George Howe, Dominique Lubar and Christopher Nevile. Our thanks to Gian Franco Brignone for allowing us to include photographs of his house Tigre del Mar. Special thanks to Gareth Richards for his reconnaissance work, to Jan Eaton for proofreading and to Antony Wood for the index. For their speed and cooperation we thank Servis Filmsetting.

FLL = Frances Lincoln Limited,
d = designed by, p = painted by,
t = top, b = bottom, l = left,
r = right, c = centre

PHOTOGRAPHS
Cover *The World of Interiors*/Jacques Dirand, d + p Gonzalo Gorostiaga
2 Tim Imrie © FLL d Christopher Nevile p Fiona Sutcliffe and Richard Sleeman
6 Ingalill Snitt
10–11 *The World of Interiors* Peter Aprahamian
14 Stephen Humphreys
15 Arcaid/Richard Bryant
18–19 James Mortimer © FLL d + p Graham Carr
22 Peter Aprahamian © FLL
26 Arcaid/Richard Bryant
30 Tim Imrie © FLL p Jocasta Innes
31 *t* Judith Watts d + p Suzanne Bellehumeure *b* Andy Boulter d + p Mauro Perruchetti
34 Ianthe Ruthven
35 Tim Imrie © FLL d Christopher Nevile p Fiona Sutcliffe
38–39 *The World of Interiors*/Jacques Dirand d + p Gonzalo Gorostiaga
42 Tim Imrie © FLL p Jocasta Innes and Angeles Blasco
43 Stylograph/Yves Duronsoy
46 Tim Imrie © FLL d Christopher Nevile p Fiona Sutcliffe and Tania Backhouse
47 Tim Imrie © FLL d Christopher Nevile p Fiona Sutcliffe and Tania Backhouse
50 Tim Imrie © FLL d IPL Interiors p Nicholas Fer
50–1 Tim Imrie © FLL d IPL Interiors p Nicholas Fer

55 James Mortimer © FLL
58–9 Michael Dunne © FLL p Patricia Boulter and Toby Kalitowski
62–3 Tim Imrie © FLL d Christopher Nevile p Fiona Sutcliffe, Kitty Beamish and Tania Backhouse
66 Ingalill Snitt
67 Derry Moore
70 Elizabeth Whiting and Associates/David George
70–1 Jan Baldwin © *Country Living* The National Magazine Co. Ltd
74–5 *The World of Interiors*/James Mortimer p George Oakes
75 Tim Imrie © FLL d IPL Interiors p Nicholas Fer
78 Lars Hallen
79 Paul Ryan
82 Lizzie Himmel d + p Lucretia Moroni
83 Ingalill Snitt
86–7 Bay Hippisley © FLL d Stewart Walton
90 Tim Imrie © FLL d Christopher Nevile, Fiona Sutcliffe, Saul Greenberg and Steve Marsh
94 Ingalill Snitt
97 Tim Imrie © FLL p Emma Hardie
98 Tim Imrie © FLL p Emma Hardie
99 *tl + bl* Tim Imrie © FLL p Emma Hardie *r* Peter Aprahamian © FLL
102 Michael Dunne © FLL p Nemone Burgess
103 Tim Imrie © FLL p Emma Hardie
104 Bay Hippisley © FLL p Stewart Walton
106 Bay Hippisley © FLL p Graham Carr
107 Tim Imrie © FLL p Cicely Gattagher
110 *t* Lizzie Himmel d + p Lucretia Moroni *b* *The World of Interiors*/Tom Leighton
111 Bay Hippisley © FLL p Graham Carr

114–5 Tim Imrie © FLL d Christopher Nevile p Fiona Sutcliffe and Richard Sleeman
118 *t* Thomas Lane d + p Thomas Lane *b* John Hall
119 Ingalill Snitt
122 John Hall
123 John Hall
126 John Hall
130 Fritz von der Schulenburg © The Condé Nast Publications Ltd/p Jim Smart
130–1 Fritz von der Schulenburg
134 Robert Harding Picture Library/James Merrell
135 Bay Hippisley © FLL p Stewart Walton
138 Derry Moore
139 Arcaid/Richard Bryant
142 Bay Hippisley © FLL d + p Jocasta Innes and Stewart Walton
143 *t* Tim Imrie © FLL d + p Thomas Lane *b* Andrew Siddenham d + p Colleen Bery
146–7 Hugo Glendinning d + p Gonzalo Gorostiaga
150 Hugo Glendinning d + p Gonzalo Gorostiaga
151 Tim Imrie © FLL d + p Ray McNeill
154 *r* Fritz von der Schulenburg *l* Rachel Macfadyen d + p Rachel Macfadyen
155 Peter Aprahamian © FLL d + p Thomas Lane
158 David Brittain © *Good Housekeeping*/The National Magazine Co Ltd
159 *Schöner Wohnen*/Camera Press
163 *l* Peter Woloszynski *r* Marianne Majerus
166 © E.P. Dutton
166–7 John Hall
170 *l* Rachel Macfadyen d + p Rachel Macfadyen *r* John Hall
171 *l* Tim Imrie © FLL *r* Tim Imrie © FLL p Sarah Delafield Cook
174 Tim Imrie © FLL p Jocasta Innes
178 *The World of Interiors*/James Mortimer p Georges Oakes
179 Bay Hippisley © FLL p Graham Carr and Stewart Walton
182 Tim Imrie © FLL p Jocasta Innes and Angeles Blasco
183 Tim Imrie © FLL p Jocasta Innes and Angeles Blasco
186 Bay Hippisley © FLL p Jocasta Innes and Stewart Walton
187 © E.P. Dutton
190 Tim Imrie © FLL p Cicely Gattagher
191 *tl* Bay Hippisley © FLL p Stewart Walton *bl* Bay Hippisley © FLL p Graham Carr *cl + r* Tim Imrie © FLL p Cicely Gattagher
194 Tim Imrie © FLL p Sarah Delafield Cook
195 Bay Hippisley © FLL p John Fowler and Graham Carr
198 John Hall
199 Bay Hippisley © FLL p Jocasta Innes
203 William Waldron
204 Tim Imrie © FLL p Jocasta Innes
206 Andreas von Einsiedel
207 Tim Imrie © FLL p Sarah Delafield Cook
218–9 Bay Hippisley © FLL d Roger Walton p Stewart Walton
222 Tim Imrie © FLL d Christopher Nevile p Christopher Nevile and Fiona Sutcliffe
227 Tim Imrie © FLL
230–1 Tim Imrie © FLL

ARTWORK
Cover Gonzalo Gorostiaga
41, 48, 56, 61 Alicia Durdos
68 Miranda Innes
72–3, 81, 85, 92, 93, 100 Jennie Smith
109 Alicia Durdos
128 Tim Foster/Aardvark Design
132 Jennie Smith
142, 181 Tim Foster/Aardvark Design
197, 201 Alicia Durdos

35